THUMBS UP

Ken Wachsberger

THUMBS UP

Memoir of a Joyful Organizer

by

Ken Wachsberger

Published by Azenphony Press, 2025

Published by

Azenphony Press
PO Box 130884
Ann Arbor, MI 48113-0884 U.S.A.
info@azenphonypress.com
(734) 635-0577

Thumbs Up: Memoir of a Joyful Organizer
Copyright July 14, 2025 by Ken Wachsberger
ISBN 978-0-945531-23-4 (ebook)
ISBN 978-0-945531-24-1 (pbk)
ISBN 978-0-945531-25-8 (hbk)

Cover by Digital Content Creators
www.digitalcc.us

Text design by Caligraphics
http://www.caligraphics.net

All rights reserved. Without limiting the rights under copyright reserved above, no part of this publication may be reproduced, stored in or introduced into a retrieval system, or transmitted, in any form, or by any means (electronic, mechanical, photocopying, recording, or otherwise) without the prior written permission of both the copyright owner and the above publisher of this book.

What you're hearing about *Thumbs Up*

"Ken Wachsberger's memoir is a captivating journey through the evolution of a gentle, courageous, and often hilarious man. His storytelling brings each moment to life, whether he's dodging (or falling on) authorities at protests in the 70s, navigating the chaos of a catering business, or empowering others to share their stories through authorship. The book is well-written, blending vivid imagery with sharp wit, making you feel as if you're right there alongside him. His experiences are not just entertaining but also deeply inspiring, showcasing resilience, activism, and a passion for making a difference in the world. The puke-in had me ROLLING!! This memoir is a must-read for anyone who appreciates a life well-lived and well-told. I LOVE IT!"

—Anne Bonney, keynote speaker and author of *Get Over It!* and *Get Them Over It!*

"As a long-time fan of Ken Wachsberger's books, I give this remarkable memoir my heartiest Thumbs Up! Finally, he dishes all the "dirt" his admirers longed to know. From the transfixing tales of his ancestors, to his funny/not-funny stint in solitary as an "accidental revolutionary," he goes on to find the love of his life and a career in the world of publishing. Wachsberger's galloping prose traces the journey of a '70s activist through at least nine lives on his way to the 21st Century. His is a life and a book to be jubilantly celebrated and honored."

—Sue Katz, wordsmith, rebel, and author of *Lillian in Love* and *A Raisin in My Cleavage*

"[S]pins a Kerouac-worthy tale of an adventure-filled life well spent. Full of fight and fun, THUMBS UP delivers on a beautiful family legacy and monumental archivist triumph with an irreplaceable volume of priceless people's journalism."

—Harvey "Sluggo" Wasserman, activist, author of *Solartopia, The People's Spiral of US History,* and other green-inspired works, from his foreword to *Thumbs Up*

"For decades, Ken Wachsberger has done heroic work in archiving the truly independent media of the 20th century—newspapers filled with anti-war, LGBTQ+, Native American, Black, and feminist voices—and the stories behind them. In *Thumbs Up*, which bursts with love and hope, he candidly tells his own inspiring story—and explodes the notion that activism recedes with age."

—Sean Howe, author of *Agents of Chaos: Thomas King Forçade, High Times, and the Paranoid End of the 1970s*

"This memoir is a gift, a cultural outbreak of joy in the dark time of the 1970s for our own dark time."

—Roxanne Dunbar-Ortiz, feminist historian and author of *An Indigenous Peoples' History of the United States*

"Ken Wachsberger's Thumbs Up is a joy to read and far more than just another life's tale of one man's journey. It is a fascinating behind the-scenes account of how thing really got done during his days as a wet-behind-the-ears activist marching through to his dogged—and successful—efforts to preserve much of the great array of material produced by the underground/alternative press during the Vietnam War. Wachsberger shares his hard-learned lessons that our intergenerational peers, the folks who are the age now that we were then, can apply as they pick up the struggle from us. And to give them confidence that when we organize we win."

—Dennis Giangreco, author of *Truman and the Bomb* and over a dozen books on historical and sociopolitical subjects under D. M. Giangreco.

Dedication

To David and Carrie

Thumbs Up: Memoir of a Joyful Organizer

TABLE OF CONTENTS

FOREWORD by Harvey Wasserman 1

INTRODUCTION 5

PART 1: I FALL OFF THE LADDER 7

Chapter 1: Making It in America 9

Chapter 2: I Become an Accidental Revolutionary 17

Chapter 3: The Trial of the MSU 132 and I Drop Out 33

PART 2: THE YIPPIES, THE ZIPPIES, AND THE
UNDERGROUND PRESS 39

Chapter 4: I Join the Underground Press 41

Chapter 5: Busted with Davey at May Day 1971 47

Chapter 6: Joint Issue Becomes Free 63

Chapter 7: I Hit the Road to Madison 69

Chapter 8: The Short One with the Curly Hair and Beard 77

Chapter 9: Miami Beach, Summer 1972 87

Chapter 10: I Score in Cleveland, Then
Write Lansing History 103

PART 3: I FIND TRUE LOVE 111

Chapter 11: Emily 113

Chapter 12: Emken Is Born 119

Chapter 13: Francine Hughes and the
Burning Bed 129

Chapter 14: We Get Married 133

PART 4: REDISCOVERING JUDAISM IN LANSING 139

Chapter 15: Return to Lansing 141

Chapter 16: McGoff Off 151

Chapter 17: We Change Congregations 155

PART 5: LIFE BEGINS IN ANN ARBOR 161

Chapter 18: The Move to Ann Arbor 163

Chapter 19: I Organize Non-Politicos at Arbor Meadows 167

Chapter 20: We Leave Arbor Meadows 181

Chapter 21: Emken Arises Again 191

PART 6: THE UNDERGROUND PRESS GOES DIGITAL . 193

Chapter 22: Brainstorming with Ed Wall 195

Chapter 23: "He'll Cover the Underground Press" 203

Chapter 24: The Underground Press Digital Collection 225

PART 7: ON THE ROAD AGAIN 249

Chapter 25: EMU Lecturers Make History with First-Ever Bargaining Unit 251

Chapter 26: Writing for Healing and to Preserve Your Legacy 277

Chapter 27: Temple Beth Emeth Joins the Sanctuary Movement 285

Chapter 28: On the Road Again 319

APPENDIX 325

Stories from the Underground and Alternative Press

- "My Waitress: I Think I'll Tip Her": I wrote after watching how hard our waitress was working one hectic evening while the guests were being obnoxious and rowdy
- "Fisherman's Tale, part 1": Two suburban kids spend the summer as fishermen in Sebasco, Maine
- "A Fisherman's Tale, part 2: Yo Ho Ho—Ulp": Because not everyone can get their sea legs their first day out on the sea
- "Story Time: A Fable": Because the end of the story is what we make it

Saying Goodbye to Two Key Influences

- "Goodbye, Dad. You Will Always Be Missed"
- "Goodbye to a Tough Broad"

Temple Beth Emeth and the Sanctuary Movement

- "Temple Beth Emeth Declaration in Support of Becoming a Sanctuary Congregation"

Acknowledgments

First and foremost, to David, Carrie, and Emily. Knowing you are with me drives me to be better. Emily, if I taught you to be an editor, I did an amazing job because your corrections and suggestions were superb and brilliant.

For your valuable comments throughout the manuscript as well as in certain key parts: Sue Katz, Jerry Gorde, Brother Bob, Shoshana Mandel-Warner, Rabbi Josh Whinston, Jon Curtiss, Martha Kransdorf, Sonia Alverado, Mary Gray, Kathie McDonald, Emilie Breuer, Peggy Glahn, Anne Bonney, Seam Howe, Harvey Wasserman, and Roxanne Dunbar-Ortiz.

And for being an unsung hero:

> Geraldine Jensen, my business coach and web advisor. She holds the record for the most Hero of the Day awards.

> Every Panera that tolerates me for as long as I want to be there for the cost of a medium iced tea and a bagel.

Apologies if I missed anyone. I can't say enough how grateful I am to all of you.

Foreword
Harvey "Sluggo" Wasserman

It's a good sign when a good friend's memoir title includes the word "joyful."

Ken Wachsberger's THUMBS UP is just that: funny, informative, impactful, and...well...JOYFUL!!!

Ken is one of those rare individuals who, even in tough times (like NOW!), can keep an even keel, a happy face, and tell a life story that's full of fun while also changing the world in a good, kind, and gentle way.

That he's a helluva writer and editor also helps.

With this unabashedly quirky and adventurous autobiography, Ken paints the portrait of a guy born with the greatest of all advantages any human being can have: great parents.

Raised in the Jewish "greena" (immigrant) suburbs of east Cleveland with a big, brainy, functional family that includes many siblings, cousins, aunts, uncles—the whole 9 yards—Ken sets out in life as a "normal guy" soon to be swallowed by the Great Sixties Tsunami of social change.

Initially apolitical at Michigan State, he finds himself—as did so many of us back then—in police custody. The issue, of course, is the war in Vietnam. The milieu is a campus demonstration. The outcome is the kind of eye-opening, life-changing time in jail that shaped a generation.

Ken Wachsberger

The modus, gratefully, is the bracingly undoctrinaire zeitgeist of the Yippie/Zippie counterculture.

While hitchhiking back and forth across the country, Ken's dizzying travels called out for a spiritual odometer plunging deep into netherworld. But his experiences tend to center on the midwestern meccas of the "mistake by the lake"; East Lansing; and, ultimately, that countercultural paradise we call Ann Arbor, where he's been a pillar for many decades.

Beautifully centered, empowered with a wonderful wife, Ken uses his unique talents as an editor and archivist to establish a comprehensive digital collection of countercultural newspapers. These "Voices from the Underground" rocked the world of the 1960s and '70s, providing irreplaceable alternative reportage and countercultural celebration that Made America Great Back Then.

As the pivotal archivist of the time, Ken reminds us that "the underground press was the voice of the largest, most diverse antiwar movement in the history of this country."

It changed, he says, "society's understanding of our unholy war in Vietnam and forced it to an embarrassing halt. At the same time, it created a peace community around the many issues of the period that it embraced."

It's no surprise, Ken adds, that "corporate historians and political leaders wanted to write it out of history or just let it be forgotten."

Thankfully, there's been a Ken Wachsberger to keep that from happening.

But not without its pitfalls. "Many papers I was unable to reach before we ran out of money. Others, I did reach and even obtained

THUMBS UP

permission to include, but we lacked the financial resources to digitize them. May the work continue."

In a fascinating piece of reportage, we learn that Ken's work has included the admirable—and mind-bending—organizer's pursuit of a union for part-time "adjunct" professors at Eastern Michigan University.

He's also taught writing at Michigan State, Lansing Community College, and in Jackson State Prison...not to mention his own "School for Compulsive Communicators," where he continues as a "book coach" for the growing self-published multitudes (including myself). His invaluable guide, *You've Got the Time: How to Write and Publish That Book in You,* is "for anyone who has a book in them."

"It's time to make the media the issue," he adds.

This memoir does a great job of doing just that. But along the way, it also spins a Kerouac-worthy tale of an adventure-filled life well spent.

Full of fight and fun, THUMBS UP delivers on a beautiful family legacy and monumental archivist triumph with an irreplaceable volume of priceless people's journalism.

Thanks, Ken. As the Yippie/Zippies used to put it, "History's no mystery: blast the past." In this lovely volume, you've done just that!

Author/activist **Harvey "Sluggo" Wasserman**'s books extend from *Harvey Wasserman's History of the United States* (introduced in 1972 by Howard Zinn) to *Solartopia* (with a theme song by Pete Seeger) and *The People's Spiral of US History*. He continues to write, fight, and convene Zooms for a green-powered Earth with reliable, protected elections (www.grassrootsep.org).

Introduction

I came of age during the most vibrant, colorful, metaphysical, creative, intellectual, spiritual, musical, stressful, liberating period in our young country's history.

Some called it the Age of Aquarius. Others say it was *b'shert*, Yiddish for "meant to be."

My generation, the baby boomers, were welcomed into the world as a Madison Avenue concept and shaped by young post-World War II married couples from what was being billed the Greatest Generation. They couldn't wait to move into the suburbs, start having us, and give us everything we needed to "make it" in our chosen careers.

In that way, many of us were blessed.

But those benefits came with a cost.

We were called upon to embrace a war with a country that had never harmed us and, in fact, wanted to be like us. Supporting the war, we were taught, would demonstrate our patriotism.

Not supporting it made us traitors.

Our mandate, unfortunately, became to change society's self-perception.

But how do you tell a generation of heroes, still basking in the glow of being democracy's savior and thinking they can do no wrong, that they are now the bad guys?

Ken Wachsberger

You build a broad-based long-term movement with support from all generations and you create your own media. Everyone's story matters!

Like the darkness that has descended on the landscape since Trump was re-elected, conditions were right to create the largest antiwar movement in our country's history, and launch some of our country's most important social movements at the same time. Baby boomer activists came to our activism from every suburb, ghetto, barrio, reservation, campus, and military base the country had to offer. Some of us, the "red diaper babies," had radical parents, including members of the Communist Party. By the time they got to college, they already had read Marx and Lenin and had developed a political analysis.

Others of us were radicalized by personal experiences that forced us to question everything we knew and open ourselves to new conclusions. These were the accidental revolutionaries.

PART 1
I FALL OFF THE LADDER

CHAPTER 1
MAKING IT IN AMERICA

I was an accidental revolutionary. I grew up in the post-war middle-class Jewish suburb of Beachwood on the east side of Cleveland, Ohio. Many of the early settlers in Beachwood and the surrounding suburbs had family members who fled the pogroms of Russia and Eastern Europe and immigrated around the turn of last century. Others arrived after fleeing the Holocaust.

My Family Make It to America and in America

Wachsbergers, Pollacks, Dratlers, and Kroshinskys followed both waves and spread all over the world from their hometowns throughout Galicia (now Poland), Marmarosh-Sighet, and Minsk. Hundreds of family members from all branches died in the Holocaust. At least four Wachsberger survivors wrote books about their experiences, including one who survived by being a translator for the Nazis in Auschwitz.

Some Jews came to this country to raise hell and organize politically for better labor conditions for workers. The same shtetls that gave birth to the Zionist movement in Palestine also gave birth to the Jewish-American socialist labor movement in the United States.

Others came to put the past behind them. They gave themselves Americanized names; and only spoke Yiddish, Jewish street talk, around us when they didn't want us to know what they were talking about. They didn't share stories about the Old Country because that was all in the past.

My folks belonged to the first generation in my family to be born in this country of immigrant parents. They weren't radicals by any means. But they were legendary community organizers, and among a handful of pioneers who built Beachwood.

- My dad, Si Wachsberger, was part of the team that built the school system. He was president of the school board, president of city council, and co-founder of the Little League, to name a few of the associations he led. He was the owner of a menswear retail store in nearby Shaker Heights that was a regular sponsor of my Little League team, which he managed and coached.
- My mom, Shirley Pollack Wachsberger, was president of the PTA (Parent-Teacher Association) and the women's auxiliary at Menorah Park, the Jewish senior citizen community in Beachwood.
- Together, they co-founded and were co-presidents of the Beachwood Arts Council, co-hosted a foreign exchange student from the Netherlands one year, tutored inner-city children while they were in their eighties, and raised four sons.

Both of my parents were tolerant and receptive to new ideas. My dad was the first Wachsberger on my branch of the family to earn a college degree. Then he became the first in his class to sign up for the army. He served in the Philippines in army medical administration and made it to lieutenant. One of his tasks was to toe-tag dead soldiers and ship them back to the States.

I wish I could say more about his military experience but, when I could have, I didn't think to ask questions; and he seldom shared stories on his own.

THUMBS UP

He was a Republican at the turn of the sixties and voted for Barry Goldwater for president in 1964. But he also hired a gay man to be principal of one elementary school. When I began working on the underground press at the end of 1970, I sent my folks every issue and they read them. Dad voted for Barry Commoner in 1980.

My mom would have been a feminist if such a thing existed in the fifties. Instead, she was forced into being a suburban housewife. Nevertheless, she was driven to be educated, like her mother before her. She read *Ms.* magazine and earned her college degree from John Carroll University at the age of 50, the first woman in my family to graduate college.

Edgewood Road

We lived on Edgewood Road, a beloved brick road until the city council, before Dad's tenure, unceremoniously paved it with blacktop. Edgewood was known throughout the city of Beachwood because a hundred kids lived on it. You held a certain higher status at school if you were an Edgewood kid. At least we acted that way.

Every summer, our family had cookouts with the Oppers, the Goulders, and the Freibergs, who shared adjoining backyards with us.

Our house was built by Mom's father, my Grandpa Harry Pollack, and his partner and brother Frank. In the Old Country, Máramaros-Sighet in the kingdom of Hungary, Hermann (pre-Harry) Pollak (only one "l" then) was a skilled craftsman, a cabinet maker, who served as the house carpenter in the Kaiser's army, a preferred position because he didn't have to go on maneuvers and he lived in the servants' quarters.

I loved my brothers and was proud to be one of Si and Shirley's boys. Don was my older brother by five years. I have fond memories of listening to the top 100 songs of the year and watching the ball drop on New Year's Eve with him and my Uncle Norman, who was only a few years older than Don, in Don's bedroom, a tradition we repeated every year until Norm started dating. Another highpoint was walking to school with Don every day when I was in kindergarten and he was in fifth grade, the one year we went to the same school.

Jeff, two years younger than me, was my best friend growing up. We shared a bedroom. We played baseball and football in the street with our friends, always watching for on-coming traffic and hoping to not break any windows. Together, we took regular trips to downtown Cleveland on the Shaker Heights Rapid Transit to hang out outside Cleveland Stadium and grab incoming players from both teams for what became two extensive autograph collections. Later, he found a spiritual side; he introduced me to the Moody Blues when he wrote a high school paper comparing *In Search of the Lost Chord* to the *Bhagavad-Gita*.

Bob, six years my younger, was the dreamer and, although we were all A-students, he was the smartest. The eyeglasses that he's worn most of his life accentuate that image. He was known for shouting out esoteric facts at random moments. We finally began responding, "Footnote!" and he would be required to provide the source of his fact. He always did. In high school, he photographed for the newspaper and was seldom seen without a camera hanging from around his neck.

One More Telephone Pole

I was a chosen one—that's how I felt growing up. I was a straight-A student and member of National Honor Society, a math whiz, class spelling champion, basketball team statistician, first-chair drummer in the band, president of my class twice, and proofreader for our school newspaper. (That's how long I've been editing.)

THUMBS UP

I ran cross country and distance track in high school. I was never good at either. I overcompensated for being too short for football or basketball. I ran the two-mile event in track because no one else wanted to run it so I was the default best two-miler on the team (until someone else ran it).

But I earned four varsity letters and two captainships, which was important back then. And I learned a valuable lesson from my first cross country coach, Mr. Mercer.

Cross country, unlike track, is not run on a standard course. Every course is unique. Four laps seldom equal a mile. Our two-mile course took us one mile up a hilly main street running on the grass against traffic; down a big gulley; up and down a small hill; up the other side of the gulley; then a mile down the main street again running against the traffic, sunshine, rain, or snow. Every race was an endurance challenge. Phone poles lined both sides of the street.

"Run as many telephone poles as you possibly can," he taught us. "Then run one more pole." That elusive second wind kicked in many times during that last length.

Exceed your self-limitations, even if it's just one telephone pole. Mr. Mercer knows you can do it.

In my freshman year, Dad was president of the school board, Mom was president of the PTA, and I was president of junior high student council. Dad was president again when I graduated; he signed my diploma.

Great things were expected of me. It was assumed I would become a lawyer and work my way up the ladder. Parents said to their kids, "Why can't you be like Ken?"

Ken Wachsberger

But I didn't know what I wanted to be when I grew up. The pressure to declare a major and choose a career that would define me as a success for the rest of my life became a major reason why I chose an out-of-state college. It became a dominant theme in my first book, *Beercans on the Side of the Road: The Story of Henry the Hitchhiker.*

I Take First Step Up the Ladder

In the summer between my junior and senior years, Dad and I visited Michigan State University. Dad fell in love with the educational opportunities in the living-learning dorms. I loved the co-ed dorms. So, I sent in my application to MSU as soon as we got back home. I was accepted later that summer, becoming the first student from the class of '67 to be accepted. I could have screwed around my entire senior year but I didn't want to ruin my record.

In the fall of 1967, I began my first year at Michigan State. I was one of 1,200 students who lived in Wonders Dorm, where the women occupied the six floors on the west wing, the men did the same on the east wing, and we met in the middle for classes and meals.

But I couldn't focus. No career path called out to me. Years later, I would learn that I had ADHD but I didn't know that then.

So, I floundered around. I entered college as a math major because of my math expertise. Then I imagined myself losing my ability to converse normally after four years of math classes, and changed my major to business. Next, inspired by heavy uses of marijuana, hash, kif, mescaline, and LSD, I transferred to Social Science. What do you do with a Social Science degree? You stay in college and get a Master's.

I was still living in the dorm in my junior year, 1969-1970. My friends hated dorm life and left for apartments as soon as they could.

THUMBS UP

I loved having all my basic needs provided for me along with the opportunity to meet so many people from so many countries.

"The Titsest Jew"

Wonders was one of the jock dorms. Residents included players from every MSU sport. One of my thrills was bench pressing double my weight in the weight room while two members of the football team spotted me. Another was getting high with a basketball player who was on the B team of the Harlem Globetrotters.

I supported being good to others and people liked me. One junior at the end of my floor, 6E, during my first year called me "the titsest Jew" he ever met, a backhanded compliment that I welcomed because he was popular but that actually meant he was surprised to like me because I was Jewish.

I read *Newsweek* because it arrived for free in my mailbox but I had no concrete political analysis.

That's pretty much where I was when May 1970 began.

CHAPTER 2
I BECOME AN ACCIDENTAL REVOLUTIONARY

Then, four days into the month, four students were killed by members of the Ohio National Guard at Kent State University during an antiwar demonstration. Their deaths hit me personally, even though I didn't know any of the victims, because I had friends who attended Kent.

Solidarity with Kent State

So, when campus leaders at Michigan State called for a student strike, I supported it. I didn't consider myself a hero or radical or revolutionary. I just believed how could I not support it?

I began attending rallies and teach-ins to learn more.

I was shocked to learn that the CIA's number one undercover program to colonize Vietnam during the fifties and early sixties went through Michigan State and had been responsible for the campus's exponential growth from a cow college to a mega university during that time.

I witnessed and participated in the meeting at the auditorium, where over six thousand students and outside agitators democratically determined the strike demands: US out of Vietnam, ROTC off campus, Free Bobby Seale, and solidarity with students at Kent State.

Ken Wachsberger

Rena Yount, a strike leader and staff member of *Bogue Street Bridge*, one of Michigan State's two underground newspapers at the time, recalled the event:

> Thursday night, there was a strike meeting that packed the auditorium. It was amazing to see 6000-7000 people debating and voting on the strike issues, in a meeting that was 6 hours long, confusing, exhausting, sometimes frustrating, sometimes emotional. There were microphones on the floor; anyone could speak. And people did, seemingly endlessly. It was great—the only time at MSU that I have seen a group anywhere near that size come together, not as spectators at some "event," but as people working something out together. It was a good feeling.

I remember one speaker. He was a member of ROTC (Reserve Officers' Training Corps), the military group we were trying to ban from campus. He stood at the open mic in full uniform and announced that he was from a military family, he had enlisted in ROTC because it had been expected of him, and now he was here to resign his commission. He resigned it there on the spot. What a hero he was, I thought. How courageous to confront and then reject every expectation of his upbringing.

Seven months later, I would drop out of school and move in with Davey Brinn, who I'll talk about soon. One day, I was alone in the apartment when I heard a knock on the door. I answered it and I saw the same guy who had resigned his commission. His name was Bill Clack and he was here to see Davey. I said Davey wasn't here and invited him inside to wait. By the time Davey got home, Bill and I were life-long buddies. He began coming to *Joint Issue* meetings with us and became a valued member of the team.

But I'm jumping ahead.

THUMBS UP

I began hanging out at Strike Central in the basement of the Snyder-Phillips dorm. I helped to write and distribute flyers, and met with travelers from other universities who hitchhiked into town to spread the word on what was happening on their campuses.

Discussing Racism at the Student Union

Then one evening, two weeks after the Kent State murders, on Monday May 18, I was handed a flyer for an upcoming teach-in on racism at the Student Union by a bearded, fast-talking freak. Only three days before, on Friday May 15, two black students had been killed and twelve injured by police at Jackson State College (now University) in Jackson, Mississippi. The event made barely a blip on the mainstream national consciousness. The purpose of the meeting at the Union was to plan campus protests against the murders of students at both campuses.

I asked him what time it was now and was alarmed to learn that the meeting had already begun. I rushed over, and was the last to arrive. The room was packed, standing room only. I stood in the back by the door.

These were glory days for Michigan State. Or, they could have been. MSU had just welcomed a new president to campus: Clifton Wharton. Wharton was a veteran establishment insider, with a job resume replete with prestigious positions on numerous task forces, executive committees, and associations that perpetuated our country's interference in Vietnam and other Southeast Asia and Latin American countries. Foundations and institutes he led were named for the Rockefellers and other members of the wealthy and powerful elite.

But he was Black. In fact, he had just become the first Black person to be named president of a major university.

So, when the usual 11:00 p.m. closing time rolled around, one of the leaders asked the Union assistant manager, Jack Ostrander, who was in charge that night, if he could extend the hours. He noted the peacefulness of the gathering and the educational relevance of the topic. In fact, rather than leave, he suggested how appropriate it would be to discuss racism with President Wharton. He beseeched Ostrander to contact the president with our personal invitation. It all seemed appropriate to me

Rick and Leslie, of the Action Group to Combat Racism, relate in Generation, MSU's other underground newspaper, what happened next: "Our representative was informed that the decision was no longer in his hands, that 'higher-ups' were making the decision, but that Ostrander would keep us informed of the decision."

Standoff at the Student Union

We heard nothing until 1:30 a.m., May 19, when Ostrander suddenly appeared, bullhorn in hand, and announced, "Everyone must leave the building immediately."

Unfortunately, we couldn't. Unable to attend in person, Wharton had sent his friends, representing the MSU, East Lansing, Lansing, Ingham County, and State police departments. They surrounded the entire building, including all doors and windows. They entered through the doors and filled the length of the back wall.

I didn't see any hints that anyone planned to leave but any effort would have been futile because there were now more police than students and we were surrounded. The police were dressed in full riot gear and gripped their billy clubs with both fists as they stood at attention. None of them wore badges.

An awkward moment of silence filled the room as both sides waited for the other to act first. We had no collective strategy. The police did.

THUMBS UP

I saw a TV screen framing this scene that I was now a part of. I waited for Walter Cronkite to tell me how it was and what happened next.

"Who's He?"

I was standing next to a woman who I recognized from Strike Central. She had never said a word to me to make me think she even knew who I was let alone cared, but she was pretty and intelligent and my hormones had a way of screaming to me even in politically inappropriate times when they saw her. I whispered to her, "I wonder what they'll do next."

I looked up then to see two policemen, each at least 6'8", marching angrily toward me. Was it because I dared to whisper? To this day, I don't know why they nabbed me first. Then, I was bewildered. I flinched as they grabbed me, each at one elbow, and pushed me toward one of the wagons with a billy club jabbed into the crook of my back to keep me moving. My armpits seemed about to tear as my legs stretched toward the ground so I could walk.

"Officer," I pleaded, "I was just listening." "Shut up, kid. That's what they all say," he responded, and I was frightened for my future. As they led me away, I heard someone whisper to someone else, "Who's he?"

Anyway, I was forced to fill out a questionnaire and then they hauled me away along with 131 other students, which was how many they could fit in the eight paddy wagons. I was lucky some of the women had their purses with them because, as soon as the truck I was in drove off, they pulled out a leaflet that gave instructions on what to do if you were busted. I got hold of a copy as soon as I could and read it and reread it so many times I nearly memorized it. Even then, I would have reread it again if the guy next to me hadn't said, "Hey, Bro, I'm busted, too."

But I didn't give it a lot of thought after I gave the instructions to him because everyone else was having a great time laughing and chanting "Off the Pig" and "Smash the State" and calling each other Brother and Sister, and in that company how could I feel alone or scared?

Poked by Officer Grunt

When we got to the station, the women were separated from the men and I never saw them again until I got out. We could hear them, though, and they could hear us, so we shouted at each other to keep our spirits up and we passed notes through holes in the walls wherever we found them. I was having a grand old time and so was everyone else. One Brother pointed to the cops, who looked shook up and confused, and noted the irony. "Funny, they're the ones with guns and we're the ones behind bars," he said. Someone else shouted, "Prison is a state of mind," and that was followed by a chorus of "Right on"s.

The mood became suddenly solemn then—relative to the previous pandemonium, that is—when Officer Grunt (my name for him) appeared with three other younger cops and shouted at us to shut up. Then, one by one, he called our names and directed us out of the cell to be arraigned. I was the first one called, probably because I was the first one who had been busted. I was handcuffed by a cop who was a foot taller than me and ordered to face left. Then Officer Grunt poked his gun in my head like it was a cattle prod and said, "Get going." I got going.

My Defense Beats Sergeant Nostrel's Offense

We followed a series of right-angle hallways and blank walls until we arrived at the front desk, where Sergeant Nostrel (my name for him) sat, flanked on either side by a young patrolman. All three wore thin mustaches and sideburns that were trimmed evenly just above

THUMBS UP

the ears. The two patrolmen had Princeton haircuts. The sergeant was bald and smoked a cigar.

Like I said earlier, I had never been busted before so I had no experience to draw upon, and, since I was the first bustee they called, I had no one I could talk to to find out what to expect. I clung to the memory of the instructions for security. So, when the sergeant said to me, "What's your name?" I recalled the line that read, "Don't answer anything without your lawyer's consent unless you have to."

"Do I have to answer that?" I asked.

"Yes, you do," he said, so I told him.

Then he said, "Is this your correct address?" and he showed me the questionnaire I had answered before I got thrown into the truck.

"Do I have to answer that?" I asked again, and he said, "Yes, you do," so I said it was correct.

Then he said to me, "Are you single, married, or divorced?"

"Do I have to answer that?" I said, and he said, "Yes, you do," so I said, "I'm single."

Anyhow, the sergeant was clearly getting fidgety. I could tell because he broke the point of his pencil and had to get another one out of his desk. I knew he thought I was a smart-ass, but he looked like a high school jock so I thought he would at least respect my good defensive strategy. He might have at first, but respect turned to hatred when my defense beat his offense. It was about to happen.

With his free hand, he turned the form around so that I could read it and he pointed to an X at the bottom of the page. One of the patrolmen removed my handcuffs. Then the sergeant handed me the pencil and said, "Sign here."

I saw the next line on the bust manual: "Don't sign anything without your lawyer's consent unless you have to."

"Do I have to sign?" I asked.

His face turned as red as a communist, but I swallowed the irony. "Now look, punk," he said. The cigar fell out of his mouth, but no one dared to move. "No, you don't have to sign, but I'm getting fed up with your shenanigans. I've been real patient, but we don't like your kind in America and you'll sign if you don't want any trouble."

Well, of course, I didn't want any trouble, but the manual didn't cover what to do when threatened by angry sergeants and I was too new at this to improvise, so I decided to play out my original strategy and just do what the manual said. Also, I figured no one else was going to sign anyhow, so I didn't sign. I just said, "Hey, I would, ya know, but my lawyer said I shouldn't sign anything unless I have to, and, well...."

I shrugged my shoulders like I was a victim of circumstance, but the sergeant didn't buy it. "You pinko lovers think you're pretty cute; don't you?" he said. He stood, and the force of his rising body against his swivel chair sent the chair crashing into the filing cabinet behind him. "Well, I don't like pinko fags." Six foot-eight of mass stomped over to where I was standing then, said, "Get going," and ordered me to follow him.

You're Kidding!

When we got to the gate that led to the cells where the men were, I thought he would open it up and order me in, but he kept walking and so I kept following. Ten feet ahead, he stopped and opened a

THUMBS UP

gate on the other side of the hall. Then he pushed me inside. A long hallway stood before me. On the right side was a blank wall. On the left were eight empty cells.

"Move," he said. We walked to the farthest cell from the gate. He opened the door and pushed me inside, then locked the door. Thirty-two angry steps led him back to the gate. I heard two more sounds, a slow grating "Creak" and a sudden "Crash." His footsteps faded into solitude.

As for me, I wasn't scared a bit—at first. I just stood there in disbelief and thought, "Naw, who's he kidding? Solitary? Me? For not signing my fingerprints?" He had to be bluffing, I thought. I figured he'd come back in five minutes, hoping to see me cowering in a corner ready to sign my fingerprints, a complete confession of guilt, and anything else he pushed in front of my face. I even thought he might have tiptoed back to the gate and was standing there right then listening in on me, waiting for me to scream submission.

So, I did the only appropriate thing I could think of. I shouted, "Fuck you, pig," to show him I could take anything he dished out. I figured he'd come in soon to get me anyhow because he had other things to do and he couldn't wait all day. I guessed he'd probably rough me up a bit and call me some threatening names to try and scare me so he could act like he'd gotten the best of me even though he couldn't get me to sign, and then he'd throw me in with the others and I'd be on my way.

I Analyze the Situation

Twenty minutes later, I suspected I was wrong.

Thirty minutes later, I thought I heard footsteps.

Forty minutes later, I knew I was wrong, so I sat down on the cold concrete floor to analyze the situation. Being in solitary doesn't offer much scope for analysis. Basically, you're there and the world is somewhere else and that's how it stays unless the cops let you out or the French storm the Bastille. It dawned on me that the odds of both were about even.

But then I heard the shouts and chants of my brothers, and I came alive and cried, "Liberté, Egalité, Fraternité!"

An hour or so later—it was impossible to keep track of time because there were no windows in the cell or in the hallway connecting the other cells, so I couldn't even tell if it was day or night, but it must have been an hour or so at least—there was stark silence and I just cried because everyone was gone and I was still there and I was certain they had forgotten about me.

You Know How Adrenalin Is

I had to find something to do to help me keep my cool and also to keep my body active so my mind didn't get carried away with fear. First, I did 200 pushups. Straight. Then I did 200 sit-ups. I was so sore I could barely think, and I wanted it that way, because if I had thought I would have been scared. When I couldn't do another sit-up, I stood up and shouted every obscenity I could think of at the guards because I didn't know if the walls were bugged or not, but just in case they were, I wanted to show them that I was more angry than scared. Then I started walking around the cell. I paced 430 laps and my adrenalin was flowing and the only times I stopped were when I had to pee.

Well, you know how adrenalin is. The first five times, I peed in the little hole in the far corner of the cell, but it was already stuffed up with toilet paper from the last person to occupy the cell so the pee flooded the hole and dripped out around the edges. I felt dizzy from the odor, or from 430 laps around a tiny cell, or from both, and I thought I saw blood splattered on the wall. It looked like my blood. Oh shit, I thought. On the wall. Shit on the wall? And people don't

THUMBS UP

flush. What do people think handles are for? How do you say to someone, "Uh, excuse me, but, uh, are you gonna flush the toilet?" "It's none-a your goddam business if I flush the toilet." "Well, uh, yeah, okay, uh, I'm sorry if I hurt your feelings." "Well, fuck you." Oh, but there was no handle. Oh shit.

I shivered, like it was New Year's morning. I leaned over the hole because I thought I might throw up, but I held in the urge because the thought of puke combined with piss was criminal to my senses. It was criminal. Criminal.

The Wet, Yellow Y

Of course, I thought, though the revelation didn't dispel my nausea. No wonder there was no handle—a criminal could unscrew it and use it as a possible weapon.

But I'm no criminal. I haven't done anything wrong. Aren't I innocent until proven guilty? I'm an American! My father pays taxes! And he flushes! Why can't they buy automatic flushers for those who don't?

My mind proposed legislation for automatic flushers on all restroom pots. Sergeant Nostrel sat down on one and it registered. Then he leaned forward because he was nearsighted and he couldn't read the police report that was on the floor in front of him and the toilet flushed. Then he sat up and it registered again.

I burst out laughing when I thought of that, but when a wad of toilet paper burst out in flames and would not be consumed, I remembered where I was and I started screaming, "Why? Why?" And so the next time I had to pee, I peed right through the bars as far as I could send it, and I did it in the shape of a wet, yellow Y.

How do I describe what happened next? Did I have a vision? I don't know what else to call it unless I called it a dream, but I was awake when I had it. I mean, I don't claim to be a Jeane Dixon or anything but I saw a scene in my mind that left an imprint as clear as that of a hot iron brand on the ass of a stallion.

There I stood and before me was a yellow brick road leading to an intersection of one-way paths that veered off diagonally to the right and to the left. To the right was an ivy-colored building whose back door led to a smoothly paved concrete road that ran indefinitely through a barren forest. To the left was a road so wide it ceased to look like a road and appeared to me as a massive void. I didn't recognize it as being part of anything I had ever experienced. Straight ahead in the distance on the second road, tiny but visible, was a wonderful oasis, and then another void.

I didn't know what it all meant but I became scared and exhausted and fell asleep for the first time in solitary. Only the recognizable grunt of Sergeant Nostrel calling my name woke me.

"Still here, eh?" he laughed, as if he didn't know. He had gone off duty soon after locking me up by myself and he didn't tell anyone I was there.

"How do you like being a pinko now?" he asked.

"If I told you, I'd spoil it for you," I answered.

He pushed me and told me to move. Then he led me back to the cell I had left eighteen hours before. Arraignments had continued throughout the night. By the time I re-arrived, everyone else had been arraigned, except for one guy. I introduced myself.

Greeted Like a Hero

"So, you're Ken Wachsberger," he said. "We gave up on you long ago." His name was called then and I was left alone once more. Meanwhile, something remarkable had been happening all night.

THUMBS UP

As the bustees were released, they did not return to their homes and dorms. They stayed outside the courthouse in a show of solidarity, so every time someone was arraigned, the crowd size increased by one. In addition, the townsfolk heard about the bust, spent the night raising bail money, and then joined us at the courthouse. The crowd filled the plaza. By the time I was arraigned, word had spread that I had spent the night in solitary, the only one, it turned out, who didn't sign their fingerprints.

I was met with a huge applause and greeted like a hero.

That night, I got it on with the Sister from Strike Central. I was turned on to her by the way her hair hung down over her shoulders from under her headband, but that seemed like a pretty non-revolutionary reason to be turned on to somebody, but I didn't know how to approach her without appearing sexist.

I thought of hugging her as a comrade, but I didn't want her to think I was putting the moves on her. I thought of slapping her rear like the guys on the football team, but I didn't want her to think I was macho.

I finally just said to her that I appreciated her support of the bustees. She liked that I wasn't aggressive and said she wanted to sleep with me.

Later, at her apartment, when I tried to take her clothes off, she stiff-armed me and said she wanted to get to know me better before we had sex. Then she asked me what I thought about the Israeli government because she knew I was Jewish.
I couldn't figure out what that had to do with having sex, but I didn't want her to think I was treating her like a sex object, so I tried to answer her question. During my rap, I mentioned some pros and cons about erecting a bi-national state and was sure she saw through my Freudian slip.

She did. In fact, it turned her on and she attacked my body so fast she ripped the buttons off my flannel shirt.

I got nervous and came as soon as I was inside her. I was embarrassed and said, "Not much of a fuck, eh?"

"We didn't fuck; we related," she said, "and I'm satisfied."

This being non-sexist is real tricky, I thought, but I think I'm gonna like it.

The Ladder Wobbles

During the entire time we were on strike, I worked as manager and cashier at the Wonders basement snack shop, the Grill. Only one other student from Wonders was among the bustees, my friend, Davey Brinn, who I mentioned earlier, and he dropped out immediately, so I was the only bustee from the dorm who residents saw. As they came down the line to pay for their food, they grilled me with questions about the war and the strike. (So that's why they called it the Grill.) They exclaimed their reasons for not being able to support it. They challenged my convictions in order to justify theirs.

Either I could answer the question on the spot, or I would remember it so I could research it after shift and be ready the next time I heard it. In either case, I was forced to expand my understanding and my convictions intensified. I was beginning to believe that I could no longer remain in school. I had to enlist full time in the Movement.

But drop out of school! A degree was the next step up on my ladder to success. By dropping out, I would be getting down off the ladder. What would I do instead?

I thought about the pros and cons of both decisions throughout the summer. When September came, I decided to give school one last

THUMBS UP

chance. My folks were, on one hand, relieved. On the other hand, the war and my arrest had presented them with a new and unfamiliar paradigm. I was relieved that they trusted me. At least, I chose to believe they did.

CHAPTER 3
THE TRIAL OF THE MSU 132 AND I DROP OUT

At the time of the arrest in May, we had been charged with loitering and trespassing. However, in a countersuit filed by our own MSU 132 Board of Bustees in Grand Rapids District Court over the summer, we had gotten the judge to drop the loitering charge. The Trial of the MSU 132 to determine the fate of the remaining charge also began in September.

What Is Really Relevant?

The state had divided us into groups of eight or so to better manage the actual case. One group was chosen to go on trial. We all understood that if this group lost and was convicted, the state would then claim precedent and proceed to pick us apart one group at a time.

But if they won, charges for the rest of us would be dropped.

So, I took a natural interest in the proceedings. I attended every trial session. I participated in meetings with the MSU 132 Board of Bustees. I got high with fellow bustees and our topnotch attorneys from the Detroit Chapter of the National Lawyers Guild (NLG). I started hanging out off campus.

School became no longer—this was one of the superstar words of the period—"relevant." I knew I needed to drop out.

Ken Wachsberger

During the week before Thanksgiving vacation, a note appeared on our hall door leading out to the elevators. It was a reminder to all residents who were not returning for winter semester that they had to declare their intentions at the front office before they went home or it would be assumed that they were returning.

That became my deadline. I waited for the last minute as my arguments for staying in college evaporated.

I left the note with Mrs. Cooper, the kindly dorm receptionist, on my way out the door.

I Make It Official

I no longer remember how I announced my decision to drop out to my family. While many of my friends saw their families abandon them over their antiwar activities, I never had to justify my opposition to the war. For that I'm grateful. Politically, we all leaned left. We loved each other as family members.

I know Dad must have had strong feelings about my decision but I don't recall talking about them with him. He was a giving man, never too busy to lend a hand. If I wanted to play catch, he would bring together our Little League team, which he managed and sponsored, and we would have a team practice. But sharing feelings wasn't his strength. I didn't ask permission. I just stunned everybody with the announcement and he didn't challenge me.

In looking back at that period, I can't say for sure how I would have responded if he would have objected. I believe, though, that in his wisdom he knew any objection would have simply created a rift between us because I was totally committed to facing this new—can I say it?—career path.

THUMBS UP

Also, I'm convinced a part of him supported my move. Neither he nor my mom ever rejected me, and that's no light statement, and for that I have always been grateful. This was a period when parents and children were living in two worlds. Remember "the generation gap"? The war was part of it (along with drugs, music, clothing, long hair, and other standard features of the counterculture).

Whenever I hitchhiked into town to visit my family, I would stop in at The Oxford Shop, my dad's clothing store, and then join him and his fellow shopkeepers for lunch at Sand's Delicatessen. I was always greeted like a local hero and persuaded (okay, not hard to do) to regale them with my latest adventures. One time, I hitched into town with five women on our way to a women's march in DC. We spent the night, Mom fed us breakfast in the morning, Dad drove us to the freeway, and we continued to the march. My folks were loved by my friends, many of whom had been disowned by their parents.

But I'm getting way ahead of myself.

I don't recall specific conversations about my decision with my brothers but I'm sure they were baffled or intrigued by their brother's unsettling actions. I had shown passionate interest in sports while growing up. I knew all the statistics. Now, all I talked about was politics. I was ensnared by the events of the times, and my brothers missed it. I couldn't share what I was feeling with them. Or maybe I just didn't know how.

As a fraternity member from Purdue, Don knew how to be cool around girls. He taught me to always have a pack of matches with me in case I was trying to score with a smoking girl. I was secretly ecstatic when he drove me to Michigan State one year, and another time when I visited him in Columbus, Ohio, where his friends called me Little Wachsie. But he was five years older than me. He missed the counterculture. Still, he was politically liberal. I was convinced he didn't get what I was doing but I always believed he admired it.

Ken Wachsberger

Jeff missed the counterculture that was all around him at University of Michigan and instead evolved from the Moody Blues and *Bhagavad-Gita* to Scientology. Kudos to him for calling a family meeting and then putting himself on the hot seat to explain his attraction and answer our questions, but we still didn't get it. When I sent him a package of anti-Scientology articles and then learned that he had never received it, I came to believe that Scientology HQ was reading Jeff's mail from me, didn't like what I was saying, and might take it out on Jeff. I had no idea if I was right or not because the group is such a mystery but a divide grew between Jeff and me that remains. He had been my best friend growing up. Now we were distant and couldn't even speak the same language. We still call each other on our birthdays and at random other times, but the walks we used to take in Beachwood to discuss our deepest thoughts are memories.

Years later, Bob would drop out of college and credit me with giving him the courage. As he recalled about my decision: "It just sort of happened. I do remember it was shocking because nobody did that back then in our community. But I must thank you for paving the way." For a spell, he lived in Los Angeles where he edited scripts and found TV and movie walk-on parts, most notably in *Frankenstein: The College Years*. Today, he is a practitioner of alternative healing. I imagined that he got what I was doing when I dropped out but he was my little brother, still in high school at the time. I don't recall having an adult conversation with him about my decision.

One person who did challenge me was the mayor of Beachwood, who lived across the street and four houses down. He took me out to dinner to convince me to remain in school and "work within the system." He tried to get me to endorse the young handsome liberal who he was promoting as the future of the Democratic Party; I tried to get him to renounce capitalism and join the Socialist Labor Party.

THUMBS UP

I heard for the first time a mother tell her children: "Don't you dare be like Ken!"

After the Thanksgiving break, I returned to Wonders for the last time as a resident, passed my final exams, and left college, thirty-four credits short of graduation. Call it karma but thirty-four is my lucky number.

I handed my Smith-Corona typewriter to my parents when I got home from East Lansing. "Here, I won't be needing this anymore," I said.

PART 2: THE YIPPIES, THE ZIPPIES, AND THE UNDERGROUND PRESS

CHAPTER 4
I JOIN THE UNDERGROUND PRESS

After dropping out at the end of fall semester 1970, I moved in with Davey, who lived with three others and a small dog in the upstairs of a house behind the neighborhood bar. Davey's job was to guard the parking lot that was owned by our landlord, who paid Davey with free rent. Davey and I, fellow bustees, became inseparable as best friends.

As a non-student back in my college town, I was in a new psychic zone. Exhilaration is a feeling that comes to mind. Freed from the requirement to read boring books for classes that meant nothing to me, I was able to browse the bookshelves of my new community of political friends and select books that piqued my curiosity. Poetry, history, philosophy, fiction, religion: No topic didn't fit my new major. I was introduced to Jack Kerouac and the Beat authors, Alan Watts and Zen, Leonard Cohen, Rachel Carson, the Black Panthers, Dee Brown, John Steinbeck, and other literary legends.

I read one hundred books during that first year of freedom. Exactly. I kept a list of titles. For the first time in my twenty years since birth, my life had a purpose: to end the war, and, while I was at it, to eliminate racism, sexism, age-ism, and all the other ills that plagued society. I had to learn about them.

Money Problems from the Start

I was introduced to the East Lansing underground press in October when I accompanied Davey to a meeting of *Generation,* one of two campus- and East Lansing-based underground papers. Davey was a member of the staff.

I was in awe of Davey and the other staff members. To me, they were political heavies, experts on all the issues that mattered, like the war, gender and ethnic studies, the environment, organic gardening, rock and roll, and the cost and quality of available drugs. I previewed Davey's article on the state of the Movement.

I was welcomed onto the staff and began attending meetings. The other staff members, like me, were searching for their answers. Many had been influenced by Kent State and the strike. Almost all were dropouts. Staffers who did not get high were the exception but I don't recall anyone being ostracized for being "straight." We were all committed fully to the Movement. Working on the paper was our contribution though many staffers belonged to other community groups as well. The articles they contributed were reports from their groups.

I especially admired Nelson Brown, meeting host, who, as co-founder of both *Generation* and *Swill & Squeal* before it, was naturally seen by me as the leader of the group. He sported a full beard, smoked a pipe, and was easily as brilliant as that stereotype would lead you to believe. When he asked you a question, you dug deep for the answer. He became a mentor.

The hot issue around that time was finances. Michigan State claimed forty thousand enrollees but the radical community was pretty modest. Supporting one underground paper was a challenge. Supporting two papers that covered the same basic topics and appealed to the same audience didn't make practical or political sense.

Where *Generation* favored off-campus news, the articles in *Bogue Street Bridge* were predominantly campus-based—that was the primary difference between the two papers. Both displayed a high countercultural awareness and a sensitivity to the sexual liberation movements. Both provided alternative news coverage to that of the Establishment press. Both served as forums for communication and debate among people concerned with change.

Also, unfortunately, both understood the publishing limitations of a newspaper that had no funds.

An Experimental Joint Issue

So, the decision was made to combine staffs and equipment and publish an experimental "joint issue." The first *Joint Issue* came out October 17, 1970. The cover showed the *Generation* and *Bogue Street Bridge* mastheads facing each other from opposite ends of the front page. Between the two was a hand holding a joint and the name, *Joint Issue*. On the inside cover, the *Joint Issue* logo, including the Zig Zag man and the words "Qualite Superieure," appeared for the first time.

Nelson noted the emergence of two trends. "A cultural understanding was beginning to develop on the paper which I think came to fruition in *Joint Issue* in terms of lifestyle questions. Issues such as women's liberation and gay liberation were starting to creep into the paper. At the same time, the paper was becoming more focused towards local politics. Some of us who had been in the East Lansing area for a while were becoming aware of our own community, the student ghetto."

Two more *Joint Issues* were printed by the middle of November, and then financial hassles once again forced the East Lansing underground to stop their presses.

Another Merger

In February 1971, *Joint Issue* merged with *Red Apple News*, the first Lansing-area underground paper, which had been co-founded in Fall

Ken Wachsberger

1970 by Wendy Cahill, Ted Prato, and Don Gaudard, and was now facing similar financial difficulties. Rather than go through another name change, attendees from both papers voted to keep the name *Joint Issue*. To clarify the transition for the community, they agreed that the *Red Apple News* logo—a red apple housing a gun-toting, fist-waving worm—would be incorporated on the masthead for the first two combined issues.

Red Apple News brought with it a much stronger orientation to women's liberation and gay liberation than was present in *Joint Issue*. This was at least the outward reason for much of the staff dissension. Much of the friction was the result of a rivalry between certain members of *Red Apple News* and the old *Generation* that would exist as long as any of them were still on the paper. I was an outsider to the dissension, didn't understand it, and found friendships based primarily on others' commitment to the paper's success and to the Movement.

With this second merger, *Joint Issue* was now no longer solely an East Lansing paper. Still young and innocent, with a circulation of only 3,000, the paper had begun to make inroads into the Lansing community, including the high schools and Lansing Community College. In helping to build a new countercultural community, regular features such as Seeds of Change tried to create an awareness of alternative institutions, like food co-ops and bicycle co-ops, that were in the area. At the same time, to protect this new rebellious community, descriptions and pictures of local narcs were printed at every opportunity.

A Dishwashing Legend Is Born

I began my career as a dishwasher soon after I joined the paper when I started working at Cave of the Candles, East Lansing's upscale basement night club where you went if you wanted a good lobster. The job came to me thanks to an endorsement from Nelson, who already was a dishwasher there.

THUMBS UP

My mother would lament about her college dropout son, "My son, the dishwasher." Years later, when I married Emily, who was a self-taught chef, we started Emken Baking and Catering and ran it successfully for twenty-three years. As I write these words, my son, David, is an executive chef in Palm Desert, California. My daughter, Carrie, is a specialist in gluten- and corn-free baking.

While the underground press staffed the dish room of the Cave, the waitpeople and busboys were drawn from the ranks of the Street Corner Society, East Lansing's best-known guerrilla theatre group. They included my friend, busboy Phil Heald, who is today known as actor Anthony Heald.

One of our job perks as dishwashers at the Cave was unlimited drinks from the bar. My go-to drinks during those days were the Black Russian, a two-ingredient cocktail made from vodka and coffee liqueur; and its offspring, the White Russian, which adds cream to the base.

While Nelson shared the dish room with me, we discussed politics and the hidden meaning of rock and roll lyrics on slow nights. Was "Horse with No Name" really about heroin?

Nelson's successor had no political consciousness but he was a partyer. On busy nights, we would drink throughout the night as if the bar was in the dish room; and then sweat away the alcohol and leave in the evening as if we hadn't drunk at all.

On slow nights, when I barely cracked a sweat, I staggered up the back entrance stair and hitchhiked home.

Regardless of my partner, I loved the job. It satisfied my anal-retentive tendencies, it was no match for my ADHD even when business was at peak activity, and it gave me enough money to pay my bills while I was devoting full time to *Joint Issue* and the Movement.

CHAPTER 5
BUSTED WITH DAVEY
AT MAY DAY 1971

Davey and I attended the May Day 1971 demonstrations in DC, where three days of antiwar organizing and civil disobedience led to 12,000 arrests, including 5,000 in front of the Justice Department. None of the protestors carried guns, to the best of my knowledge.

The goal, as stated by antiwar strategists, was to shut down the government to protest our continued involvement in Southeast Asia.

Saturday May 1: Setting Up Camp

We attended as part of an affinity group consisting of thirteen friends and acquaintances from East Lansing who went to DC determined to play our part.

The concept of affinity groups was new to me but I embraced it for its success in preserving safety and unity within the group. In the extreme likelihood that the police would try to create mayhem with teargas, every affinity group had its own code name that every member would scream out amidst the teargas clouds until all members had reconnected with each other and they could disperse in an organized fashion. Our favorite song at the time was Merle Haggard's "Okie from Muskogee," so we became the Okies.

Ken Wachsberger

Saturday May 1, we joined 40,000 protestors coming into the nation's capital from out of town for two reasons: to camp in West Potomac Park near the Potomac River by night; and to shut down the government by day. The event slogan was "If the government won't stop the war, we'll stop the government."

Live music played in the background: the Beach Boys, JB, Linda Ronstadt, the Band, and other headliners.

Camps were organized by state so local meetings and rap sessions could be easily organized. We Okies found the Michigan section, set up our tents, and joined a group of Michiganders passing a joint around a campfire.

All was peaceful.

Sunday Morning: Chased from the Camp

We were awakened Sunday morning at 6:30 to a bullhorn's angry command: "ATTENTION, ATTENTION: YOUR PERMIT FOR CAMPING HAS BEEN REVOKED. EVERYONE MUST LEAVE THE CAMPING AREA."

The command had a familiar ring. Oh, yeah, MSU Student Union one May past. I wasn't scared at all, but I can't say I was brave either. Adrenalin was my armor. I looked for direction from others with more experience.

In no time, the grounds were filled with activity. but it was in the form of meetings. Helicopters circling the area probably couldn't believe that instead of just dispersing we were meeting. When we finally left—except some fifty who hung around to get busted—we reconvened by state at various places in Georgetown University and American University.

THUMBS UP

The tactic was a big mistake by the government, who counted on victory through mayhem and instead forced us to become familiar with the streets we would tomorrow be trashing. At the same time, the police could no longer guard us as a group because we were spread out throughout the city. I don't remember the details of the meetings we attended or how many we attended but they deepened our sense of solidarity and determination.

Throughout the day, the thirteen of us kept together, and we had some good luck that evening. We found shelter and food from the mother of a group member, who was a resident of DC.

Monday: Hit and Run in the Streets

The Michigan contingent was part of the Georgetown group. On Monday, we did hit and run throughout the day but always in that general neighborhood. Our group plan was to resist arrest, hit and run-style. This meant we couldn't just sit in the streets and be arrested. Instead, we would throw a trash can into the street and run. Push a car into the middle of the street, lock it, and run. Break glass in the street and run.

Meanwhile, this same tactic was being employed by affinity groups from other states at strategic points throughout the city.

Later, I would hear criticisms of the action because we were causing a waste of taxpayer dollars. We justified the symbolic damage we were causing by calling attention to the real damage the United States was causing to citizens of Vietnam, with our tax dollars. I found the argument compelling and still find justification in it. We were crazy but we had to be to change the paradigm.

Police reactions ranged from just chasing to serious head-beating. Many of us were beaten and let go, and even still seven thousand were busted. Radicals who were stuffed into RFK Stadium organized themselves by state. But no Okies were among those busted.

Judges were furious that they were going to have to work round the clock for at least a week just to get everyone out.

The mostly Black local residents, likely exhilarated to see the police going after white kids, opened their doors to us so we could escape the teargas fumes and clear our throats with glasses of fresh water.

That evening, the government claimed victory because government employees had made it to work. We claimed victory because the employees had been ordered to arrive at 5 a.m.; and no work got done anyhow because the employees spent all day looking out their windows.

Tuesday: Davey and I Prepare for the Inevitable

Tuesday's activities called for street tactics and confrontations with police, similar to those that took place Monday. Slight differences, of course, were expected based on what both sides had experienced and learned from that first day.

We were at one major disadvantage: Seven thousand of us had been busted Monday. Others had probably been scared away by the tear gas and the swinging billy clubs. How many of us would be out there on the streets for a second day of the same was the question of the morning.

Within our own affinity group, eleven people remained: three had returned to East Lansing and one had joined us. Other than Davey, I now no longer remember their names but I recorded their initials. Please say hello to t, p, k, j, m, j, d, c, p, d, and myself.

We began the day with good offensive energy. Word was getting out throughout the protestor community that there would be a rally at

THUMBS UP

14th-J at 11 and then a march to the Justice Department for a noon rally in the courtyard that Attorney General John Mitchell and his staff members could not avoid.

Members of our group had mixed feelings because no march permit had been obtained and busts were inevitable. p, c, and t decided to stay back, while the rest of us psyched ourselves for another confrontation with the police.

But rumors also were spreading that protestors were getting picked up right off the sidewalks. We were advised that walking in pairs was the safest way to travel, so we walked in pairs. I walked with Davey.

During our walk, we prepared ourselves for what we predicted would happen. Davey said, "If they try to bust us, I'm not gonna fight it." I said "Farout!" because there was no greater affirmation in 1971. We made a pact that if one of us got busted, the other would get busted, too. We sealed our brotherhood.

One speaker caught my attention at the pre-march rally when he pointed out that news reports pointing out what we failed to do this second day, close down the city, were an admission of what we succeeded in doing the first day.

That's all I remember about that rally but I remember the march to the Justice Department, with several thousand people, as having significance because it was a courageous act in the face of likely arrest.

Busted with Davey in John Mitchell's Courtyard

At the Justice Department, ten thousand of us sat on the street and waited for the program to begin.

Newsweek memorialized the moment for me.

Ken Wachsberger

I never saw a program lineup so I don't know most of the speakers' names but their backgrounds and topics checked all the relevant boxes. They spoke passionately and hung their arguments around or connected them to the war. John Froines, one of the lesser known of the Chicago 7 but one of the most active organizers of the May Day activities, spoke and was later busted inside the crowd by six undercover cops just before the mass busts began.

And then came the mass busts.

Over the mic came the orders: "EVERYONE MUST LEAVE THE AREA IMMEDIATELY."

We appreciated the warning but it lacked sincerity. With walls on two sides of us and police on the other two—a couple thousand per side, I estimated—we had no chance to escape. p, d, and j found that out when they tried to leave and the cops wouldn't let anyone out. They rejoined k, j, Davey, and me, all of us having decided to be arrested peacefully.

One by one, that's what happened, except for a handful of protesters who tried to resist. As the police marched toward the crowd, we moved close together, joined hands, and waited. It became a ritual: A cop would walk up to a protester who would then get up and walk to the bus with him. When Davey got busted, I stood up to make sure I was next.

Not All Cops Are Pigs

I had the good fortune to learn that "not all cops are pigs." They weren't the enemies. They did, however, represent the enemy, which is why I tried to talk with them and establish whatever rapport I could.

I was lucky enough to be busted by a Black cop from DC who had been on the force for two years. When I asked him what he thought of the mass arrests, he answered, "It's all bullshit." He was crying. He tried his best to get me onto the same bus as Davey but, when he was

THUMBS UP

given the arrest form to fill out, he was also given the name of another officer, so I had to get onto the appropriate bus.

Also, he wrote down my name as "John Smith." Can you believe a cop did all that for me? I told him I wanted my correct name on it—I had committed myself to the cause and I wasn't concerned with faking it. We shook hands three times before I got on the bus.

Do you remember how a year ago at the Union, I was the first one busted, the only one thrown in solitary, and the last one released? This time, I was the last one to climb into the first bus to drive away, the first one out because I was closest to the door, and the first one thrown in the clink. I noted the similarity as it was happening but was too caught up in the event to dwell on comparisons.

Jail in DC

Official arrest time, according to the arrest form, was 2:50 p.m. Twenty-five minutes later, I entered an empty cell #2 at the U.S. District Court cell block.

The absence of any large items in the cell made the small appear distinctly. A roach in the middle of the floor called out to me. I scooped it up and put it in my shirt pocket.

Physically, I guessed the dimensions of the cell were 40 x 21. Two benches built into the walls extended lengthwise from the front almost to the back; in the rear on the left side were a toilet and a sink. For ten people, these amenities would have been sufficient. By the time the guard closed the door behind the last person, we could barely see the floor. Someone said the number was 106.

A handful of my cell mates were juveniles but, for the most part, they were college-age, with probably as many being dropouts as students. The vast majority were longhairs; only a few were Black.

Ken Wachsberger

I Share My Roach

I shared my roach with a high school dropout and the only two men who were no longer student-aged, a priest and a reporter.

Bruce R was one of the juveniles. At sixteen years of age, he was a high school dropout with a record that consisted of two counts of auto theft, two counts of possession, and one charge of breaking and entering and grand larceny (the haul was rifles). He was living at present with, as he said, "a man, three guys, and four gals." They sold dope that they got straight from the mafia. As he put it, "I've just got too many connections for a guy 16." His full red beard made it hard to believe his age, but his driver's license convinced me. He wasn't really politically minded, but he was definitely against the war: His brother had recently died in Vietnam.

The second person was a Catholic priest from Mobile, Alabama. Although still a priest in good standing, he had done nothing to gain the church's good favor when he opposed the pope's ruling on birth control and then asked his bishop to resign. He drove to DC in the VW bus where he lived with a nun, at the bishop's nonawareness. They traveled the country taking part in demonstrations and living on $100 a month. Next year, he said, he planned to organize a group of people to travel the country and campaign for Senator McGovern in the primaries. He asked me if I was interested but I couldn't see it.

John Mathews was the third person. As a reporter for the *Washington Evening Star*, he was surprised to find himself all of a sudden behind bars for the first time in his life. He took advantage of the journalistic mantra that nothing can be too bad if you can get a good story out of it and used the time to interview me, as a representative of the youth generation. I explained the dynamic struggle between the Life Culture and the Death Culture as I saw it for an article that appeared in the *Star* the next week.

THUMBS UP

He was arraigned after only twenty hours thanks to his irate boss. On his way out, he took down the number where I was staying in DC and gave me his. I didn't give it any thought after that.

The Extended Drum Solo

I spent time in three different cells, all equally crowded. The limited circulation of air meant less fresh air still available for each breath. Increasing levels of litter and dirt made free space even harder to find. People slept on filthy floors that didn't get swept until we had been locked up over thirty hours.

After six hours in the first cell, I began to feel dizzy. but I was too hyped up from the events of the day to notice. The lack of food didn't bother me. More discomforting were the lack of physical space and shortage of fresh air. I nearly passed out while waiting to be printed and photographed.

In the second cell, my brain was hosting an extended drum solo.

I felt better leaving the cell to be processed but, by the time I left the next cell, dynamite was being exploded in my head and my stomach felt like the ocean at high tide.

At least, I thought this time, I was on my way out. I was wrong. Instead, I was led to another cell, slightly smaller now but with about the same amount of people.

The Life Culture and the Death Culture

I was seeing the world in those days as a polarity between the Life Culture and the Death Culture, or the radical and the liberal, with the two possessing, respectively, the best characteristics of the culture we were trying to create and the worst characteristics of the culture we were trying to replace. Washington, Death Culture, was the karmic bonus to that analogy.

Ken Wachsberger

I interpreted the crowded conditions, subpar food, and police harassment as a psychological battle between the Life Culture and the Death Culture, with the former winning, naturally.

> our long captivity brought out many differences between the two lifestyles. the death culture, to begin, is an "every man for himself/every woman for herself" culture. sandwiches given to hungry people would naturally cause a "me first" battle among them; shortages of physical space would naturally cause people to fight for whatever they could get; long stays in such overall shitty situations would naturally cause people to turn on each other.
>
> but such was not the case. if there wasn't enough food to go around, whatever there was was shared. with cigarettes, it was a matter of taking a hit and passing it on, as was also true when drinking water out of the flask someone brought in. sharing was a reflex action; no one thought of hogging.

To keep our spirits up, we chanted, we rapped, we slept. Squabbles were kept to a minimum.

The Food Strike

I didn't sleep at all during my whole time as a prisoner. My ADHD mind was absorbing details from all corners of the cell and I didn't want to miss any of them. I didn't see myself as a leader. The ethos in some parts of the Movement that I inhabited was that we were all leaders; we're all in this together. I only wanted to help keep our collective spirits high. When we were chanting, that was easy. But when someone would crack up, tension found its way into the room. That happened one time.

Wednesday morning, 8:00 a.m., we had just lived through another bologna sandwich with rancid mayonnaise meal. One Brother,

THUMBS UP

a white guy with long straight hair parted in the middle, had been complaining to me about the conditions. I turned around for a minute and, when I looked back, he was hanging onto the bars yelling at an officer about our rights being denied. The officer listened calmly as he raged on. Where we had just been patriotically chanting, we suddenly became quiet.

So, I took the floor and got everyone's attention (except the Brother and whoever was sleeping). Why me? I don't know. No one else did anything at that moment and it needed to be done. I said:

> People, we can't let this happen. This is just what the pigs want. They know we're in lousy conditions, that we're uncomfortable, we're tired, we're hungry. They want nothing more than for us to crack up and turn on each other. and this is what we can't do. We have to keep our spirits high.
>
> To speak of rights is ludicrous. Did any of you actually believe that we could come to DC with the intention of shutting down the government and then be treated as guests in the prisons of that same government? The fact that we have paper rights means nothing—those only serve to influence our cases in court; and our cases are gonna all be thrown out anyhow. So, they don't have to give us anything.
>
> We were all cool until this one dude cracked up and then it all changed. We know that the pigs will continue to hassle us so that we'll all give up and never demonstrate again. This can't be allowed to happen. We have to stick together.

Then I suggested a food strike. At noon, when the guards came around with the bologna sandwiches, we started shouting, "No food! No food!" The other cells spontaneously joined in and the guards walked away.

They came back later with oranges and bananas. The strike was successful in that it brought us better food but also it gave us a cause to rally around.

As for the Brother who cracked up, I talked to him and was able to calm him down by giving him an extended rap similar to the one I gave the group.

I Am Arraigned

At 5:30 a.m. Thursday, fifty prisoners got on a thirty-six-person bus that took us to Federal Court. We were brought to a room and locked up with about eighty other people, all waiting for a lawyer to take them in front of the judge. I filled out the appropriate form and then psyched myself for another long wait. Shortly after, my name was called.

I appeared with ten other bustees in front of Judge Daly. Let me briefly introduce him. As our lawyer warned, "Don't expect any breaks from him. He's probably the toughest of all the judges. Our strategy will be to just try to stall him long enough so that he'll eventually leave and we can get an easier judge." We had all been confidently expecting $10 collateral. What a bummer it was to hear the revised edition.

Sure enough, we got what he had told us to expect. Unless you could get someone to take third-party custody or personal recognizance, he released us only on $250 bond.

But I fared relatively well. When we stopped to visit my parents on the way to DC, Dad had brought up the name of a former neighbor, h, who now lived in DC. He had said it jokingly and I took it in the same spirit. Now, I was busted in DC and h, who I didn't know at all, was who I knew best in DC. I gave the police his name and he came down to take third-party custody. Then he said to the judge, "I have some friends from Ken's hometown who are here now at a psychiatrists' convention. They're leaving tomorrow. If I promise to get Ken a ride home with them, will you let him off?"

THUMBS UP

Well, the judge didn't act quite so reasonably but, in a rare mercy case, he released me on $50 collateral.

What that meant was, if I didn't show up in court, I would forfeit the fifty bucks, but they wouldn't come looking for me. If I did show up, and we won the case, I would get it back. If I showed up and we lost, I would take whatever punishment they dished out.

Knowing that

> - the cases would all be thrown out because there were so many, or
> - they would be thrown out because of technicalities (like the fact that our rights were denied, or we weren't given phone calls, or the conditions were shitty), or
> - the cases would just be postponed indefinitely and finally dropped, or
> - we would take it to court and win,

I made the decision to stick around to see what would happen. My trial was set for Monday. What I planned to do, if the trial took place at all, was watch the ones before mine. If their charges were dropped, mine would be also and my money would be returned. If they were sentenced, I wouldn't show up and I would just forfeit my collateral.

Reunited with My People

At the arraignment, I was reunited with my people. Out of our whole affinity group, I was the only one who hadn't been given a phone call, so I was the only one they hadn't been able to locate.

Davey walked into the courtroom around 6:00 a.m., as I was still waiting to be arraigned. He had been in the courthouse all night trying to find out what was going on with p and k, who were together, and me—we were the only ones who hadn't yet been released. At the house, I was reunited with the others.

Of those of us who were arrested, I was the only one who had to stick around: p was given $20 or two days plus credit for the two days she had already served; k was given a court date in June and released under her own personal recognizance; the others paid $10 collateral. Having no reason to stick around, they all left town that afternoon.

Left Alone in DC

So, what happened to me?

Let's get back to John Mathews. I noted that he took my number and gave me his. When I got to the house, I found a message for me saying that John had called and that I should call back. He had calmly wondered when I got out and couldn't believe I had only been released in the last hour. When he heard that my trial was Monday, he welcomed me to stay with him, and I did.

John, his wife, Roberta, and their daughter, Susan, treated me like an honored guest. When John introduced me to friends, he called me his token freak. I wasn't looking for validation for what we had done, but it was clear to me that some parts of the public were on board with us.

Limbo Forever

On Monday May 10, I appeared with seventy-six other protesters before Superior Court Judge Hamilton. Most had been busted Tuesday, but several had been busted Monday and the week before. One by one, we were called up, each with no lawyer, each getting one when we got up.

I really believed the cases would be dropped, but the prosecutor tried. Six cases were dismissed outright and several were rescheduled.

THUMBS UP

After a brief break, the cases continued. I and about five others still hadn't been called when, at 3:45 p.m., one of our lawyers told us that the judge was accepting *nolo contendre* pleas, meaning that we didn't plead innocent or guilty. The fine, however, would be $10. Most defendants said they were going to take that, so he went to tell the judge, a Black liberal.

He returned with a possible deal: Under section 5010a of the Federal Youth Correction Act, anyone under 27 could get the following:

- credit for time served
- no fine
- 90-day unsupervised probation

The charge was disorderly conduct.

This offer was even better than the first.

But then the group was split up. Some of us went down to room 12 to appear before Judge Halleck. Here, the terms changed slightly:

- We still would get credit.
- There still would be no fine.
- There would be no probation.

Rather than a guilty plea being entered, we would plead neither "guilty" nor "innocent." Each case would just kind of stay in limbo forever.

"Evolution, not Revolution"

This was the best offer yet, but the good judge was really pissed at Attorney General Mitchell and President Nixon for making these mass arrests and then dumping them on the courts and he wanted to make it known. In an impromptu speech, he said in no way could the prosecutor ever adequately try more than five cases. To do so would take "forever and two weeks." He even got the prosecutor to admit it. He continued: "I believe in evolution, not revolution. I believe in this system and it's essential that we can prove that the law can apply equally to all." He referred to the necessity of being able to show us that we could get a "fair shake." Over and over, he said he was "troubled."

His speech, with which we all concurred, convinced us that we should try to get innocents rather than *nolos*, and feel confident in winning. "Remember," he warned the prosecutor, "you have to be able to prove within a reasonable doubt that each one of these people committed the alleged crime."

The prosecutor was freaked. As each defendant came up, he either dropped charges or tried to win the case. With those he tried to win, either he ended up dropping charges or the judge dismissed the case.

I got a *nol pros*, which meant the prosecutor decided to not prosecute. At 6:00 p.m., I appeared and won. It was a pleasure to pick up my $50.

Three spring issues of *Joint Issue* provided extensive coverage of the May Day demonstrations.

CHAPTER 6
JOINT ISSUE BECOMES FREE

And then came summer.

Initial Plan Bombs

Based on enthusiasm of the previous spring, the projected business plan for *Generation* at the beginning of fall semester was to appear on the streets every two weeks supported by subscription sales. Unfortunately, enthusiasm had peaked in the strike; few subscriptions were sold. For money, we had to sell ads and hawk papers on the street for fifteen cents apiece. We printed about 3,000 copies of each issue and sold about half of them.

We would go to press with a new issue when we made enough back from the previous issue to make the financial loss bearable. Then we would print another issue. This model carried over to the first *Joint Issues* and through the merger with *Red Apple News*. The trouble was, it took us a month to sell enough papers to print the next issue.

We raised the price to twenty cents, figuring we wouldn't pick up new readers by raising the price, but we wouldn't lose readers either so we'd net five extra cents on every sale. We applied the same reasoning when we raised the price to a quarter.

I enjoyed going out to sell papers with Nelson even in the middle of winter; he treated me as an intellectual equal and he analyzed every situation with facts and examples. But I hated selling papers. It was a waste of time we could be using for organizing or writing.

Roped into My Own Plan

I had an idea. I introduced it at the last meeting before summer vacation. Many staffers were leaving town. We had already resolved to begin publishing again in the fall but questioned whether or not there would be energy to do a summer issue.

I raised my hand passively; I didn't usually speak; in my mind, I was always the new kid, not as together as the others. Nelson acknowledged me.

I said, "If we raised our ad prices and sold enough ads, we could increase our circulation to 10,000 and give the paper away for free. If we raised our circulation to 10,000 and came out free, we would have an easier time getting ads. Then, once we got the ads, we'd be able to pay for the paper so that we could afford to come out free."

The idea was inspired. I anticipated a glorious reception from the heavies, who would naturally take leadership of the idea. An ad sales campaign would form organically.

Instead, my memory is of the entire staff speaking in unison in my direction, saying, "Well, sell the ads!" In reality, it might have just been Nelson offering his immediate endorsement and the others quietly agreeing but I was intimidated to compliance.

New Ad Campaign Works!

I couldn't say no. The ad campaign began the next day.

By the end of six weeks, we had sold $300 worth of ads. The printing cost for 10,000 copies of a 16-page black and white issue was $305.

THUMBS UP

For the first time in the paper's history, we lost only pocket change. We considered that a profit.

The first free *Joint Issue* hit the streets on July 14, 1971. Advertisers saw it as a good business investment.

Fall semester, for the first time ever, we were able to create a regular bi-weekly schedule to print 10,000 copies each of six issues based on advance ad sales. To the best of my knowledge, *Joint Issue* was the first underground paper in the country to come out free on a regular bi-weekly basis supported by ad sales. Underground papers in Columbus, Ohio (*Free Press*), and Madison, Wisconsin (*Free For All*), soon followed suit, directly influenced by *Joint Issue*'s success.

I was now a political heavy because I was a dynamic ad salesperson. I never felt like a newcomer again.

Controversy, Principles, and Responsibility

But selling ads created its own controversy. As I noted in *Voices from the Underground*,

> The revolutionary raps we had at that time centered around the possible hypocrisy of selling ads to capitalist businesses for a newspaper that advocated the overthrow of capitalism. Hard-line critics said it was liberal to accept any ads at all. We took their opinion seriously because, God forbid, the worst insult was to be called a liberal. In the end, however, we decided it was more revolutionary to provide a free community service by accepting ads than to be purists and be forced to fold.

But we had principles. We took ads from bookstores, restaurants, the leather craft store, the head shops, a futon store, record shops, a shoe store, some of the progressive student groups on campus, and assorted small businesses. But we avoided institutions that we saw as being counter-revolutionary beyond the level of acceptance, such as banks, insurance companies, Jacobson's department stores, and barber shops.

> With the advent of the free paper, mere survival passed on as the crucial issue. With a newfound freedom to sit back and analyze our place in the community, the staff rose to a new level of awareness and realized that we weren't just a rag anymore. We were now coming out regularly, and we were reaching so many thousands of readers that we had a—gasp—responsibility to be credible. That meant cleaning up the rhetoric and dealing with our own hypocrisies.

Yes, it came as a surprise, but not everyone knew we lived in "Amerikkka." Some people were even offended by our use of the term "Pig." Still, they read *Joint Issue* because they saw it as some kind of alternative to which they could relate.

To certain people, *Joint Issue* attained a position of extreme importance. High school students, growing up in isolated communities, far from the excitement of the campus area, but experiencing similar changes in their values, could see this professional-looking paper that was expressing the same thoughts they were thinking and they could gain more confidence that they weren't alone.

For scores of prisoners who began receiving *Joint Issue* for free in the mail, it became their connection to the outside world. Certain countercultural merchants were so behind the paper, they advertised just to be a part of it. Young factory workers at last had found a paper that was aware of and sensitive to the alienation that they felt from their jobs.

Whoever we were, we had questions—there was definitely a new consciousness in the air. We all were finding new ways to relate to our government (negatively, skeptically) and new ways to relate to

THUMBS UP

each other (positively, intimately). We were searching for new ways of living together that weren't defined by oppressive sets of institutions, such as the nuclear family, the hierarchy of the university, and the military.

Real men, we had been taught, had to be tough, competitive, power hungry. We had to dominate women, hate gays, never admit to being wrong. And for god's sake, don't express feelings or seek help. If you can't get your way, killing is acceptable. With my fellow Brothers, we looked for ways to shed those negative traits that kept us trapped in our male roles.

Today, we call it toxic masculinity. The religious right embraces it as their children murder schoolchildren, blow up religious institutions, and find the solution to every problem in weaker gun laws.

Special issues devoted centerfolds to discussing particular countercultural values and concerns that are common today but that were still new back then, such as prisons, heroin, communal living, gays, birth control, women's self-help, and organic gardening. Volume III, number 4 (February 21-March 4, 1972) featured, in addition to an ecology special, the first community handbook, which was a directory of the countercultural/New Left institutions in town.

CHAPTER 7
I HIT THE ROAD TO MADISON

The Movement years brought me a personal benefit that my best positive vision could not have fantasized. I discovered that I was popular with feminist women because I was cute, smart, funny, and kind, had bedroom eyes, and, most of all, they loved sensitive men and they saw me as sensitive.

I had been insecure around women all my life. I had been body shamed because I was short and I interpreted that to mean I was unlovable. I wasn't aggressive with women because I always believed I would be ultimately rejected. Feminist women saw that as sensitivity. I see that now as Zen.

It wasn't unusual for me to wake up on a friend's couch after a pot party with a liberated woman who I considered way above my pay grade who had been turned on by my sensitivity.

It Began with a Woman

But whenever I broke up with a woman, or, more likely, a woman broke up with me, I would become depressed. My body had to move and I had to follow it wherever it took me. In those days, when I was depressed, I hit the road. These were my hitchhiking years. Anywhere I went, in town or cross country throughout the seventies, I hitchhiked. Jack Kerouac was my role model. When I learned that the first time I ever hitchhiked was in the year he died, 1969, I believed it was *b'shert*, meant to be, and that I was carrying on his tradition for the next generation.

Years later, when I became my family genealogist, I learned that my grandfather immigrated to Baltimore at age eight with his father, moved to Cleveland where family members had already settled, left his father and abusive stepmother when he was fourteen, and never looked back. Dad was a journalist at Miami University; one summer he hitchhiked around Ohio sending articles back from every campus. So, when I hit the road, I was proudly carrying on a family tradition.

In May of 1972, I broke up with a woman in Lansing, fell into my "woe is me" state of mind, confronted my depression by hitchhiking into Madison, Wisconsin, to visit a friend, discovered the students had gone home for the summer, and was left not knowing anyone else in town.

I Meet the Yippies

The Madison community, I discovered, had a reputation for being the most radical in the Midwest. In addition, their Youth International Party (Yippie) chapter was the most active in the country outside of New York, where Yippie was born.

Thanks to the local counterculture's Crash Pad File of volunteer hosts, I found a place to crash with Michael Chance, a writer on Madison's underground newspaper, *TakeOver,* who was also active with Madison YIP (Youth International Party).

The Yippies, who four years before had become media myths in the minds of young Americans, were now embroiled in a bitter feud among leaders. The primary cause of the feud was disagreement with the amount of proceeds owed by Yippie co-founder Abbie Hoffman to Tom Forcade for sales of Abbie's *Steal This Book.*

THUMBS UP

Tom Forcade and the Zippies

Tom Forcade was the mysterious, unsung publisher of Underground Press Syndicate, the first nationwide network of underground papers from the Vietnam era, of which *Joint Issue* was a member. He was the first underground press editor to obtain press credentials. He was a major drug dealer and founder of *High Time*s magazine.

According to people who knew him, he was a genius but totally nuts. He was funny but vicious. A lunatic and a visionary. Narcissist and romantic. Crazy, irrational, and self-contradictory. "A dark cloud." And paranoid.

But he was a force of nature. He was someone who always knew he was going to play a major role in history and wanted to dress the part. I knew him for his two dress outfits: his solid black suit with black wide-brimmed hat and black shoes and socks; and his solid white suit with white wide-brimmed hat and white shoes and socks.

The disagreement had caused Yippie to split into two factions. The one led by Abbie and his Yippie co-founder, Jerry Rubin, represented the first-generation Yippies and their followers, including those who fought in Chicago 1968. The one led by Forcade represented the second-generation Yippies, those who had been too young for Chicago 1968 and were now ready to serve their country in Miami Beach 1972.

Tom had created the group as an alternative to the Yippies, claiming they needed to get out from under the shadow of Abbie and Jerry. He called them Zippies, "to put the zip back into Yip."

The young protestors who came down to Miami Beach that summer, including me, for the most part had no idea there had been a split at the top of Yippie Central and didn't care. At the campsite, Yippies and Zippies organized together, got high together, slept together, and just wanted to stop the war.

Dana Beal: Not Recognized in His Own Time

The day after I arrived in Madison, Yippie Dana Beal was released from Dane County Jail where he had done nearly a year for marijuana possession. The next day, he hitchhiked into Madison with a pound of weed for the upcoming Smoke-In. I met him the next day.

We clicked immediately. We were both hyperactive, gifted political organizers, and—the clincher—from Lansing. Our friendship was destined. It was *b'shert*. He was a few years older than me and a longer-time youth radical than I was so he saw me as a young him; in my mind, I was Robin to his Batman. To others, I was Dana's friend and was immediately accepted into the inner circle of the Madison YIP community.

Dana has never received the recognition that is due to him. He would be a household name today, like Abbie and Jerry, if, during the Chicago riots, he hadn't been in jail for another of his many drug busts.

Sean Howe, in his biography of Tom Forcade, *Agents of Chaos: Thomas King Forcade, High Times, and the Paranoid End of the 1970s*, quotes one former Yippie as saying, "Tom sees Dana as sort of a junior varsity leader."

That's not how the young people in Madison and Miami Beach saw him. He was a magnet of determination and commitment. I happened to arrive as the Madison YIPs were planning a Smoke-In to be held that weekend on the Capitol lawn, and I plunged into the organizing activity. At the Smoke-In, he delivered a speech he had rehearsed daily in his latest prison cell and his performance was flawless.

THUMBS UP

Tension in Madison

By the time I arrived in Madison, the community was already tense. Only two years before, in the early morning of August 24, 1970, four Madison men going by the name New Year's Gang had blown up a bomb in the Army Math Research Center (AMRC) office in Sterling Hall on the campus of University of Wisconsin.

The site was chosen because the AMRC was funded by the U.S. Army to support the war. Advance recon had told the Gang no one would be in the building. Advance recon was wrong. Robert Fassnacht, a postdoctoral researcher in physics and a father of three young children, was working late that day. Unintentional deaths hurt just as much.

While the event had happened nearly two years ago, and deeply affected the peace community, it was back in the news. On February 16, only three months before, Karl Armstrong, seen as the ringleader of the group, had been busted in Toronto after a year and a half in hiding, with a cache of weapons and radical literature.

Blockade of Haiphong Harbor Spurs Civil Disobedience

Then, on Monday May 8, 1972, President Nixon announced a blockade of Haiphong Harbor and a plan to drop mines there and on other major North Vietnamese ports that were entryways for military supplies from the Soviets.

The blockade was seen as an escalation of the war and provoked student protests all over the country. In Madison, the plan, to be implemented on Wednesday May 10, was organized civil disobedience.

We organized by affinity groups, as we had done in DC during the May Day activities, for the best defense against teargas. I was with a group of seven YIP friends. We adopted "Foonman" as our group name because someone suggested it and no one objected. I think it was an inside joke the others got because they were from Madison and that I accepted because I didn't care.

The tone for the evening's demonstrations became obvious quickly. We listened to a few announcements at the Library Mall, then attempted to march the one hundred yards to Bascom Hill. As the first of us began to arrive, the first bomb attacks hit us and we scattered. "Foonman! Foonman!"

My First Death Rush

Around this time, I felt my first death rush. We were walking down the street, low on strategy but high in anticipation, as I recall, and we reached an intersection. We noticed a police car across the street so we took a right down the side street back toward campus. They didn't chase us. But they lobbed a canister of gas.

By this time, I had learned that gas itself wasn't too bad; its value rested in its ability to disperse a crowd. So, I somehow got into the habit of fading to the rear and lagging behind until I knew everyone was headed in the same direction, and then I'd follow. Being the last to leave, I was a good target for the can of what someone said was nausea gas.

We had heard rumors earlier that they would be using this. We were warned that it would burn the skin and that it would make us nauseous—no bad vomiting, just dry heaves. I prepared for that scenario, but you can't intellectualize your way through an experience.

The bomb that landed a foot to the left of me exploded, and shrapnel flew into my mouth and into my eyes. If I had just felt the nausea, as I had anticipated, all would have been cool as the pre-planned script played out.

THUMBS UP

Instead, I couldn't breathe. I had to gasp for whatever breath I could find. I knew what was supposed to happen and I knew what was happening and they weren't in sync, and I worried. I couldn't conceive of dying but it was a death rush nonetheless; I believed I was facing imminent death. It became a test that I had to pass, like I always did in school. With my eyes blinded, I lost sight of my affinity group members. My screams of "Foonman! Foonman!!" to get their attention came out as moaning whispers. I finally just grabbed someone so someone would know I wasn't all there. Two of the women from the group saw me; I was relieved to join them.

The fear of the unknown, of not knowing what was going to happen, was the worst part of this experience. The anticipated effects, the nausea, finally did appear and I did some good gagging. For ten minutes, I struggled to breathe, but my breath finally began to come back, as did my sight. Within a half hour, I was ready to go, feeling stronger for having survived both psychological fear and physical threat.

And having no idea what was about to happen.

CHAPTER 8
THE SHORT ONE WITH THE CURLY HAIR AND BEARD

We were walking down the street away from the Capitol. I don't remember if we had already pulled off any actions (aka, thrown garbage cans into the street). Out of nowhere, two police trucks came tearing up the street. Two more came tearing down the street.

I don't know what street we were on at the time but we were two blocks away from the Square and heading away from it on the right side of the street, which we had just crossed. To our right were a row of stores and a parking lot. On our left were more stores and a parking lot.

No Peaceful Surrender

Our instant reaction, totally emotional, was to flee. But our second reaction, based on the realization that we were surrounded by forty police dressed in gas masks and riot gear who were swinging their clubs in wild search of a target, was to surrender. Instantly. With hands raised.

"We give up. Take us in."

But peaceful surrender was not the plan they had in mind. They lobbed a canister of teargas at us.

Ken Wachsberger

So, we took off again—this time to avoid the gas. We ran into the parking lot where, unfortunately, a high wall lined the perimeter. We couldn't scale it so, in order to avoid the gas, we were forced to run toward the police.

The Beatings Begin

And so the beatings began.

I analyzed the event the day after I got out of jail. I wrote:

> Now I suppose it's natural for individuals to ask at one time or another, "Why me?" As each club, each kick, each curse reached its target, said target asked just that same question. It seemed as if they were all after me. But no, I knew that that was just an ego thing—obviously everyone else was getting it, too. The screams seemed to confirm that.
>
> Which, somehow or other, brings up another concept, that of leadership. In an organized affinity group, togetherness should be such that there's no need for any individual to emerge as a leader. But ours was an affinity group in name only. All else was absent, and it took a loud voice to keep us from messing up worse than we already were. I didn't realize it at the time, but—well, as Maddog said later, "It really was you who kept us together." Maybe I didn't pick up on it, but the police apparently did, because, even though everyone did get beat up a little, I was the center of the action.

My memory is a little hazy as to exactly all that happened, but most of the issues where I had doubts were later confirmed by others.

THUMBS UP

I remember running away from the Capitol (upraised hands are no defense against a club-wielding cop). Hearing a scream, I stopped and turned around: Jane had fallen and a cop was coming at her. My first thought was, "She needs help." My second thought was, "I can't help her. I've got a cop headed toward me." Reversing my steps, I ran toward the Capitol and into a parking lot—which was closed off on three sides.

Riding It Out to the End

What a rush, to say the least. Did you ever experience the feeling of resignation, the horrifying feeling that something awful is about to happen and that all you can do is ride it out until the end? I fought that feeling with some fancy footwork in the lot, but one right to the head put a stop to that. With one last effort, I sought to escape by jumping over a three-foot-high brick wall to get out of the parking lot. I cleared the wall but I accidentally landed on a cop, thus accidentally resulting in my only offensive effort of the night. The rest was their show.

How can anyone justify in his or her mind beating the shit out of someone, literally trying to knock another person senseless? I had plenty of time to ask myself that and other questions throughout this, my second death rush of the evening.

"You fuckin Commie!" Whack! Right in the head.

"Why don't ya go back to China?" Oof! Right in the nuts.

Lying on my stomach, writhing in pain, with my arms covering my head to protect the places that hadn't yet been walloped, I was in a near state of shock—not so much from the physical pain as from the sight of more police still coming out of the trucks. Everyone seemed to want to take his turn—and I think most of them did.

Ken Wachsberger

"Ow, oo, groan!" The beatings only lasted about fifteen minutes but it seemed like forever. One cop maced me while I was lying there. Another walked on me. (I don't know what he was trying to prove.) Others were content just to club. When it suddenly dawned on them that I might be dying, they stopped. I didn't realize until I saw my reflection in a window that my face looked like a tomato.

And so I laid there, with a circle of fifteen satisfied police officers looking down at me: "That'll teach ya to disobey the law." "Next time you'll think twice before bothering people."

"I gotta admit," I confessed as I looked up at them, "you guys did a good job tonight."

"What Do We Do with Him?"

That was it for the beatings. Figuring that the police would be harassing and arresting any individuals or groups of two and three, we had invited other people to join us so they wouldn't be alone. After the beatings, one of the guys in our group was seen getting into one of the police cars.

I was finally told that I was under arrest and I was ordered to get in the truck. I was pretty out of it when I sat down. I could barely lift my hand to sign the arrest sheet. Swaying back and forth with my hands on my knees to prevent me from falling over, I stared blankly at the wall and groaned. "Handcuff that guy," one officer ordered. "He gets me nervous."

As they drove away, I became the subject of a team strategy meeting. The first question to answer: "Should we arrest him?" Options became:

> a "Let's dump him back on the sidewalk and leave him there."
> b. "Let's drive for a few blocks and let him out where he'll

be separated from his group."
c. "Arrest him."

"c" was the correct answer.

Second question: "What should we charge him with?" That was easy: disorderly conduct, the old catch-all.

Third, question: "Who should be the arresting officer?" Some confusion followed. Who got him first? Who got him last? Who got him best? They finally settled on Sergeant Robert A. Behnke because he was the cop I had landed on. (I was lucky they didn't get me for assault and battery.) With their decision, they added the charge of resisting arrest.

They had to call Sergeant Behnke so we could have our pictures taken together. According to the Criminal Complaint [with my comments inserted]: "The defendant jumped to the top of a wall approximately four feet high and was approached by Sgt. Behnke [waving his club], who informed the defendant that he was under arrest for disorderly conduct. The defendant then jumped from the wall on top of Sgt. Behnke and began fighting with him. [Can you imagine me picking on one cop while fourteen others are headed right at me?] Sgt. Behnke subdued the defendant, who then again began struggling and kicking, getting partially away from the said officer, who subsequently succeeded in apprehending the defendant and placing him under arrest." [No mention anywhere, naturally, of the teargas or the bloodbath.]

The fourth and final question to be posed: "Should we take him to a hospital?" After a quick debate that centered on logistics more than morality, it was decided that I would be booked first and they would see how I was then. Two hours later, still bleeding from two head wounds, they took me to Methodist Hospital, where I was given stitches for a one-inch gash on my forehead and a two-inch gash on the top of my head.

Ken Wachsberger

I Deviate from the Stereotype

If I had any feelings at this point, I had fully compartmentalized them and put them in a drawer. I was strictly in my head, experiencing what was happening but at the same time observing it and creating a narrative. I was Yippie playing to the media.

During the ride to the jail, I told myself the police didn't hate me; they hated the stereotype I represented: "Fuckin Nigger! Fuckin hippie! Fuckin Commie!" So, I deviated from the stereotype whenever I could. As a longhaired hippie protestor, I was expected to be loud-mouthed, but to their surprise (and mine) I came on mellow, really mellow. Talking slowly and softly with one, I was at my mellowest best:

> Him: "I fought in the war."

> Me: "Wow (I always said "wow" when I talked mellow), the shit they're using in Vietnam wasn't even invented then."

> Him: "You should see the streets here."

> Me: "Wow, can you imagine what the streets are like in Vietnam?"

He was almost in tears. When I was taken to the hospital, he came along; I was relieved to have a non-hostile cop with me at that time.

I made the most of my appearance wherever they took me: in the truck, at my booking, in the hospital, in jail, at my arraignment. The message I hoped to convey was, "Nobody could have done anything so bad as to deserve what he got." It got to some people.

THUMBS UP

Best line of the night, which also fell the flattest. When the booking officer asked me what color my hair was, I thought a second and said, "Red."

Ollie Steinberg and the WERMs

A few hours after I was busted, in the early morning of Thursday May 11, 1972, in another part of town, "3 'hippie-garbed' wig-wearing policemen," according to the May 10, 1972, issue of *TakeOver*, Madison's underground newspaper, approached a home at 131 North Bedford Street that was the hangout for a well-known group of five Madison radicals called the WERMs (Wild-Eyed Revolutionary Movement).

According to *The Capital Times*, Madison's liberal daily newspaper, the WERMs were thought to be afraid of a Neo-Nazi group that had made its presence known in the Mifflin Street area and might have believed the police, who didn't identify themselves, were Neo-Nazi members.

Regardless, the police claimed they were shot at because they had prevented the WERMs from burning the offices of an insurance company in a Madison suburb earlier that night. By the time the shooting was done, three police officers had allegedly been shot, the WERMs were overpowered and beaten, and all five of them were in jail.

Ollie Steinberg was charged with three counts of attempted murder and one count of conspiracy to commit arson and was facing a possible 105-year prison stretch; the three other men were charged with conspiracy to commit arson; and the one woman was charged with criminal obstruction.

My path crossed with Ollie, whom I had met briefly the week before, when he was marched handcuffed past the cell where I was incarcerated. We acknowledged each other, though at the time neither of us felt like smiling. Dried blood from my forehead had sealed my right eye shut.

Seven months later, Ollie copped a plea of guilty to two lesser charges of "conduct regardless of life" with a maximum of five years each (the third attempted murder charge was dropped) and was incarcerated in a minimum-security institution. He was released in the summer of 1975 after serving a total of three years.

Fat Julie

Whether or not that guy from our affinity group who got in the police car was an undercover cop I'll never know for sure. I don't remember anything about him anymore other than that he existed and he was someone we invited into our group because of our concern for his protection.

But history has shown that there was one other person in the group who definitely was an undercover cop.

Julie Maynard was her name but she was known as Fat Julie. I don't ever recall that name being used in a derogatory fashion, however. She was called Fat Julie because you can't carry 300 pounds on a 5'8" frame and be anything but fat.

But she had a warm smile that she always wore when she saw me. She was well liked by others as well, and generous with her ample economic resources, so I know other members of our affinity group shared my sadness that she would be unable to share in our upcoming righteous street activities.

We understood, though, that no heart in an obese body like hers could withstand the pressure of running from police and breathing in mass quantities of teargas. Before we went into the streets, we said goodbye

THUMBS UP

to Julie. I know I kissed her on the cheek and we hugged. Then I said I was sorry she would be unable to be with us.

Years later, a friend sent me an unsigned article from the February 9-26, 1976, issue of *TakeOver*. In the article, called "The Cow That Came in from the Cold," the author details how Julie's cover as an FBI informant was blown and then provides a summary of Julie's experience. In retrospect, I now see me kissing her goodbye and going off to battle while she heads straight to the telephone, calls the police, and says, "Get the short one with the curly hair and the beard."

Arraignment

The rest is anti-climactic.

Jail wasn't too bad. I was groggy from the beatings, loss of blood, about four shots of Novocain, a pain pill, and a booster shot, but I was too hyper to sleep. Instead, I talked with the other prisoners.

Eight of us occupied the cellblock, one guy for drunkenness (he was 72), one for beating his mother-in-law, and six of us from the demonstrations. Each of the eight cells measured about 6 x 7 and consisted of toilet paper and a toilet (not just a hole in the floor in the corner of the cell), a cot with a mattress, and a sink. A walking area connected the cells, and in the front of that area, in a small room in the corner, was a shower and a mirror. The food was unmemorable except for its mediocrity.

Arraignments began at 2:00 p.m. and I was out an hour later. Bail was set at $209: $100 for disorderly conduct, $109 for resisting. I was declared indigent when my lawyer there said I only had $4.50 on me.

Later that day, Dana fixed me up with Robert Christensen, who he said was the best lawyer at the Dane County Legal Services Center. Bob got the prosecutor to drop the disorderly conduct charge if I would plead guilty and take a $209 fine for the resisting arrest charge.

I knew Madison YIPs were getting ready to head down to Miami Beach, where both major parties were holding their nominating conventions that summer. If I had fought my case, I would have missed my ride. I chose Miami Beach and rode down with them. To this day, I don't know who paid the $209.

CHAPTER 9
MIAMI BEACH, SUMMER 1972

In Miami Beach, Dana was the link keeping the Yippies and Zippies together as one. Fresh out of jail again, he hadn't been forced to choose between Yippies and Zippies so both sides were vying for his support.

We stayed with Forcade at the Zippie House in Coconut Grove. I was welcomed into the inner circle, which included Tom and his friends, because I was Dana's friend. A thrill was working on the UPS (Underground Press Syndicate) member newsletter. The underground paper where I worked in Lansing, *Joint Issue*, was a member.

Meanwhile, Tom moved constantly, whether he was writing, calling out instructions, producing and directing the guerrilla theatre demonstrations he financed, or provoking other movement groups.

Old People and Young People Unite; but Tom Is Too Dark

Occasionally he showed insight even if he didn't get credit for it. An issue in the early days of the summer revolved around the attempts of us young people to convince the city council to grant us park space to sleep and eat while we were there.

That part of Miami Beach was a largely Jewish old folks' community. Giving us a park would mean displacing the senior citizens who hung out there.

Ken Wachsberger

Local right-wingers opposed our efforts and recalled images of dirty hippies rioting in the streets of Chicago in 1968 to instill fear in the hearts of the local senior citizens, many of whom were Jewish and whose average age was 63. The city council threatened us with more police and more weapons.

Old people began to avoid us. More than once, a senior citizen walking toward me on the sidewalk crossed the street so she could avoid passing me. We were shocked and humbled. Old Jews in the South Beach area were residents of the low-cost housing there. Many had only one meal per day. But our youthful arrogance had prevented us from seeing them—because they were Jews, whose stereotype had them all being rich—as an oppressed minority.

Tom realized we needed to begin doing outreach and gave Joyce Hodges and me $10 to do something. We began introducing ourselves to senior citizens' groups. I saw my grandparents in all of them. We allowed them to touch us. A young people-old people alliance began to emerge.

We realized that most of these old people had probably never met a hippie other than through the media, let alone touched one, so we visited the parks where they spent their afternoons and the free lunch programs where many of them ate their only meal of the day. We sang songs, spoke, and passed out leaflets telling who we were and why we were there.

Meanwhile, we petitioned them for signatures to demand that city council give us a campsite.

We won and were given Flamingo Park, one of the senior citizen hangouts. During the days that followed, they offered their homes to us as refuge from the teargas that filled the streets and they fed us chicken soup to replenish our energy. They visited us every evening.

THUMBS UP

But somewhere along the way, Tom's darkness began to snuff out my passion with the Zippies. I heard enough about how awful Abbie and Jerry were. I drifted away and became part of the Yippies. I'm pretty sure Joyce did, too. Yippie took ownership of senior citizen outreach.

Yippie's "Wedding of the Generations"

The symbolic highpoint of the summer leading up to the conventions was Yippie's "Wedding of the Generations," which was held at Lummus Park on the Sunday before the Democratic Convention began. Joyce represented the young people. An old couple from Miami's poor downtown Jewish community represented the senior citizens.

Abbie recited a Yiddish poem that only he and the senior citizens understood that he wrote on the plane down to Miami Beach called "Nixon *Genug*," which is Yiddish for "Enough Nixon Already." Jewish poet Allen Ginsberg, acting as "rabbi," married us. We voluntarily changed the slogan of credibility to "Don't trust anyone over 35 and under 60."

My article about the young people-old people alliance appeared in Miami's underground newspaper, *Daily Planet*.

As I look back at it with the eyes now of a senior citizen, I see that thread as a highpoint of the pre-convention half of the summer.

I Free Martha Mitchell with Jerry Rubin

The night before the first convention opened, the Zippies sponsored a Smoke-In at Flamingo Park. I sat in the lotus position next to Allen Ginsberg as he led a large circle of Brothers and Sisters in "Om!"

Ken Wachsberger

Later, I was sitting in the Zippie tent with a few others. We were passing a joint around while we drank electric Kool-Aid from a pitcher. I got restless and decided to take a walk.

I was walking alone through the heart of the park toward nowhere in particular and I saw Jerry Rubin in the distance. He called to me to join him. Let me tell you about Jerry.

I met him when we were still fighting with city council over the issue of a campsite. The federal government's response to the debate was to deny us money for camping space and porta-johns, claiming none was available. Not unnoticed, however, was the fact that they were pouring megabucks into the police department in the form of guns, helicopters, and extra people power.

So, to kick off our summer campaign, we planned a march "to protest the militarization of Saigon and Miami Beach."

The day before the march, as Yippie media coordinator, I repeated, it seemed like a hundred times, until I had called all the names from the Yippie phone list of media people who were streaming into the city, "Hi, this is Ken from the Yippies. We're having an action to protest the militarization of Saigon and Miami Beach." I gave them the time and place and told them to join us.

Meanwhile, Martha Mitchell, the wife of Attorney General John Mitchell, had in three years in DC become a media darling because of her habit of sharing John's secrets with her media contacts. In the days leading up to the 1972 Watergate burglary of the DNC headquarters, she warned them of "dirty tricks" being committed by the Committee to Re-Elect the President (CRP) to win the election. John was the head CRP. He denied the allegations, then enlisted the FBI to keep her ignorant of the break-in and away from her media contacts.

THUMBS UP

That same night before our march, she eluded her FBI captors long enough to call UPI reporter Helen Thomas and complain that she was being held a political prisoner.

When the news broke, we immediately changed the theme and staged, instead, a "Free Martha Mitchell" march.

At the organizing meeting that evening at the Albion Hotel, where Abbie, Jerry, and the other Yippie insiders and their best friends were staying, I talked briefly with Jerry during a break. We were standing in the hallway just outside the apartment. I don't remember how I ended up alone with him at that moment but he had come to like me. He saw me as a young him. I didn't share the Lansing connection with him, like I did with Dana. But he and I were both Jewish. All three of us were ADHD and gifted organizers.

I was a kid then, relative to any level of radical sophistication, and I was slightly overawed in the presence of a living myth, but even from that perspective I noticed that he looked somewhat forlorn. He was 32-years old at the time and obviously, in a culture that didn't trust anyone over 30, feeling old.

When he said to me, in a way that made me feel like he was talking out loud to himself and thinking this thought for the first time, "It's kind of scary to feel your life has peaked at 28" (his age during the Chicago '68 demonstrations), I felt sad. The next I heard of him after that summer, he was going in and out of every therapy of the Me Decade that he could get his head into. He wrote his autobiography, *Growing (Up) at Thirty-Seven*, about his experience in therapy.

I Meet Norman Mailer

So, we're at the park now. He sees me from a distance and calls to me to join him. He was walking with Norman Mailer, who was the most famous male author of the time. I caught up to them.

Ken Wachsberger

"Norman," he said proudly as he put his arm around my shoulder and drew me in, "I want you to meet the Yippiest Yippie of them all."

I was still tripping. The smell of the colors was outrageous. Thoughts collided with each other as they competed for my attention. My mind was racing to manufacture the perfect opening line to meet a literary legend. I fell into groupie mode and almost said, "Gee, Norman, you're my favorite author." But I imagined him asking, "Oh, what's your favorite book?" and I had never read one of his books. I couldn't even think of a title. I didn't know what else to say and the clock ran out. I just stared at him.

And that was the day I met Norman Mailer.

The Yippie Puke-In

The Yippies and the Zippies represented the youngest, zaniest, most idealistic, and funniest segment of the broad mosaic of voices that was the antiwar Movement. We were media-driven guerrilla theater actors when the idea was new. We organized outrageous street theatre performances all summer that were designed to "get the media," which meant get a story about us somewhere in print media, radio, or TV.

The events had to be funny and unexpected. Sometimes, they were controversial and deliberately offensive. At times, they were seen to challenge the bounds of decency.

The Zippies can claim "Wheelchairs for Wallace" as their funny dig at a Southern racist where the joke is that he's in a wheelchair.

The Yippies had the Puke-In.

THUMBS UP

The Yippie Puke-In was held in front of the Fontainebleau Hotel after the cops chased nine of us out of the hotel on the day the Republican National Committee was slated to meet there.

Following the meeting was a reception, the perfect venue, we decided, to show Richard Nixon and the Republicans how sick their policies made us feel.

The day before, a pharmacist had sold us each a bottle of Ipecac, a non-prescription medicine that induces puking for those who need such an outcome. He told us it would take about five minutes to take effect.

On our way to the hotel the next day, we met at a pizza joint for Cokes and pizzas with green pepper, sausage, and extra cheese. Once we got to the hotel, we figured it would take about five minutes to sneak into the hotel and position ourselves outside the meeting room so we could meet the delegates on their way to the banquet and serve them the appetizer that we were about to prepare for them. We chugged the contents, snuck around the hotel, and entered from a side door.

Unfortunately, we were now the only ones in the hotel dressed in cutoffs and T-shirts. The Secret Service agents couldn't figure out who we were so they trailed us from behind. When we got to the meeting room, a suspicious guard asked us to show our room keys. We started fumbling around in our pockets like we couldn't find them. Then we noticed the Secret Service agents, and the guard started shouting, "Out, out," so we split immediately before they could nab us.

Outside the hotel, a group of Zippies were demonstrating for a righteous cause that I don't remember. A woman was shouting chants into a megaphone and the crowd was repeating them. Media from around the world were capturing every detail, to be broadcast on the evening news.

Ken Wachsberger

Meanwhile, five minutes had long since passed.

But I figured we couldn't have long to wait before the Ipecac took effect on at least one of us, so I borrowed the megaphone from the woman. Then I turned to the crowd and the cameras and I said:

> People, I have an important gut-level statement to make. We're from the People Uptight about Killings Everywhere (PUKE) and we want to talk to Richard Nixon and to all you Republican Fat Cats. We want to tell you that we're tired of your lies and your deception. You promised us jobs and you gave us the wage-price freeze.

The cameras were on me the whole time. I kept looking to the side to see if anyone was beginning to look nauseous. Everyone just looked befuddled so I kept talking:

> You've wired all our phones so we can't even make a private call. And now you've just finished your National Platform Committee meeting, where we all know you made plans to bring us more CIA heroin, more bombed dikes, more drowned babies, more napalmed innocent citizens.

And then I caught a glance of the one guy in our group who we thought might be an undercover cop. He might have been but he was the hero that day. I could see him turning pale and starting to gag so I led into my conclusion:

> And now you celebrate. Feast. Banquet. Eat all you want — you can afford it. After all, it was paid for with our tax dollars. But don't ask us to join you; we've eaten enough of your shit.

The cameras were all on me watching my every move, so I pointed my finger at the focal point of the whole camera crew and said as I waved it angrily:

THUMBS UP

We've had enough, Richard Nixon. We've had enough, Republicans. Your obscene acts are more than we can handle. And all I can say is …

My finger drew an arc from where it was to our hero's stooping figure. The cameras followed.

… we're just sick about it.

"Ulbleeeh!"

Four spectators turned white.

Another Yippie lost it, and the cameras turned to her. Then another. Then another. Between the nine of us, we puked for a half hour, and every time someone heaved, someone else grabbed the megaphone and gave another reason why the Republicans made us sick. The cameras had a field day.

But then the editors got hold of the stories and censored the whole event. The *Miami Herald* gave us one word: "disgusting."

I couldn't figure it out. What Richard Nixon and the Republicans did every day was far more disgusting and they got all the press they wanted.

Stew Albert

I met Stew Albert that morning. Stew was one of the mythical first-generation Yippies, a co-founder, in fact, and a brilliant activist theoretician. If he was lesser known than Abbie and Jerry by the general public, it was only because he didn't stand trial.

During the summer of 1972, when we of the second generation were still coming of age, Stew was there often, giving generously of his name, his energy, and his vision to the cause.

Ken Wachsberger

I was walking beside him on my way to an early lunch before the Puke-In when he shared his words of wisdom with me. What I remember most: "They can't beat us. We're having too much fun."

Enter Jerry Gorde

At some point in the summer, which neither of us can pinpoint, I met Jerry Gorde. Later, he would become my on-the-road partner. We were Neil Cassady and Jack Kerouac of the seventies. Jerry even did most of the driving, like Cassady, while I sat shotgun with my journal open, like I imagine Kerouac would have done.

But we're not there yet. At this point in the story, Jerry and I are both feeling our way around the upper levels of Movement leadership. We don't know each other yet. Allow me to introduce him because he was an unsung hero of the summer.

Jerry Gorde Joins Yippie National Collective

Jerry was a native of nearby Hollywood, Florida. He became the liaison to Miami Beach for the Yippies. The timing couldn't have been better for him. Henry King Stanford, the president of University of Miami, had just invited Jerry to depart the university after he shut down the Administration building; and his dad had cut off his funding because of his activities. He was leather smithing to raise money to eat, and crashing in a friend's apartment:

> This guy just shows up in the Student Union, and he says, "I'm Brad Fox, from the Yippies, I'm the advance man. We're all moving down to Miami for the Democratic and Republican conventions. I checked in with the underground press and with some media people and asked who we should be working with in Miami. Who's got the lay of the land? Who's got some files and intelligence? And your

name just came up repeatedly. So would you like to share with me how you can help us out?"

Jerry impressed Brad with his files and rolodex, then took Brad to his apartment. Brad asked to use the phone.

> This was when long distance was, you know, a charge. I said sure, because it was my friend's roommate's phone. He gets on the phone and he dials a number, and he's all excited talking to whoever it is on the other end of the line. "Yeah, I found our guy. This is gonna be great." And then Brad hands me the phone and it's Abbie Hoffman. He says, "Brad's filled me in on what you got. We're excited to be working with you. Seems like you've got the lay of the land. Do you have a car?"

Jerry did, his Ford Falcon. Over the next 72 hours, he became the airport runner:

> I picked up Abbie and his bodyguard, Rick Stern, who was later exposed as an undercover cop. Next was Jerry Ruben, and then Lee Weiner, who was like the money conduit and the treasurer. Then Allen Ginsberg and Patty Oldenburg, Claes Oldenburg's first wife. Then Gabrielle Schang, and John and Yoko's liaison, Kathy Streem, because John and Yoko were still under threat of being expedited out of the United States.

> I didn't pick up Judy Gumbo because she was protesting the way the white primarily Jewish males were conducting themselves.

For his good work, he was invited onto the Yippie National Collective. His first assignment was to find them a place to live with at least eighteen rooms as close to the convention center as possible, and a suite of offices. He found them the Albion Hotel, an old shabby retirement hotel that overlooked the convention center. "They were quite willing to give us two floors, because the summer is their low period in terms of renting the rooms."

Then Ed Sanders showed up, and Jeff Nightbyrd, and some others, and they filled out the rooms and began the process of preparing for the convention.

> There was nothing deliberate on my part. I mean, I'm just making some key chains and leather goods and friends are handing me their meal cards for the cafeteria so I can sneak out meals.
>
> And I had no fucking clue what I was going to do with the rest of my life. You know, Dad's going to come for the car. I know that's going to happen. He's going to tell me to go fuck myself. I'm going to tell him that, when the revolution is over, he'll be on his knees, and then we will be estranged for the next quarter of a century.
>
> Which kind of happened, except for the fact that the Yippies gave me a path forward. It was like, wow, yes, I can't believe this is happening. All my heroes are dabbled together, and they've just put me on the letterhead.

I Meet Jerry

I can't remember when I actually met Jerry. He can't either. But it became inevitable, especially after he became the Yippie liaison to all the political groups. As he recalls, his role was to insulate the Yippies from Forcade but he was empowered to agree to nothing.

> So, I went to the Zippie house in Coconut Grove and I discovered that the people who are hanging with the Zippies are more like me than these exalted ones that I was living with. Meeting you and some of the other Zippies beyond Tom, I found that there was much greater alignment than Jerry and Abbie led me to believe. I mean, I did not have the capacity or the knowledge to understand why there was a distinction between Yippies and Zippies. To me, we're all in it to end a war and to fuck with Nixon.

Jerry Rubin, in particular, irritated him:

> I was the Miami connection, so they nicknamed me Miami Jerry so I would never be confused with him. Jerry was the only one who treated me like a fucking go-fer. His attitude was, "You're not really a national collective leader. You're the Miami guy who knows how to make things happen. You know all the press, so we have a press conference. You know how to reach out to everybody and get them to show up, that kind of stuff. And, by the way, go get us lunch."

Jerry was not highly involved in the work of the young people-old people alliance; the initial efforts came from the Zippies and Zippie expatriates. But he did represent the Yippies in negotiations with the city over where we could set up camp: "I followed my script: Give us Flamingo Park adjacent to South Beach or we will take the Miami Beach Golf and Country Club by any means necessary. It was an easy decision for the powers that be."

Ken Wachsberger

Jerry Busts Salt and Pepper

Other than being embraced by his heroes, Jerry's highpoint of the summer was his role in exposing two black-op operatives of Nixon's operation, one white guy, Jerry Rudolph, and one black guy, Harry Crenshaw, whose code names were Salt and Pepper.

> Fred Francis, who was with NBC, pulled me aside and told me that he had gotten intelligence that Salt and Pepper had infiltrated the VVAW and were living in the VVAW encampment. They were going to be planting munitions in the encampment and then executing a search that would lead to indictments, and they were doing this because VVAW had a level of credibility that the other groups didn't have.

> I went to the head of the VVAW and told him the story. And he told me that he was unwilling to call out brothers in arms without clear evidence.

So, Jerry concocted an idea.

> I said, well, since I know their real names and that they will be working together and hanging together, if you would assign somebody to walk around the encampment with me, if we see a white guy and a black guy hanging really tight with each other in front of us, and I yell out, 'Hey, Jerry! Hey, Harry,' if they respond to their real names and turn around, then isn't that enough evidence to identify them as this black-ops team?

And it worked. Jerry and Harry's cover was blown, the indictments were canceled, and they were thrown out of the VVAW.

THUMBS UP

The day after the Republican Convention ended, they pulled over in an unmarked car, threw me against the car, and told me that, now that my protection was leaving, you don't want to be sticking around in Miami anymore.

They were assigned to the Nixon team because they were detectives in mainly the police department, which meant they were going to be here long term.

"You don't want to fuck with us. You need to get the fuck out."

So, I was scared, and I needed to get the fuck out, and there was nothing left for me there. I mean, what the fuck am I going to do, anyhow?

CHAPTER 10
I SCORE IN CLEVELAND, THEN WRITE LANSING HISTORY

After the summer activities ended, I hitchhiked back with Red Bear, a friend from the Lansing area who sported, no surprise here, a bushy red beard. Although we had been friends of the same friends in Lansing, we didn't become friends to each other until Miami Beach. We were ready to return home after a long summer.

Jerry, who was in self-preservation mode because of Salt and Pepper, was happy to accept our invitation to join us. "I needed to find a new path forward. You became my Dharma buddies and turned me onto the road."

Red Bear and I helped him pick out his camping gear and his first backpack, an orange full-length beauty, which Jerry later bequeathed to me and for the past thirty years has been an indispensable part of my basement inventory.

On the Road to Lansing

We left Miami Beach with three hits of acid and some pot, which we kept in a tin can, so when we got harassed by cops, it was in the can on the side of the road.

The first day, we made it to Atlanta, Georgia. I remember walking down Peachtree Street and feeling the presence of the *Great Speckled Bird*, one of the legendary underground newspapers from the Deep

South that would later be one of the stories in the Voices from the Underground Series.

Jerry adds: "We kind of as a joke stopped in at a storefront for a home rental company of some sort—called something like Find a Home—so, we went in and told them we needed a home...yuk yuk... and the owner was taken by us and took us into his home. We did a few odd jobs, a combination of painting and entertaining him with stories and experiences well beyond his own grasp. We stayed for a day or two and then headed back out on the road."

Jerry's memory of day three is vivid:

> We got close to being accosted in Cleveland, Tennessee, by some Rednecks. Red Bear saved the day because you and I had no clue what to do. He just presented himself like, "Do you want to fuck with us? Come on. Bring it on," because Red Bear was huge with a scary, bushy red beard.

Our final stop was Cherokee, Tennessee. None of us had ever been there:

> We headed up into the mountains, and we realized why they were called the Smoky Mountains: because it was sucked in with fog. It was wet and it was cold. We couldn't even get enough dry wood together to build a fire so we couldn't cook the rice. So, we decided to just drop the acid because we wouldn't care about eating at that point. And that's when we realized that we had left the acid on the side of the road on our last pickup into Cherokee. So, we didn't get to do the acid, either.

Instead, we came out of the mountains and slept in our sleeping bags on the front porch of a tourist shop in Cherokee. The next morning, we continued on to Lansing.

THUMBS UP

"So that was the beginning of on the road with Kenny and Red Bear."

Jerry Moves On

Back in Lansing, Red Bear and I began working on *Joint Issue* again.

Jerry stuck around for a few weeks, then moved to Madison, where he became a co-founder of *Free For All*, the first free underground paper in Madison, which Jerry modeled after *Joint Issue*—except for the method of financing. He recalled:

> Other than Lansing, New York, and Berkeley, Madison was the ongoing seat of the Yippies. Karl Armstrong and his brother were from Madison. I was invited there by my friend, Julie, and her husband, Steve, to stay at a safe house that they ran.

Julie was the same Fat Julie who had gotten me busted in Madison and would later be exposed as an undercover cop. She had spent the summer being the front office secretary for the Yippies in Miami Beach and that's how she had gotten to know Jerry. Jerry became best friends with Steve.

He remembered Steve as being a Yippie at heart. "He was just this character that was living with Julie."

Then one afternoon: "I don't know where Julie was at the time. We were in the living room. He took out this big knife and he started throwing it at this piece of wood that he had melted onto the wall. And as he was throwing the knife, he was talking to me about how important it is that we remain in solidarity and secret and you don't get to tell anybody anything that you hear going on and all of that."

That set off his sniff meter: "I was thinking that this was going to be my Dharma. Then one day I just packed up my backpack and decided it was time for me to get back on the road, to disappear out of Madison and continue this journey, whatever the hell it was. What helped was, being a Miami boy, I didn't have the right clothing for winters in Madison. But it wasn't right for me anyway. I had never lived in a four-season environment. You know, it was brutal."

Underground Gives Way to Alternative

In the summer of 1973, I attended a conference in Boulder, Colorado, hosted by the *Straight Creek Journal*. The 150 attendees represented over fifty underground papers, including many from UPS.

They were all financed in their own unique ways. One staff I remember financed their paper by selling pot, but never heroin or speed. Other papers guilt-tripped rich liberals into supporting them or found rock groups to hold fundraising concerts. One way or the other, they got the money because the papers were more than labors of love. They were mission-oriented, and that mission was politically, economically, artistically, spiritually, and culturally anti-the officially sanctioned viewpoint of the corporate press. And that was what had made them underground.

But by 1973, increasing numbers of Americans had come around to our antiwar arguments, and the government was being forced to wind down the war. Ideas that had appeared first in the underground press were everywhere on the pages of the corporate press, which, of course, were claiming the stories as their own.

For instance, release of *The Pentagon Papers* by Daniel Ellsberg nearly scandalized the government and inspired charges of "treason" because of the supposed sensitivity of the information; in fact, the substance of those revelations had long been known by readers of the underground press.

THUMBS UP

What we discussed at the conference was that our ideas were no longer underground in even a romantic sense. A vote was taken and it was agreed to change the name of Underground Press Syndicate to Alternative Press Syndicate. The underground press of the Vietnam era in name ceased to exist.

Driveaway to Cleveland Stadium

I left town after the conference with Steve Vernon, from *Joint Issue*, Tim Wong and Marie, from *Free For All* in Madison, and maybe someone else whose name I don't remember. Our mode of transportation was a driveaway.

The driveaway was a favorite way to travel around the country at little or no cost. Car owners who wanted to transport their cars without driving them made them available as driveaways. Then, hippies would drive them either for free or for just gas money.

The challenge was to find a driveaway to your desired location.

From Boulder to Madison to Lansing, the best available driveaway ended up in Cleveland. Since I was from Beachwood, an eastern suburb of Cleveland, I volunteered to bring it the final five hours from Lansing to Cleveland, visit my family, and then hitchhike back to Lansing.

My instructions were to meet the owner at Cleveland Stadium, home to the Indians. The owner was Herb Score, legendary fastball artist with the Indians who became an announcer after his career was cut short by a line drive to his eye!

We were the second attempt to get his car back to him. The first had driven about halfway before being stopped and busted with a cache of weed in the trunk. The car was returned to Boulder and that's where we picked it up.

Ken Wachsberger

Joint Issue's Legacy

Joint Issue served the Lansing-East Lansing community until the end of the Vietnam War and even beyond. We were usually organized anarchistically; everyone did everything. Sometimes we called ourselves a newspaper; at others, we called ourselves a magazine. Sometimes we focused more on international news; at others, our focus was local.

We always strove to be as open as possible and encouraged other community members to become involved. Individuals in other organizations wrote their own articles if they wanted them to go in. We reprinted articles from other UPS-member papers and from Liberation News Service, the AP and UPI of the underground press.

We wrote peptalk slogans for the counterculture to live by and printed them running up and down the margins and upside down:

- Don't talk to the FBI!
- Pick up hitchhikers!
- Sisters pick up sisters!
- Boycott grapes and lettuce and all wines from Modesto!
- Chop down cars!
- Tip the dishwasher!

If nothing was happening locally, we organized a rally and wrote about it from the first-person perspective. One example was our Impeach Nixon rally that we organized and that liberal Democrats then tried to take credit for.

I wrote about national boycotts and about local news and about my growing understanding of how to be a real man in a nonsexist world. When I was hitchhiking and organizing and going to conferences around the country, I wrote about antiwar activities and political

THUMBS UP

arrests in Washington, DC, and Madison and Boulder and Miami Beach and other communities I visited.

One of my more memorable articles, about the time I dropped acid and went to hear Leighton Ford, Billy Graham's son-in-law, was called "I Dropped Acid and Saw God." Another, called "Got One on the Pig-O-Scope," was about a game some friends invented that required the driver to follow a police car and try to not get caught. That one irritated hard-line, left-wing politicos, who thought it was irresponsible. I interviewed United Farmworkers founder Cesar Chavez. Another article, called "My Waitress: I Think I'll Tip Her" (a takeoff on the Geritol ad tag line, "My wife, I think I'll keep her"; see appendix), I wrote after watching how hard our waitress was working one New Year's Eve while the guests were being obnoxious and rowdy.

Like me, staffers came and went. I headed out west. I headed out east. In 1976, I worked for part of the summer with Jerry on a gillnetter in Sebasco, Maine, and then for a spell with him in the tourist trap town of Bar Harbor, the Tijuana of Maine (see two stories in appendix). We found jobs in a souvenir shop making belts, wrist bands, and other leather products. Jerry, it turned out, was a master leather craftsperson, a skill he had picked up during a childhood sickness when he was laid up in bed for an extended period. I had no such skill, just a talented friend. I imitated his moves but not as skillfully.

JD Asks Me to Write Local History

I came back to town and found a place to rest my backpack in the basement of John "JD" Snyder, the editor of the *Lansing Star*, the successor paper to *Joint Issue*. I don't remember how long I stayed there but it was just a brief stay while I got acclimated to being back in town.

Ken Wachsberger

From there, I moved into one half of a small duplex just this side of the railroad tracks on Kalamazoo Street. My first morning there, a train roared by the house just past midnight. My body involuntarily levitated six inches and then crashed to the floor, where I woke up. The next morning when the train came by, I didn't hear a sound. I never did again.

When I joined the paper, I found myself the only staff member on the *Star* who had been on *Joint Issue* during the paper's heyday. JD asked me to write a local history of the underground press.

He wanted one thousand words but to write a piece that short required distance and time away from the event so I could begin sifting out words that didn't fit the shortness. I was still living the history. It was still happening. I had no distance.

When the deadline came, I was already beyond a thousand words and just getting started. John published it as part 1. I said I would have the rest for the next issue but I couldn't finish it then either. It became a four-part series.

And then I met Emily.

PART 3:
I FIND TRUE LOVE

CHAPTER 11
EMILY

After the house by the railroad tracks, I moved in temporarily with my friend, Mary, a former girlfriend who was now a dear friend. I was on my way to New York, at least in my mind. The underground press had been a mission but, unfortunately, it wasn't a career. I loved being a writer, though, and there was no place better to be, I imagined, than the book publishing capital of the world. Publishing and lodging connections? I figured I'd figure that out when I got there.

Good Thing Mary Wasn't Home

So, I was doing yoga one evening in Mary's living room. I was sitting on the floor in the lotus position, barefooted, in my underwear, meditating. A candle flickered four feet in the distance. My mind was exploring all corners of the room. A cobweb in the corner of the ceiling captured my attention but only fleetingly and then it disappeared.

Suddenly, a harsh ring shattered my silence. Then another. My scattered thoughts shattered to the floor as my right hand reached out dramatically and grabbed the source of the disturbance.

A woman's voice on the other end said, "Is Mary there?" I said no.

She introduced herself as Emily. Further, she knew I was Ken because she worked with Mary and Mary had told her about me.

Ken Wachsberger

What I remember next is her pouring her soul out to me. My mind hadn't fully adjusted from my meditative state; but what I picked up was that a plant on the TV had fallen over and water had spilled into the back of the TV, shorting it and blowing out the lights.

She told me she lived on Elvin Court, by where the Army Reserves met, only a few blocks from Mary's home on Jerome. I offered to take a look.

I Bluff

Okay, that was my first bluff of the night. The truth is, if the problem had required any act more complex than plugging in the cord, I wouldn't have known what to do. But I was feeling refreshed from my yoga now and I was attracted to her voice. I wanted to meet her.

I put on my pants and shoes, stashed my bag of weed in my back pocket, and walked to her home on Elvin Court. I knocked on the door, she opened it, and I was instantly blinded by the most wondrous flash of beauty I had ever seen. I didn't see that coming. My defenses were down.

I was transfixed.

Meanwhile, Emily returned to the subject of our phone call as seamlessly as if we had never hung up the phone. I was barely paying attention to her words. All I said was, "I understand. I'm Jewish, too."

According to Emily, she fell in love with me the moment I said that. I don't remember saying it. It was the best line I don't remember saying that I ever said.

I was too stupid to recognize love when it was staring me in the face. But I recognized lust and instantly could not see myself ever not being with her.

THUMBS UP

The rest of the evening, we drank Emily's Chablis, smoked my Michigan green, laughed, and loved/lusted, and it was codependence at first sight. We never did get to looking at the TV.

Emily Meets the Family

Emily was at the time separated but not yet divorced from her husband. A photo of a rebound partner was on her night stand next to her bed. In the morning, she placed the picture face down and buried it with a formal declaration.

As fate would have it, we woke up Passover morning. I asked her what she was doing for the Seder. She said she was from New York, so nothing.

I was from Beachwood, Ohio, less than a five-hour drive from Lansing. I was going to celebrate with my family, as we did every year. I said, "Why don't you come with me?"

And she did. She met my family the day after she met me. I was too stupid to know about protocols concerning introducing girlfriends to parents. I just didn't want to give Emily any time to forget about me while I was gone.

We stayed in Cleveland for a week, then returned to Lansing where I stayed with her again, and then again, and then I finally officially moved in with her. I never did make it to New York but I am forever grateful that New York came to me.

The evening we met was March 30, 1977. We celebrate it every year.

I Help Emily Get Divorced

Michigan is a no-fault divorce state. I obtained a template for do-it-yourselfers to type up divorce papers from an area women's legal aid group and then typed up Emily's divorce papers. She submitted them when she appeared before Circuit Court Judge Raymond Hotchkiss.

The good judge was known to be a political liberal but, in the student ghetto of East Lansing and Lansing, he was known as a slumlord. I had written articles about him for *Joint Issue* and *Lansing Star*. He was Emily's landlord. We caught him snooping around the yard one day.

But he couldn't argue with my typing artistry or my textual accuracy. He granted Emily her divorce, while stating the fact that he was Emily's landlord into the official record.

Working at the Halfway House

While I was living with Mary, a friend connected me with a job at a halfway house for a half dozen teenagers, four boys and two girls, who had been abused or rejected by their parents and now were considered troubled kids. When I moved in with Emily, I was still working there.

The house was run by a married couple, the house parents, whose names I don't recall. They had landed the job because they had the right certification and, as far as I could tell, were the only ones who had applied for it. They took care of the kids during the day.

I was part of the team who watched the kids in the evening while the couple were sleeping and during the day when the couple needed a sanity break. We also took the kids on occasional outings. My specialty was talking local businesses into giving the kids free movie passes and tickets to gyms so they could work off steam. We ended one outing early when I caught one of the boys doing flips on a trampoline with a lit cigarette in his mouth.

THUMBS UP

The house where the kids lived was located in the middle of a neighborhood street, so one responsibility was to make sure the kids stayed in line in public. They always did.

I enjoyed the job. I felt I had a good rapport with the kids, who for the most part respected my authority. It was a short drive from Mary's and then from Emily's. It paid a decent salary. I believed I was giving back to the community.

I Lose My Job for Love

By the time I met Emily, her dad, David, who was 54, was dying from cancer. I offered to drive Emily to New York to see him because I knew she would not have too many more opportunities.

I drove Emily in my Sport Suburban, which I had bought from a newspaper ad for $400 a few months back. The transmission had recently sprung a leak. The fluid circulated throughout the transmission while the car was moving, but it began a steady drip as soon as I stopped. So, I packed a kitchen pan for the trip. Every time we stopped, I would jump out of the car and quickly position the pan under the leak to catch the fluid. When we were ready to leave, I reloaded the fluid into the transmission, hopped in the car, and turned on the ignition.

The day after we arrived, I described the condition of my car and my attempt to keep the fluid in the transmission to David, who was not yet in the hospital. That was the only one-on-one conversation I shared with him and the only time I met him when he was still alive when I left.

That adventure, Emily later told me, endeared me to David. I was too dumb to know about protocols but I was the guy who brought his little girl to see him when he was dying. Although he and I never spoke of it, I know he died knowing that Emily had made a good decision. I knew from Emily that he had had a vicious temper in his prime but he was always mellow and kind around me. I mourned in advance what I knew would never be the opportunity to form a deeper bond with him.

Unfortunately, I lost my job in the process. I announced at work that I was going to miss some time at work because I had to drive Emily to New York. I explained the urgency of the situation and assumed the staff would unanimously support me given that we were feeling people in a feeling profession. As a show of good faith, I recruited a friend, who was as equally qualified as I was for my position, to substitute for me while I was gone.

The staff did support me.

However, my supervisor, a young punk with oversized glasses who thought he was on a fast track to the top of the counseling world and is the reason I dislike the name Wally, ignored my good faith, said I hadn't known her long enough to love her, and fired me.

During my second visit, David died and we held his funeral. Emily flew there while he was still alive; I drove Sport Suburban and met her there. Emily, even then the project manager, handled all the funeral details.

Before David died, Emily, her mom, her brother and his first wife, and I were all at the hospital. At one point, I must have been in the restroom. David asked Emily, "Where's Ken?" To Emily, that was a sign that he knew I was going to be a part of her life.

CHAPTER 12
EMKEN IS BORN

Emken Baking and Catering was born in a hustle one day in early 1978 when I made a promise only Emily could keep.

My Friend Eva Lacto

I was working as an auto mechanic, an unlikely choice given that I had never worked on a car growing up. I took two classes in Lansing Community College's renowned auto repair department, one each in wheel alignments and brakes. Then I took the certification tests and passed both because I was always a proficient test taker.

I applied for a job as an auto mechanic in the Sears garage and got it, as a tire banger. I fixed flat tires, installed new ones, and made sure every tire on every car was filled with the appropriate amount of air pressure before the car left the lift. That was it. If the job was any more complex, like actually requiring a wheel alignment or new brakes, it was sent on to the next bay.

Every shift I got a 15-minute break.

A friend of mine, Eva Lacto, rented space on the display floor of Sears to run a health food shop. Healthy food was Eva's calling. By night, she taught nutrition in her living room. She harvested three acres of organic vegetables behind her farm each fall.

I visited her shop regularly during my breaks.

Ken Wachsberger

I was talking to her one day. She was telling me about the Natural Food and Health Spring Fest that was being held the following weekend.

A Proud History

The Lansing area's organized health food and alternative community already had, by 1978, a proud history that went back at least eight years, to 1970, when the Green Earth Buying Club held its first meeting.

By 1978, portions of the East Lansing counterculture community were already actively migrating westward into Lansing and eastward into Okemos. Many had been students during the period of the Vietnam era antiwar Movement. Now, they had graduated or dropped out. Proximity to the Michigan State University campus was no longer an advantage, while high rents to rip-off landlords were certainly a disadvantage. The moves reflected the common desire to remain in the community without paying the high rents.

Various locations in East Lansing reflected the attempts of Green Earth Food Coop, as it came to be known, to gain stability, but by 1973 the coop strained as the community grew in population and expanded in area. In addition, members wanted access to coop goods on a daily basis rather than the weekly schedule that had been the style all along.

In 1973, the coop moved to a new location on East Michigan Avenue in Lansing and changed its name to Wolfmoon Food Coop and Natural Bakery. In moving, it became the first storefront coop in Lansing. Three years later, East Lansing residents, supporting Wolfmoon in spirit but unwilling to travel to Lansing to shop there, started East Lansing Food Coop (ELFCO).

THUMBS UP

First-Ever Natural Food and Health Spring Fest

By 1978, the community was spreading throughout Ingham County. As the final hibernating days of winter approached, members of that community were hard at work preparing for the first annual Natural Food and Health Spring Fest, which was to be held April 15 at East Lansing's Martin Luther Chapel.

The event was expected to be the largest gathering of healthy and health-conscious individuals in the area in memory; and members of the planning committee, including Eva, were meeting daily to work out last-minute details. Already, specialists were lined up to speak on and demonstrate such consciousness-raising topics as polarity therapy, massage, home birthing (no demonstration promised here), yoga, herbal healing, and the advantages of distilled water. A tempeh demonstration and a lecture on how to make compost promised to begin the afternoon session with a spiritual lift. Two scheduled bicycle tours were being sponsored by the Community Bicycle Cooperative for those who wanted to be part of the festivities without having to stay inside. A network of young fathers and mothers promised to handle daycare arrangements.

I happened to notice on the poster that a vegetarian buffet meal was included with the ticket price.

"Eva," I asked, "who's doing the catering?"

She was handing a Health Fest brochure to a customer at the time so she couldn't answer right away; but, when her baby daughter cried for more of the pureed brown rice Eva always fed her for lunch, Eva didn't respond as quickly as she usually did. When she finally spoke, her words were carefully chosen, her tone perplexed. "I don't know. We forgot about that. Do you have any ideas?"

Ken Wachsberger

I Make a Promise Only Emily Can Keep

A mystical force spoke for me. I don't know its origin. It said, "Emily and I can do it."

"Do you do vegetarian catering?"

I couldn't believe she didn't know that I was one of the premier brown rice aficionados in the world. I scrambled brown rice with eggs for breakfast; I mixed it in tomato soup for lunch; I combined it with sauteed vegetables for dinner. It was I, didn't she realize, who challenged the cynics who believed brown rice and peanut butter did not go well together? They were right, of course, but only I tried it and could speak with a conviction born of experience. Yet even my abilities paled before those of Chef Emily.

Emily was my secret weapon. She was legendary beyond the borders of the Lansing area. Emily did not prepare a brioche of salmon as her first entree delight: It was a fried egg. And she was four years old, not two. However, she did indeed prepare her first complete meal at six; and by ten she had taken over the family kitchen chores.

In grade school, while her classmates were growing up to Dick and Jane and Dr. Seuss, Emily studied Julia Child for pleasure and automatically converted recipes she read to her own proportions "Emily, why don't you read something practical?" her mother complained. But Emily rebelled early.

Like me, she grew up Jewish. Her next-door neighbor was an Italian gourmet-cooking Mama. Her brother worked for five years as a number two son in a popular Long Island Chinese takeout restaurant. When she met me, she met vegetarianism. Later, she received pastry training at a vegetarian restaurant where she was the soup chef and pastry chef apprentice. She learned from all her teachers and grew beyond their abilities. Emily could do anything, or so I believed at that moment when I was tinged with both mystical daring and hallucinatory bravado.

"Who do you think you're talking to?" I asserted.

"It's got to be fructarian," she said.

"No problem."

"For 150?"

"Give me a break."

Desperation convinced her.

Emily Defines Fructarian

That night over dinner, I said to Emily, "Emily, what does 'fructarian' mean?"

"It's a kind of vegetarianism that doesn't use milk or egg products," she said.

If you're thinking that sounds a lot like veganism, your hearing's fine. Somewhere between then and now, the name changed. But we weren't there yet.

She had recently begun reading up on vegetarian cooking. Emily didn't just follow recipes, or even just improvise on recipes and follow the revised versions. She researched. Emily knew the nutritional value of every food she prepared and the best ways to preserve it in preparation. Emily knew the caloric weight of every food and ingredient on the chart because she considered calorie guides light reading.

Ken Wachsberger

"Could you cater a fructarian meal for 150 people?"

"I don't know. My brother and I threw an anniversary party for our parents for fifty people."

"Could you?" I repeated.

"I suppose. Why?"

"Phew!"

We Pull It Off

Three days later, we met with the members of the planning committee over a miso soup and saltless rice chips brunch and proposed our menu, which the committee accepted after careful scrutiny. Our menu consisted of fried rice casserole, broccoli almondine, a fifteen-item salad bar with homemade croutons and two homemade dressings, banana cake with surprise topping, and a choice of herbal tea or iced lemonade to drink. Any calls for butter were filled with margarine as a non-dairy substitute. Our Thousand Island salad dressing used an eggless brand of mayonnaise. The other was homemade Italian.

And then there was the surprise topping. Originally, in our brainstorming, we had thought of whipped cream as an appropriate topping for the banana cake. Unfortunately, the fructarian requirement prohibited dairy products. Not to be topped in her search for a topping, Emily discovered, one evening while I was trying to get her mind off her work, a health food substitute for whipped cream that was made with soy powder. But it didn't exist in prepackaged form. It had to be made from scratch and discovery.

The planning committee, which had censorship power over all our recipes, approved it so we added it to the menu. "But to be honest,"

THUMBS UP

Emily confided to me, "I'll be surprised if it works." "I'll be surprised if anyone likes it," I added.

Hence the name.

But we pulled it off, though not without averting a few near disasters. I wouldn't be telling you this story if we hadn't.

The door on the chapel's oven was blessed with a loose hinge so we were able to bake the banana cake only by leaning a chair up against the underside of the door handle to seal in the heat. The brown rice nearly burned, but not in vain. A serious post-event criticism/self-criticism session, in the truest spirit of Chairman Mao, convinced us that fifteen pounds of brown rice should be baked in pans in the oven, not boiled and simmered in one deep pot on the burner.

The Surprise Topping

Emily's quick thinking gets credit for saving our surprise topping. Despite our best electric beater's best efforts, we couldn't get the recipe to foam up to the right consistency. "Add cream of tartar," Emily ordered, even though we hadn't brought any. "It works with eggs. Maybe it'll work with the substitute." Luckily, the kitchen had its own supply. We added a pinch. Then another pinch. Then another pinch.

Finally, it began to foam. Soon it resembled shaving cream. I prayed it would taste better.

We were too late to dab the decorative swab onto each piece of cake before setting them all out because the pieces were already out on the table and the people were already moving down the buffet line. So, I took the whole pan to the end of the line and played the role of host asking each person if he or she would like our surprise topping.

Ken Wachsberger

"What is it?" they all asked.

"It's a surprise," I answered and winked my eye à la "Chefs don't tell recipes." "But it's not whipped cream," I hinted, "because that would be dairy." They were impressed with my mystical knowledge.

People congratulated us all evening because it looked so much like whipped cream without being whipped cream. Did it taste like whipped cream? If carob tastes like chocolate, our surprise topping tasted like whipped cream. "It tastes very healthy," was a favorite compliment. Only later did our more rational minds realize that the "cream" in "cream of tartar" meant our lifesaving additive was dairy. We were young then.

Emily was so happy with our success she let me do all the dishes myself.

We Gain a Reputation

We became Emken Baking and Catering. Our tagline was, "But only if you want good food and service."

We were famous for our fifteen-item salad bar at a time when salad bars were a cutting-edge buffet item. We were salad bar pioneers.

Because vegetarian cooking was new in those days, we gained a reputation as vegetarian caterers. The reality soon collided with the economics of trying to maintain a vegetarian food business in a meat-and-potato society. As a full-time business, we made whatever the customer wanted—except veal, which we boycotted; but we continued to claim vegetarian and organic cooking as one of our specialties.

In looking back at our success of that day, I became convinced that Emily could make anything. So, I made a practice, in selling our services, of promising whatever the customer wanted.

THUMBS UP

"Can you make...?" they would ask, and I would answer, "Are you kidding? We make the best ... west of the Cuyahoga River." Then I would run home to Emily and say, "Emily, can you make ...?" and she would say, "I don't know. I've never done it before."

But she never failed to come through and so I continued to make daring promises, and she continued to make me look good. As a result, even after we stopped actively promoting ourselves, Emken continued to do a steady word-of-mouth business.

My article. "Hiring Your Reception Caterer," appeared in the August-September 1988 issue of *Bride's Magazine*.

I also returned to Michigan State to take my final thirty-four credits and earn my BS in Social Science.

CHAPTER 13
FRANCINE HUGHES AND THE BURNING BED

In the middle years of the nineteen seventies, three women killed their male abusers and forever changed our understanding of domestic violence. These cases were precedent setting in the attention they brought to the plight of women who were victimized by their husbands and other male assailants. They laid the foundation for a new awareness of self-defense. They inspired a movement to create a system of life-saving shelters.

Joan Little

The first, Joan Little, was a Black woman who, on August 27, 1974, murdered a white prison guard and known abuser at Beaufort County Jail in Washington, North Carolina, who attempted to rape her.

Little was charged with first-degree murder, which was later reduced to second-degree. As a Black woman facing an automatic death sentence in the state that hosted one-third of all death penalty cases in the United States, her case attracted the attention of anti-death penalty and prisoners' rights advocates, as well as voices in the civil rights and feminist movements.

On August 15, 1975, when a jury of six whites and six Blacks ruled her not guilty, she became the first woman in United States history to be acquitted of murder using the defense that she used deadly force as self-defense to resist sexual assault.

Inez García

Inez García's story is murkier because it involves heroin and guns but the feminist part is clear.

García was a Puerto Rican-Cuban woman from Spanish Harlem who shared an apartment in Soledad, California, with a drug trafficker, Fred Medrano, so she could be close to her husband, who was imprisoned in Soledad. On March 17, 1974, two men came to buy heroin from Medrano and ended up raping García. García hunted them down and killed one of them while the other got away.

García was represented by famed Black Panther lawyer Charles Garry, who argued that the trauma caused by the rape plus a history of mental instability had caused her to act with diminished capacity. Feminists felt he sold out the self-defense defense; and the jury didn't buy the story anyhow. She spent two years in California Institution for Women on a charge of second-degree murder before her appeal was heard.

During her retrial, her feminist lawyer, Susan Jordan, argued that going after the person who had sexually assaulted her was García's right as a form of self-defense. She was exonerated.

Francine Hughes

The third case was local and Emily and I were part of it, though as minor characters. It happened in Dansville, some 22 miles southeast of Lansing. On the evening of March 9, 1977, just three weeks before I met Emily, Francine Hughes, the mother of four young children, three of whom were home that evening, gathered her children in the car and told them to wait. She went back into the house and poured

THUMBS UP

gasoline around the bed where her live-in ex-husband was passed out drunk. Then she drove to the police station, with the children in the car, and cried, "I did it!" He died of asphyxiation.

In her trial, it was revealed that Francine had left the home of her alcoholic father when she was sixteen to marry the man who became her abuser for the next thirteen years. By the time she killed him, they were no longer even married; but she had allowed him back into her home and nursed him back to health after he survived a serious car accident. When he recovered, he began beating her again, burning her school books, and threatening her life. That evening, he had beaten her, burned her books again, and raped her. Then he passed out.

Francine's defense committee argued for a landmark interpretation of women's self-defense: "But he was drunk on his ass!" Yes, and that was the only time she had the advantage.

Her lawyer told the defense committee he was going for temporary insanity. We feared that strategy would eliminate the opportunity to establish a legal precedent for self-defense.

Her lawyer said he just wanted to keep her out of jail.

At trial, the prosecution charged her with first-degree murder. Francine's lawyer argued temporary insanity, as he had said he would do. His argument won. She was acquitted on November 4, 1977.

No one was totally angry at the outcome.

And no one doubted that, as the third of the three cases involving "battered-woman syndrome" as a defense, it changed our understanding of spousal abuse.

But first it had to gain national attention.

Ken Wachsberger

Rally at the Capitol

Sylvia Chase, reporter for ABC, heard about the work we were doing. She contacted the committee and said, "I want to break the story nationwide but I can't report on a committee meeting. What can you do?"

We said we could put on a rally at the Capitol, the standard approach when you were a Lansing activist.

Emily and I attended committee meetings regularly but we were by no means leaders of this passionate group. My main contribution was helping to organize the rally at the Capitol and getting the word out by distributing flyers all over town.

My highpoint of the rally was watching Emily play her guitar and sing the song she wrote for the occasion, "The Francine Song," on the Capitol steps. To this day, it is one of the most haunting, inspirational songs I have ever heard.

The Francine Hughes adventure was my first time doing political organizing work with Emily. The experience led me to two discoveries: Any woman who was going to be a long-term part of my life would have to be an advocate for social justice; and Emily was an advocate for social justice.

Sylvia Chase was there to cover the rally. Her story played a powerful role in getting the word out and it led to the movie, *The Burning Bed,* starring Farrah Fawcett. The movie helped to inspire the national domestic violence prevention movement.

CHAPTER 14
WE GET MARRIED

Those were on-the-road days for Emily and me thanks in part to Emily's dad's Vega, which Emily inherited after he died. Our catering was part time or full time, depending on whatever else was going on with our lives. We catered first in Lansing, then in upstate New York, then in Austin, while always holding other jobs as well.

I Commit

While we were in Austin, I proposed. The timing was right. I don't know what force says to a man, "It's time to commit," but it said it to me while we were in Austin. Emily was smart. She was funny. She had good energy and loved to travel. She even liked to hitchhike; we had already hitched together to Cleveland and New York. Politically, we leaned far left. We were a team. Being Jewish like me was a convenience, but that was only one factor, like the others.

Emily says I got down on one knee when I proposed. I swear I tripped. We celebrated with margaritas.

I was slow to commit. Previously, we had been together because we wanted to be and only for that reason. Getting married meant we had to be. The word had a dark jail-cell feel.

But every morning, I would wake up and think, would today be better or worse if Emily was no longer in it. And it was always worse.

Ken Wachsberger

Since my Cleveland family was large, Emily's New York family was small, and we didn't have any family in Austin, we decided to move to Cleveland, import Emily's family, and get married there.

Our invitation showed a picture of Emily and me standing on the side of the road on I-35 in Austin. Emily is holding Ernestine-Hemingway, our cat at the time. I'm wearing my full-length backpack. Both of our thumbs are out. The headline says, "Emily and Ken are finally getting hitched."

When my Aunt Sue read the invitation, she said, "It's about time," because we had been living together for so long already. She was among the relatives who met Emily at the first Seder.

Below the picture, we wrote, "Now that you've said it's about time," and then provided the critical details.

Fairmount Temple

We were married April 7, 1979, at Anshe Chesed Fairmount Temple, in Beachwood.

Fairmount Temple was one of the largest Reform Jewish congregations in the country, with roots going back to 1842 in Cleveland. The congregation multiplied in size and changed locations to accommodate growth spurts. Then the post-war migration of members into the suburbs forced congregations to follow.

Anshe Chesed, which had been located on Euclid Avenue since 1912, purchased the 32-acre site on Fairmount Boulevard in 1948; but it took a nine-year court battle that ended up in Ohio Supreme Court before the City of Beachwood was forced to change their zoning laws to permit construction of the temple. The site was dedicated on May 31, 1957.

THUMBS UP

I was in fourth grade by the time my family joined Fairmount Temple. Previous to that, we belonged to Park Synagogue, whose members were largely from the Old Country and leaned Conservative and Orthodox. Fairmount Temple members were Reform Jews, politically community-oriented.

And the temple was located in the backyard of our neighbors across the street. Goodbye carpools to Park.

Unfortunately, the membership was so full they weren't accepting new members. But, Dad learned, staff members and employees could belong and their kids could attend school there. So, he became a teacher. Years later, he became the temple's executive director.

The head rabbi when we joined was Arthur Lelyveld, an internationally known peace activist who had marched with Martin Luther King, Jr., and been shot in the process. Rabbi Lelyveld was a controversial figure among the congregants. The board of directors said rabbis shouldn't be political. I saw him as a model of a Jewish leftist intellectual.

Rabbi Lelyveld married us.

Our Wedding

Our wedding was joyous and shared with 140 relatives and friends. One friend of my folks called it a "three-hanky wedding."

We walked down the aisle to the tune of Judy Collins' "Since You Asked." We walked together to protest the symbolism of the woman being given to the man as property, and also because we were already living together. We wrote and recited our own vows. Then, to Woody Guthrie's "This Land Is Your Land," we walked up the aisle together, symbolizing that we were still living together but now we were legal.

Ken Wachsberger

At the reception, we welcomed our guests.

I had written "The Ballad of Ken and Emily," my poem about how we met, as a gift on our first anniversary. Emily had written a song, "I Take Thee," to express her love for me. We told Rabbi Lelyveld we wanted to perform them at the ceremony. He said, "Knock your socks off but I'm not coming on stage until you're done because my portion is going to be eighteen minutes."

Eighteen is the numerological value of *chai*, the Hebrew word for "life," as in "*L'chaim*." An eighteen-minute service, he explained, would bless us in advance with a life filled with *mazel* (good fortune), strong family ties, warm friendships, love between the two of us, loving children, peace, harmony, a vacation once or twice a year, and maybe even a healthy retirement.

But all that was lost if the service ran into nineteen minutes.

So, we held them until the reception.

The Reception

Emily and I planned the reception with my mom. She clenched her lips when we insisted on a vegetarian buffet but gave in when we agreed to a roast turkey exception for her Uncle Ben, who would not have known how to navigate a vegetarian buffet spread.

But she swore no way to our attempt to cater the wedding ourselves. We gave in when she found a caterer friend who agreed to follow Emily's recipes. The bar offered unlimited soft drinks, beer, and wine, and a champagne toast.

For the wedding cake, a carrot cake, Emily emphasized to the baker that it could not have any nuts in the recipe because my older brother, Don, had a deathly nut allergy. The baker agreed. But as a way to

THUMBS UP

keep the tiered layers from sticking to each other, he sprinkled on a layer of coconut. At the cake cutting ceremony, Emily tasted the cake that symbolized our love and exclaimed, "Oh, shit!" Her sudden observation probably saved my brother's life.

We contracted a local rock and roll band—whose name was a line in a Rolling Stones song—until midnight but I kept them stocked with beer and joints and they played until 2. By the end of the evening, the lead guitarist was lying on his back, writhing out a guitar solo and my ninety-year-old Grandpa Al was on the dance floor swinging his pretty young partner.

We spent our first evening in a dive that hookers rented by the hour because we wanted a water bed, which was becoming the rage at the time. We told the owner we were newlyweds. He said, "Yeah, sure. Here's your key."

That night, Emily had a headache.

PART 4: REDISCOVERING JUDAISM IN LANSING

CHAPTER 15
RETURN TO LANSING

We stayed just over a year in Cleveland and spent the time in two homes.

Our Homes in Cleveland

Our first home was on Coventry, the legendary hippie street in Cleveland Heights, where the artsy Heights Art Theatre had just begun what would be a ten-year run of *Rocky Horror Picture Show*.

We lived in an apartment above a hardware store. Our neighbors were *refuseniks*, among the wave of Jewish immigrants who were fleeing Russia and being brought to America and resettled by Jewish communities. We seldom socialized but we greeted each other warmly and they taught us *dosvedanya* (until we meet again).

Then we moved to a home in Shaker Heights owned by one high school friend, who reconnected me to another high school friend, who honored us by hiring us to cater a party at his home. That turned out to be the only major job we did in Cleveland.

Emily and I Find Work

Emily found two jobs in downtown Cleveland through Mom's friends' temp agency, as a receptionist at the front desk of an advertising firm, where she used an early-1900s switchboard; and then as a paralegal with a high-priced law firm. She disliked them both. Then she walked into Earth by April, the number one vegetarian restaurant in Cleveland, stated her credentials to the head chef and owner, told a few stories about Emken Catering, and she got the job she loved, as their soup and pastry chef. Lucky break for them.

Meanwhile, I found a job at American Greetings writing poems and limericks. I thought that would be a fun, creative job but it turned out to be so mundane I left after a month. Through the temp agency, I found a job at the Cleveland Clinic as a secretary because I could type eighty words a minute. I worked in the office of a surgeon who was famous for planting shunts in patients' brains to relieve pressure, a procedure that was both praised and condemned and about which I understood nothing. But his forms and correspondence had no typos.

I decided I wanted to get into radio so I took the appropriate class at the Specs Howard School of Broadcasting and gained certification from the Federal Communications Commission (FCC), because I was a gifted test taker. The certification qualified me for a job for which I was totally unqualified, maintaining and operating equipment at radio station WBBG-AM.

But it led me to legendary Cleveland disk jockey Jay Lawrence, who had recently become WBBG's 6 a.m. to 10 a.m. morning drive deejay. Jay was in a running feud with another local deejay legend, pioneer shock jock Gary Dee. When Dee's marriage to TV celebrity Liz Richards ended in a highly publicized domestic violence drama, Jay jumped right in and hired me to write short, funny scripts of Dee and Richards in unusual conflicts, usually caused by Dee himself.

I was paid in bragging rights. Each one took about a minute to write and, I'll be humble, the quality reflected my effort. But Jay loved them as first drafts. Whatever I gave to him, he changed to fit his mood at the moment.

THUMBS UP

Bill Randle was another local legend and a pioneer from the fifties who dj'd at WBBG while I was there. His segment where he explained to listeners how to train a cat to flush a toilet likely did not further his legend status.

Short Stay in Detroit

I accepted an opportunity from friends in Detroit to run their catering hall, with the condition that Emily would run the kitchen. They didn't believe a husband and wife could work together, largely because they couldn't, but I insisted on that condition and they relented. I moved out there first and Emily followed.

We left Detroit in the summer of 1981, after less than a year of stress and unhappiness, because Emily believed she wasn't welcomed or respected because the owners refused to accept that we were working well together:

> Not only was I not respected but they were verbally abusive and harassed me. When I applied for unemployment, I told the entire story to the worker there and they absolutely insisted that my unemployment payments would be acceptable. There are very few reasons why anyone who quits a job gets unemployment benefits, but this fit the bill. In today's world they could have been sued or perhaps, been in violation of rights acts.

We returned to Lansing, which was the safe space we needed after the debacle in Detroit. Our old landlords had a place for us.

Settling In

That summer, I began an MA program in Creative Writing and nabbed a grad assistant job teaching basic writing to future farmers in the agricultural technology (ag tech) department. Emily worked as a pastry chef at Roma Bakery, the premier bakery in town.

And Emken Catering picked up our first steady contract when the Okemos Kiwanis Club hired us to cater their weekly meetings, thanks to a connection from our landlords. Working with the Kiwanis Club gave us no opportunity to practice gourmet recipes. The thirty men who attended each meeting were a meat-and-potatoes group. Each meal included a meat, a starch, frozen vegetables, a pastry, and a drink. We gave them a cut-rate deal; I was okay if we had to open a box or frozen bag.

We served their meals family style and took home sixty dollars a week in profit. It paid for most of our groceries for the week.

They were kind men and we always felt appreciated. When David was born, they gave us gifts.

Coming Back to Judaism

During the time I was meeting Emily, I was experiencing a return to my Jewish roots. I had rejected Judaism during the Vietnam era because I associated it with the evil middle class, which I had rejected. But then I spent the summer of 1972 in Miami Beach and found myself surrounded by heroes of mine who were largely Jews: Abbie Hoffman, Jerry Rubin, William Kunstler, Allen Ginsberg, Stew Albert, and others. I met senior citizens in the poor downtown Jewish community in Miami who had fought the Fascists in the thirties.

I was already attending services at the Conservative Shaarey Zedek Synagogue by the time we met. Shaarey Zedek was Lansing's main Jewish congregation. Its membership ran from extreme Reform left to moderately extreme Orthodox right. Emily began attending with me. We were "adopted" by a well-to-do group of friends and

THUMBS UP

welcomed into their group. We became "the nice young couple." They promoted us throughout the congregation. For their continuous friendship, I am still grateful.

Don't Stack Glasses

A mantra among dishwashers is "Don't stack glasses" because when water gets between them it seals them together. One evening, while washing dishes after the Kiwanis dinner, I was trying to separate two glasses that had been stacked. I applied what I thought was delicate force trying to twist them apart. The glasses shattered and cut one of my tendons.

We went immediately to the hospital and found out that it was hanging on by about a quarter of an inch. If it tore, we were told, it would shoot up my arm like a rubber band and the surgeon would have to cut into my arm to retrieve it.

But the cost to repair it now was $500. We had nowhere near that amount of money and no insurance.

If memory serves me, this was the adventure that taught me self-massage and how to visualize, because those were the only tools I could afford. And it did heal!

But while it was healing, we were at a catering job at a congregation member's home. We were prepping in the kitchen before the job and my Band-Aid slipped off my finger while I was mixing a dip. Oy. It wasn't on the counter. I didn't see it on the floor.

I searched the dip, horrified at the possibility, then searched again, and then again. I spooned the dip slowly into another bowl so I could inspect the product a spoonful at a time. I never found the Band-Aid. But I kept my cool throughout the job. One expression of shock by a surprised guest could have put us out of business forever but it never materialized.

We Hit the Road and I Change the Base

We made enough money between 1981 and 1982 to hit the road for six weeks in our Chevette, which we bought in Lansing. We went first to Austin to visit friends, then through El Paso, where we spent the night in a hotel. The next morning, we crossed the border on foot into Juarez and toured the touristy part of town. Then we continued on to Phoenix and San Diego, to visit with my father's twin brother, my Uncle Sandy; my Aunt Kay; and their family.

In Beverly Hills, we were lavished with hospitality by Dad's wealthy Miami University ZBT fraternity brother, his anorexic wife, and their illegal-alien maid. Think *Down and Out in Beverly Hills*.

In Oakland, I introduced Emily to my *Joint Issue* friend, Steve Vernon, and his wife, Dee.

Our next destination was Portland, Oregon, to visit Emily's cousin, who was a state police officer, and his family. We got lost trying to find the house so we were driving around desperately looking for clues. A police car noticed our aimlessness and came up behind us with the lights flashing.

"Oh, shit," I thought. Two out-of-state hippies driving suspiciously through their town in the middle of the night was not a good look. So, I hopped out of our car and walked eagerly to theirs before they could turn off the ignition. "Officers, I'm so glad you're here," I said. "Can you tell us where Bill D. lives?"

I explained that my wife was his cousin, we were visiting from out of state, and we were lost. The surprised driver called Emily's cousin to verify our identity. We got a police escort to the house. Strategically, what I did is known as "changing the base."

THUMBS UP

Coming Home

On our return trip, we spent three days and nights in Yellowstone National Park with elk, moose, and Old Faithful. We shared our site with a French couple who arrived after the last site was taken and had nowhere to stay. A site was not in sight.

We welcomed them to share our site. In gratitude, they invited us to visit them in France and gave us their address. That information is long since lost.

In Madison, we stayed with a high school friend of Emily and his wife.

Then we returned home.

Emily was pregnant within a month. David Joel Schuster-Wachsberger was born July 5, 1983. He was named after Emily's father, David Schuster, and my favorite older cousin, Joel Gray. The attending nurse handed David to me. I held him until he stopped crying for the first time.

The Corner of Saginaw and Newton

We lived in a rental home on the corner of Saginaw and Newton.

Our neighbor directly across the street on Newton was the former head of the Michigan State University police department. He was the guy who had arrested me at the Student Union in May 1970. I never talked to him about the bust. I wasn't ready to confront him, but I appreciated the irony.

When David turned two, Emily went through an existential crisis and decided she needed a more stable career. She earned her MA in counseling in 1987 and immediately got a counseling job at

Ken Wachsberger

Olivet College, a forty-minute drive from Lansing. I was working at MSU at the time, teaching ag tech students basic English; and also teaching Freshman Composition at Lansing Community College's downtown campus.

Meanwhile, as Lansing caterers, we never had a legal kitchen. We worked out of our kitchen. Because a legal kitchen was the first requirement for being able to advertise ourselves as caterers, we could never legally advertise ourselves as caterers. So, we used word of mouth and were successful.

We had an unspoken agreement with the landlord, a large realty company that included among its many land holdings a catering hall. In other words, our landlord was our competition. But we paid our bills on time, took good care of their property, and kept an eye on it, so they looked the other way. Or they just never knew. We never talked about it.

We Avoid the Health Department

We didn't have such an agreement with the health department, so we just laid low and avoided most display ads to avert attention from the fact that we weren't working out of a legal kitchen. We weren't allowed to advertise in the Yellow Pages. We kept a clean work space though and we made sure Ernestine-Hemingway, our cat, washed her paws before we let her cut vegetables. We took out liability insurance just in case a customer got sick but we never had to use it.

The idea of sanitation laws carries with it a positive connotation. We think of Upton Sinclair novel, *The Jungle*, which exposed unsanitary conditions in Chicago's turn-of-the-century meat packing plants, and we thank God for them.

THUMBS UP

In reality, though, they were to us a means by which large food establishments limited their competition. For thirty thousand dollars or so, we could have gone into partnership with a bank.

But then we would have had to mass produce meals in order to keep a steady cash flow and we didn't want to compromise our quality. As Emken Catering, our food was exquisite and our prices were affordable.

CHAPTER 16
McGOFF OFF

In 1977, publisher and movie producer Michael Moore created the alternative newspaper, *Flint Voice*. Six years later, he changed its name to *Michigan Voice* and shot for statewide visibility.

A few long-time veterans of the Lansing-area peace community met with him when he came to town. We liked his energy and statewide vision, and we became the Lansing branch of the paper. That relationship was short-lived due to personality clashes, but while we were on board I wrote three articles.

Muldergate

One was a piece about publisher John McGoff. McGoff was the owner and publisher of a string of over seventy weekly newspapers across the United States.

In 1972 in apartheid South Africa, Eschel Rhoodie, former managing director of the right-wing magazine, *To the Point*, was appointed secretary of the South African Department of Information under Minister Cornelius Mulder, a member of Parliament since 1958 as well as Minister of Immigration and the Interior.

Together with General Hendrik van den Bergh, who was head of the Bureau of State Security (BOSS), they conceived of a scam that, when the South African press found out about it in 1977, became known as Muldergate, South Africa's contribution to the

Ken Wachsberger

English language's campaign to make the word "gate" a suffix for "government scandal."

Judge Rudolf Erasmus headed the three-man investigation into the scandal that led to the downfall in 1979 of Mulder, Rhoodie, and Prime Minister John Vorster. According to the Erasmus Commission report, their plan was to plow money into a public relations campaign to change South Africa's world image by bribing major influencers from major newspapers in Europe, England, Japan, the United States, and South Africa to write favorable stories about South Africa and the apartheid regime.

McGoff was the number one connection to the scandal from the United States. He lived in Williamston so that gave me a Michigan angle.

But that happened in 1977. What was the current events angle?

The Current Events Angle

In Fall 1982, construction was completed on the Clifton and Delores Wharton Center for Performing Arts, a glorious addition to what was already one of the most stunning campuses in the country. It was named after President Clifton Wharton, the first Black man to be named president of a major university, and his wife.

In an effort to rehabilitate his horrible reputation as a racist, McGoff donated a million dollars to the university with the stipulation that the Festival Stage be named after his wife. The university gladly complied and the Festival Stage took the name of Margaret Ewert McGoff in 1981.

The grassroots Southern Africa Liberation Committee (SALC) rose in anger and demanded "McGoff Off."

THUMBS UP

My article, "John McGoff and the Fine Art of Apartheid," was the cover story in the August 1983 issue.

The next year, the campaign succeeded and her name was removed. Members of SALC gave my article credit for pushing the issue over the finish line. I'm grateful for any help I was able to give.

CHAPTER 17
WE CHANGE CONGREGATIONS

Another article for *Michigan Voice* I wrote about the Peace Now movement in Israel. I had no idea when I wrote it how far-reaching its effects would be on the lives of Emily and me.

I Hear My Voice

Peace Now was a federation of peace groups that was founded in 1978 to advocate for a two-state solution in Israel/Palestine. In 1982, they brought 400,000 people onto the streets to protest after the Israel Defense Forces (IDF) sat back and watched while Christian Lebanese forces massacred some 3,000 innocent civilians in Beirut's Sabra neighborhood and the Shatila refugee camp next door.

I was amazed. An antiwar movement in Israel? In the United States, Jews were expected to support whatever Israel's government did in the name of "showing unity." We were pressured to cheer all Israeli moves and change our minds only to the extent that they did. Any deviation from mainstream thought and we could be shunned as "self-hating Jews" or "naïve."

Like young Americans who opposed the U.S. government during the Vietnam era but did not consider themselves anti-American, American Jews like me supported Israel's existence but were appalled by its politics. No mainstream Jewish organization spoke for us.

Ken Wachsberger

Suddenly, for the first time in my awareness, I heard antiwar voices shouting from within Israel. Peace Now was the first evidence I saw of any kind of major antiwar movement in Israel that was led by Jews.

So, when one of the leaders of Peace Now came to town to speak at MSU's Hillel in early 1983, I went there to interview him.

I told him I was excited to meet someone from Israel's first antiwar group. He corrected me with a nuance: "We refer to it as a peace group." Okay, I was a veteran of the Vietnam era antiwar movement; we worked for peace in Vietnam. So "antiwar" and "peace," according to my activist experience, were pretty much synonymous. But I respected his distinction. I was happy to know him, know about Peace Now, and, as a result, actually became involved in the local Friends of Peace Now chapter.

I Meet Julie

I told a friend of mine from the peace community, John Masterson, about the article I was writing. John said to me, "You've got to interview Julie Petry."

Julie was the acknowledged leader of the Palestinian-American community in the Lansing area. She was among the Palestinian Muslims who fled Ramallah in 1948 during what the Palestinians called Nakba, which was the displacement of their communities during the time when the State of Israel was being established.

She consented graciously. She was cordial from the start, a gentle soul with a warm smile, but a determined intellectual whose opinion mattered.

What I wanted to hear her say was that what Peace Now offered was at least a good-faith step forward in the peace process. She was hesitant to outright agree even to that because she knew her words could be taken out of context and I hadn't earned her trust.

But I returned to the question more than once looking for nuances.

Finally, she responded, "It's step one."

That was all I needed to end the interview. I saw the title of my article: "Peace Now: Step One to Mideast Peace."

Meanwhile, both of us were coming to see the humanity in the other. I was a Jew whose family fled the pogroms at the turn of the last century and came to America; Julie was a Palestinian Muslim who fled Ramallah in 1948 and came to America. I was the interviewer; she was the interviewee. We maintained those formal roles throughout the interview.

The moment I clicked the off button on my cassette tape recorder, we stood and embraced. We cried in sadness, joy, and relief.

The article appeared in the April 1983 issue for some reason with the revised title, "Peace Now, Begin Later."

That should have been the end of the story.

My Brilliant Idea

I mentioned earlier that I returned to MSU to pick up my final thirty-four credits. One class, called "Philosophy of the Counterculture," relied on books and events from the Vietnam era. Having returned to college after seven years as a dropout, I was now substantially older than the other students. And, of course, I was the only one who had had direct experience with the Vietnam era counterculture. I became an elder statesman.

One student who looked up to me as a role model also belonged to Shaarey Zedek. He was a teacher in the Sunday School. One day he asked me if I could substitute for him for two weeks. His class that semester was on Arab-Israeli Relations. The students were seventh and eighth graders.

I didn't want to destroy his image of me so I accepted right away. And I had a brilliant idea! What better way to teach the kids about Arab-Israeli relations than to bring in a real live Arab person!

So, during my first class, after having gotten Julie's okay, I gave the students the news that they would be having a guest the next week. I was excited because I believed I was contributing to the process of peace in the world through dialogue. I helped the kids brainstorm a list of questions that they would want to ask her and we talked about those topics.

The kids went home and told their parents.

Just a Warning

The next day, I received a call from the mother of one of the girls in my class, who I considered a friend despite her obvious serious social-climber tendencies.

She "advised" me to disinvite Julie, who was, among certain elements of the Shaarey Zedek community, the personification of the evil Arab.

Of course, she didn't believe that, she asserted. Nor did she threaten to boycott Emken Catering. But, in a masterful display of passive-aggressive, she said, "I'm just warning you that you could lose business if you invite Julie."

THUMBS UP

I Seek Wisdom

Hmm, I thought, this question calls for wisdom.

I made an appointment to talk to the rabbi. As it turned out, the community was divided in their feelings about the rabbi. It was generally agreed that he did a good funeral. Beyond that, some loved him; some hated him. The issue was taking on extreme urgency because his contract was about to be up for renewal. The renewal battle was expected to be brutal and divisive.

So, the rabbi performed an act so noble he united his supporters and detractors in admiration for him: He resigned.

When I met with him, he had already resigned and was waiting for his contract to end. When I asked if I could have his blessing to invite Julie, he responded sagely, "Well, I've got nothing to lose."

Julie and the Jews

That was good enough for me. That Sunday, Julie visited Shaarey Zedek. When I spotted her at the end of the hall, she was walking slowly, clinging to the wall as if trying to disappear. I hurried to greet her so I could escort her to the classroom.

Meanwhile, angry parents lined up outside the door. We had to walk through them to get into the room. She was scared shitless. Whatever she planned to say, she condensed into about thirty seconds and then she whispered for questions.

The kids had barely begun asking questions from their list when the parents began hurling questions at her. They were trying to protect their kids.

Ken Wachsberger

It was a perfect Zen experience. Zen: The harder you try to do one thing, the more you end up doing the exact opposite. In this case, the attempts by the angry parents to attack Julie only caused their children to sympathize and identify with her.

Next Year in Jerusalem

The day Julie came to Shaarey Zedek happened to be the Sunday before Passover. Like congregations around the world, Shaarey Zedek was hosting a model Seder for the kids to prepare them for the upcoming main event with their family. Julie sat next to me and I proudly shared whatever universal elements I spotted.

I couldn't think fast enough to avoid the awkwardness of the closing line, though: "Next year in Jerusalem." Among Jews, it is an affirmation of faith, a place in the heart as much as in the Middle East. Palestinians can be forgiven for missing that nuance. Julie smiled politely.

Not everyone at Shaarey Zedek knew or cared that Julie came to visit. We suffered no stampede of fleeing friends. But among the member elites whose bigoted thinking we had uncovered, we felt a strong chill. Our reputation as a business tanked within the community and we felt alienated. Any spiritualism we had ever felt in that holy place was crushed.

We joined a younger congregation, Kehillat Israel, that only hired their first rabbi while we were members. We remained there comfortably until we left Lansing.

PART 5
LIFE BEGINS IN ANN ARBOR

CHAPTER 18
THE MOVE TO ANN ARBOR

On a trip to New York in 1985 to visit Emily's family, I visited the office of *Present Tense*, a progressive Jewish magazine published by the American Jewish Committee, publishers also of PT's counterpart, the conservative *Commentary*. *Present Tense* was founded and edited by Murray Polner, a widely respected Jewish progressive editor and author or editor of *When Can I Come Home? A Debate on Amnesty for Exiles, Antiwar Prisoners, and Others* and seven other books.

I Panic, Then Do the Research

What I was really looking for was a full-time job. He didn't have one but he offered me a freelance assignment. He invited me to write about the Arabic community of Detroit, which was the largest in the world outside the Middle East.

I didn't know a thing about the Arabic community of Detroit. I said "Sure, no problem."

Then I panicked.

But I also began doing background research. I found a book on the Arabic community in America, which had an entire section devoted to the Arabic community of Detroit. I read it three times and took extensive notes.

Ken Wachsberger

I learned that the greater Detroit community was home to a mosaic of Arabic subcultures. Christian Palestinians lived here. Muslim Palestinians lived there. Maronites, Melkites, Chaldeans, Coptic Egyptians, and others lived in their own communities throughout the city and the surrounding suburbs. Some were largely blue-collar factory workers, others shopkeepers and professionals. The more I learned about the different communities, the more I realized I didn't know.

Then I called the co-editors, brothers Nabeel and Sameer Abraham, who taught at two local-area colleges. When I spoke to them on the phone, they could tell I was knowledgeable on the subject; I was sincere in my desire to write an authoritative, fair story; and I respected their expertise. My subsequent interview with them and the introductions they gave me to members of the different Arabic communities became the foundation of my article.

My Article Is Well Received

My article, which appeared in the August 1985 issue under the title, "The Middle East in the Middle West," was well received by PT's audience and I received two immediate offers that I embraced and then lost but that led us to Ann Arbor.

The first, a profile of the broader Arabic community, I wrote for *Detroit Jewish News*, Detroit's Jewish weekly. After I submitted a generally favorable picture of the Arabic community using leaders of the community as my experts, the editor insisted I present "the Jewish side." So, I interviewed Phillip Slomovitz, the by-then-retired founding publisher. I quoted him agreeing with what the Arabic experts had said, but the editor pulled it anyhow.

They never gave me a straight reason why they rejected it. As I tell the

THUMBS UP

story, they hired me thinking I had infiltrated the Arabic community and they had been hoping for an expose, not my friendly, optimistic profile, so they censored it.

They sent me a kill fee for $400 with a note that said endorsing the check was my agreement that I would never again use the content I had gathered. I endorsed the check and included a note that said, "What right do you have to take my property?"

Bad Optics

My second offer was to write a book on the Arabic community of Detroit for Wayne State University Press (WSUP). What an honor! But I wasn't blind to the optics of a Jewish non-expert on the Arabic community writing a book on the Arabic community for a local publisher.

So, I contacted Nabeel Abraham, who I had relied on for my *Present Tense* article, and asked him to be my co-author. He agreed and we started visualizing.

But one criterion for writing the book was that it had to raise outside funds. I may be wrong but I didn't see any signs that they really reached out to potential funders. It might have been my star power—or lack of. Nabeel, on the other hand, had actual name recognition and respect in the Arabic community. I was just a Jew who had written a nice article. In any case, they didn't raise the money and the book didn't happen.

Later, I saw that Nabeel wrote another book on the same topic but with a different co-author for WSUP. I don't mind admitting it was a worthwhile course correction for WSUP as I never had the expertise the project deserved.

Ken Wachsberger

Move to Ann Arbor

In 1987, while hope was still in the air, we moved to Ann Arbor because it was close to Detroit but with a far better school system, which became our primary bullet point after David was born.

Emily found a job as a counselor in an adolescent outpatient substance abuse treatment center in Livonia, between Ann Arbor and Detroit, so she made the initial move. I brought David a month later. I was hired as a full-time adjunct lecturer at Eastern Michigan University, teaching freshman composition.

CHAPTER 19
I ORGANIZE NON-POLITICOS
AT ARBOR MEADOWS

We lived in Spice Tree Apartments for a year and then bought a home in Pittsfield Township in the Arbor Meadows Manufactured Home Park, where we had an Ypsilanti address but were in the Ann Arbor school system. Our time there coincided with the rise of awareness among manufactured homes owners that they were an emerging constituency.

We moved in on September 10, 1988, my mom's birthday. Emily was thirty-two weeks pregnant. Carrie Suzanne Schuster-Wachsberger was born November 15, 1988. We took the C in my Grandma Ida Wachsberger's Yiddish name, Chaika, and gave it to Carrie. Her middle name was in memory of Emily's Aunt Sadie. She was the first Wachsberger girl born into the family since Dad's older sister, my Aunt Lil.

Manufactured Homes

Manufactured homes, or factory-built homes, are hybrid places of residence. In Michigan, they are a cross between apartment living and owning a traditional stick-built home.

You own the house as private property but you rent the land. Like an automobile, the property value of the physical house decreases but you signed a long-term home-loan contract with a bank to buy it so you can't up and leave, like when you lived in an apartment. Meanwhile, the land value goes up—but you don't have a stake in the land—and so do rents, over which you have no control.

We moved there because the Reagan years were about to give way to the Bush #1 years and we anticipated the economy falling apart. A manufactured home wasn't as good an investment as a stick-built home but it was better than an apartment, its location in the Ann Arbor school district gave it added value, and it was the best we could afford.

Arbor Meadows

Arbor Meadows was being built in three phases. Phase one was already finished by the time we moved there. Our home was part of phase two. Phase three was just starting to be built.

The residents of Arbor Meadows were a different community than the countercultural leftist community I had known in Lansing. They included older conservatives and younger married couples with small children. One couple in phase two was strongly religious and anti-choice. Another, in phase three, were two lesbians who were guarded in public but looser in private social gatherings. A hard-drinking trucker and his Southern gal wife who supplied me with pot lived interracially across the street with their son, daughter, and grandson. A divorced mother and her four kids lived with a member of the handyman crew two streets over.

Our best friends were a Coptic Egyptian chemist who followed us over to Arbor Meadows from Spice Tree Apartments, where he had lived below us, and his WASP wife, who he married after he moved to Arbor Meadows. His daughter from his first wife became David's first babysitter in Ann Arbor while we were in the apartments and later took care of Carrie at Arbor Meadows.

THUMBS UP

We had a beautiful one-story home built by Redman Homes. In 1,550 square feet, we had three bedrooms, a large office, a fireplace, two bathrooms, a jacuzzi, an eat-in kitchen, a living room, a formal dining room, and a utility room. When it was being built, the builder forgot to punch a hole in the floor of the utility room for the pipe that connected the clothes washer to the outside. The first time we did laundry, the room flooded.

The house rested on a surface of clay that dared plants to grow. It had 2 x 6 construction so we could have moved it onto land if we wanted, but we never did.

The kids played with their friends on the playground and in the pool.

Emily, who is bilingual, spoke English and Spanish with our kids so they could grow up learning both languages. "Da me mano," she told them whenever we crossed the street or were in a crowd. On New Year's Eve, we hiked through the snow to get snacks at the corner convenience store to welcome in the new year. "Da me mano," Emily said as we approached the parking lot. Today, Emily still speaks Spanish whenever she can. In every Mexican restaurant we visit, she is known as "La Gringa."

David Starts Kindergarten

David was once describing a new friend to me and I couldn't place him. He told me where he lived, how many brothers and sisters he had, what kind of car his parents drove. I still couldn't place him. Finally, he said, "He's black." Oh, I knew right away. If he had led with "He's black," I would have known immediately because color was a distinguishing feature in my upbringing. For David, I was pleased to learn, color was just another feature.

David started kindergarten while we were at Arbor Meadows. His school was on the traditional track where students called their teachers

Ken Wachsberger

Mr. and Ms., the kindergarten class had only kindergarteners, and, in all grades other than kindergarten, kids sat at their desks for the entire period.

For first grade, we were able to get him into the alternative school system within the public school system, ironically because they needed a white male to maintain diversity. In the alternative track, students called teachers by their first name and his first class had K-3. Kids could negotiate with their teacher to walk the halls if they needed to work off energy and regain focus, which David often did.

We got a call one day from David's first-grade teacher who said he had climbed up onto the roof and she thought we should know. We laughed as we told her he was fearless on the stairs. He shocked my mom when he jumped from the sixth step in her living room and landed on his feet when he was two years old.

When David turned eleven, while we were still living at Arbor Meadows, he earned his black belt in karate. We celebrated his achievement in the clubhouse.

Carrie Begins Kindergarten

Carrie found her two first boyfriends, next door and across the street. In winter, she loved sledding down the hill next to our home.

When Carrie was an infant, I sold World Book Encyclopedias. I went mostly to homes where parents had requested information, which meant they had given advance permission for me to do the *schpiel*. I carried Carrie with me in her carrier, which I placed on the floor next to me or on the table. The mothers gave me points for being the liberated husband. I don't know how many sets Carrie's presence sold for me but I probably owe her a commission.

THUMBS UP

Because Emily and I both worked, we had to find daycare for Carrie before she was old enough for kindergarten. We were fortunate to find the Adventure Center, located in a shopping center at the end of the street where I worked by day at Pierian Press. I picked her up after work. On our way out to the car, we always stopped at the pay phone so Carrie could pick up the receiver and "call" Mom.

We were still living in Arbor Meadows when Carrie began kindergarten, As David's sibling, she won automatic admission to the alternative school that David had nabbed by fate and begun in first grade. She came with us when we visited David, though, and so she only knew of one room. When she and I walked into the same room on her first day of kindergarten, she exclaimed, "This is my room!" She was immediately at home.

I Learn That Reincarnation Is Real

What happened after that absolutely taught me that reincarnation is real.

We were standing in the classroom, which, with all the kids and at least one parent apiece, was filled to capacity. A buzz was in the air as we all waited for the program to begin. The kids were surveying the crowd excitedly, looking for familiarity or to make sense out of the stimulation overload. A girl and her mother stood next to each other ten feet to our left.

And then, randomly, she and Carrie made eye contact. At the same time, they screamed recognition. They ran to each other and embraced. I don't remember if they called each other's name at that moment but I wouldn't be surprised if they did.

They knew each other. They must have.

I looked at her mother, who I had never met. She was as baffled as I was. We smiled and, of course, were drawn to introduce ourselves. Her name was Cathy Martin-Buck. Her daughter's name was Christine. From that moment on, Carrie and Christine became best friends and sisters.

But I think they already knew each other.

I believe Christine is the only person in the world who has known Carrie longer than Emily, David, and me.

Jim McDonald Airs a Grievance

One day in the summer of 1991, we found an invitation in our screen door. It was to a meeting in the clubhouse to discuss grievances. I don't recall if Emily and I had any at that time but, as members of the community, we wanted to know the issues that mattered to other members. We both attended.

The invitation came from one eccentric member of the community, Jim McDonald, who, with his wife, Kathie, became two of our best friends. Jim had been cited by the manager of the park for running his hose on his roof constantly to cool the house. He called the meeting to air his grievance.

Jim died on October 24, 2022. At his funeral, his daughter, Emilie, recalled that experience from many years before:

> As a teenager I had to explain to my friends why there was water pouring off the roof of our house when the sun was shining with not a cloud in the sky… Dad had found a way to cool the house down by removing the heat from the shingles! The only problem was that the park management where we lived did not approve. I mean… Ask them to

THUMBS UP

explain why they had to go to court to make him remove the garden hose from on top of the roof! Well... he fixed that! He simply put a high-powered sprinkler in the back yard and aimed it up onto the roof! Yes, my teenage years were pretty rough.

The First Meeting

Sixty people attended that first meeting, which took place in the early evening hours of Tuesday June 11, 1991. Residents came to get acquainted, to share concerns, and to find support.

If Jim had hoped to find resolution for his grievance at that first meeting, he was way off.

Rather, he tapped into a well of anger and irritation among the residents. We discovered that many residents had similar grievances, including about

- inadequate drainage along the sides of the road;
- wet ground underneath homes;
- sunken lawns that flooded after rainstorms;
- scrubby, poorly maintained grass in the medians and common areas; and
- decaying or cracking roads even though many were less than four years old.

Other concerns included

- pet fees especially for indoor pets;
- ambiguity and perceived unfairness in determining "premium lots"; and
- penalties assessed to households with more than a pre-determined number of family members.

Ken Wachsberger

Residents demanded to understand the park's regulations regarding size, location, appearance, and content of "For Sale" signs so we could suggest revisions to make homes for sale more visible.

So, they took turns airing their grievances and attracting waves of sympathy from each other. A sense of catharsis was in the air. But as the evening wore on, the energy began to dissipate.

I Call for a Survey

Dad became my moral compass and my strategist. He was the consummate grassroots politician. As a kid, I walked with him as he went door to door introducing himself as a candidate for whatever local office he was seeking or as a campaign manager for an ally. We passed out flyers, bumper stickers, and yard signs. We gathered signatures for ballot initiatives and issues he supported. He wrote letters to politicians.

I realized that if we were to organize, which was the only logical solution I could imagine to our shared concerns, we had to have a reason to come back and, so far, we had none. So, I proposed a survey. I said, "We'll get the survey to every member. Ask what they like and dislike about Arbor Meadows. What are your main concerns? What improvements would you like to see? How important is it to you that residents organize?"

I thought of the questions off the top of my head. They weren't what mattered. The survey gave residents the assurance that they were being listened to; and it gave us a reason to come back, to hear the results. We set a date for the next meeting. That turned out to be another bitch session.

In my invitation to residents in advance of our third meeting, scheduled for October 27, 1991, I wrote, "Tensions were high, matched only by frustration."

THUMBS UP

However, as an ADHD, I had the exact opposite reaction. I was energized by the stimulation overload. While some blamed the meetings for causing negativity, I credited them for bringing the negativity into the open.

Then I called for volunteers to amend the pool regulations, to draft guidelines for our new basketball court, and to learn how to bring recycling into the park.

A Community Is Born

For the next seven months, an emerging leadership continued to do outreach to the residents. David walked by my side when I visited the residents' homes to listen to their concerns, like I had walked with Dad.

I suggested ways residents could get involved, including becoming block reps, attending general meetings, organizing block meetings, and spreading the word about what we were doing with friends who lived in other parks.

We formed committees. Emily became a leader of the Rent Committee, which was charged with compiling the data we had accumulated in our survey and interpreting it.

The Legislation Committee educated residents about legislation being debated in Lansing that affected our community; and about how we could mobilize to influence it.

We began identifying residents who were showing up to meetings and volunteering.

We promised the moon. If you had a problem, we could fix it. So, people supported us and we made their lives better.

Ken Wachsberger

Almost Meeting with Rob

Meeting with management was an early demand. It took us a year to bring it about. In the interim, AMRA came into existence.

Shortly after our July 24, 1991, meeting, I announced that Rob Rutherford, Arbor Meadows manager, had told me he would be happy to address us all at an open meeting. That generous offer inspired what was to be the agenda at the October 27 meeting—a question-answer session where Rob could respond openly to concerns that individuals had been voicing to each other.

Many of these concerns, ironically, had arisen as a result of Rob's well-intentioned but obviously flawed "open-door policy," which found tenants meeting one-on-one with Rob, comparing notes, and discovering that they had received different answers to similar concerns. We hoped that a group meeting could clear up some of these problems.

In accepting my initial invitation, Rob added two suggestions: that his boss, regional manager Jim Hoekstra (of Lautrec Management in Farmington), accompany him; and that they meet with just three or four tenant representatives rather than at an open meeting.

I told him I would ask tenants about Hoekstra attending but meeting with three or four tenants was premature until we had a formal structure in place to help us choose representatives.

To allay Rob's concern that an open meeting would be "unruly," I said tenants would submit questions to me so I could weed out duplicate questions and organize the others. I promised to personally read each question at the meeting so my voice could filter out any hostility on the part of question writers.

Rob agreed to check with his boss.

THUMBS UP

Not Meeting with Rob

In the coming days, I got total affirmation from tenants that Rob's idea would be met favorably so I called him back and accepted. Unfortunately, Rob's boss refused to address a large crowd and urged Rob to not attend either.

I reminded Rob that to renege on what was his own offer might now be seen as an expression of bad faith. Rob insisted an open meeting would cause too much tension. I said the tension was already there and facing it head on was the way to relieve it.

We repeated our respective arguments about his "open-door policy" as his chosen method for dealing with tenant concerns. He said he would get back with me.

When next we spoke, Rob said he was "going to pass" and repeated his open-door invitation.

Result: A major blow to our hopes for good-faith discussions between residents and management. It was a tense period for those of us who knew Rob and his family as friends and neighbors.

Major Silver Lining

Nevertheless, Rob's reasons for not attending the meeting became one more reason why residents at Arbor Meadows needed an active tenants' organization.

Seven months after our initial meeting, by a vote of 300 to 10, we turned our vision of becoming an official residents' organization into a resounding reality. Residents from Saline Meadows, Westland Meadows, and Battle Creek, who were already looking to us for leadership, accepted my invitation to join us in celebration and to soak up our energy.

Ken Wachsberger

One issue we faced as we were coming together was whether or not to call ourselves a tenants' "union." Personally, I preferred it to any more benign term. But, in deference to some of the older, more conservative residents whose active support we wanted but who attached only negative connotations to the term, we opted for being known as Arbor Meadows Residents Association (AMRA).

AMRA Elects First Officers

Three months later, on Saturday April 11, 1992, exactly ten months to the day after that first meeting, Arbor Meadows Residents' Association (AMRA) elected our first officers. I was honored to be elected president, formalizing the leadership position that had been informally bestowed upon me because I had suggested the idea that brought us back for our second meeting.

My fellow officers were Tim Thiry, vice president; Ted Dodasovich, treasurer; and Dawn Stanton, secretary.

Kathie McDonald became editor of our newsletter, *The R.A.P. (Residents' Association Publication)*. We distributed copies free to all residents. Like the model I used when I made *Joint Issue* free in 1971, we accepted ads from residents and local businesses. Volume 1, number 1 was the May 1992 issue.

In my first President's Notes, I envisioned an association built on high-level resident participation. And I raised the righteous cause of solidarity with apartment dwellers to bring rent control.

Unfortunately, that mountain has never been scaled in Michigan.

By September 1992, all twelve of the twelve block rep positions had been filled.

THUMBS UP

The Grievance Committee, whose chair was the oldest, most conservative resident in the park, successfully resolved its first resident grievance.

We formed a Building & Grounds Committee and put the call out to residents who felt strongly about the appearance and maintenance of our community.

Senator Pollack Visits Arbor Meadows

Emily, as the chair of the Rent Committee, invited State Senator Lana Pollack to tour Arbor Meadows and hear our concerns. In accepting her invitation, Senator Pollack became the first elected official to visit Arbor Meadows as a guest of AMRA.

Senator Pollack, one of the most well-known consumer advocates in state government, noted that she supported State Representative Sharon Gire's bill to create a mediation and arbitration board for management and residents to resolve disputes.

We educated her about the redlining that we faced when banks lowered their interest rates for home mortgages to revive what was then a comatose economy, but routinely denied applications from manufactured home owners.

CHAPTER 20
WE LEAVE ARBOR MEADOWS

On Friday June 26, we finally had our meeting with management when four AMRA representatives met in the clubhouse with Resident Manager Rob Rutherford and Regional Manager Jim Hoekstra. Being a formal organization gave us the ability to elect representatives and we did.

Management had as much of a reason to want to know who we were as we did to know who they were. What we were saying was that we were now one voice. We had many issues.

So, the meeting opened with an air of casualness. We weren't negotiating; we were getting to know each other. We had submitted a list of questions in advance to defuse tension. Now it was their turn to provide answers. We proceeded with good faith; so did they.

Kathie and Hoekstra Summarize the Meeting

The best summaries of that historic meeting came from Kathie McDonald's article in the July 1992 issue of *The R.A.P.*, "Summit Talks a Success," and Hoekstra's response, which I received in the form of a letter on July 23.

Synthesizing the two reports:

> 1. The scrubby lawns and medians were scrubby when management purchased the property but they promised to upgrade from sod by hydra-seeding any extremely brown

areas; and also repair the standing water problems under homes and in yards, all on a "most serious" basis after they located where the problem areas were. We offered to help them locate the problem areas.

2. In the meantime, management offered free soil and seed to any resident who wished to handle their own landscaping. Emily and I took advantage of that offer.

3. Roadway, driveway, and sidewalk repair was an ongoing project, assessed and evaluated every spring. Hoekstra assured us their crew would begin working on the most serious areas by mid-summer 1992 and anticipated completion of all repairs by fall, weather permitting.

4. They imposed a pet fee primarily to limit indoor pets but would consider alternatives if most residents agreed to them. For the record, they noted, their pet fees were under the standard industry rate.

5. Industry policy supported a per-person fee for more than two people per home; but they didn't charge until the number exceeded four, and what they charged was half the industry standard.

6. Premium lots included those that butted up to woods, ponds, and neighborhoods; those that housed a double-wide home; or a single-wide home with an expand-o; and those that butted up to a common area. The premium surcharge was levied only once even if a lot met more than one of the above conditions.

7. Management reported that the current rubbish company's fees for curbside recycling pick up were "prohibitive"; and Pittsfield Township did not have a mandated recycling

THUMBS UP

program. However, they promised to seriously consider any suggestions from our Recycling Committee.

8. Management deferred the question of spraying chemicals on the lawns to their current lawn care company and promised to consider any equitable alternative.

9. The most passionate issue among residents was rent. I was urged by a number of them to begin an escrow account as a way to press our case for relief. At the meeting, Hoekstra refused to explain what factors went into determining our monthly rent, rent increases, and how much of that money went into park improvement. He promised only to take my questions back to the owners.

Meanwhile, in response to four proposals that we submitted to management:

1. They agreed to use the clubhouse to display information on homes that were for sale as long as residents provided the one-sheet descriptions of their homes.

2. They agreed to erect glass-enclosed bulletin boards with maps at park entrances.

3. They accepted AMRA's Building & Grounds Committee offer to rewrite the rules and regulations for the pool area, the basketball court, the playground, and the clubhouse.

4. They agreed to hang a bulletin board by the mailboxes so AMRA could distribute news and meeting notices to residents.

Further, Hoekstra assured us they were pressuring Pittsfield Township Police Department to enforce the 15 miles per hour speed limit; and supported the Neighborhood Watch program. He answered the crucial questions that had bothered so many of us: "For Sale" signs could be as big as 18" x 12"; and, yes, Rob consulted with him frequently regarding qualifying prospective residents.

Both summaries saw the meeting as a great success in opening up the avenues of communication. Some issues were resolved; others were opened for discussion. We established plans of action for resolving future concerns.

Kathie concluded by proclaiming to residents that it was now time "to go to work to meet our end of the agreements."

Overcoming Misconceptions

And we did. First, we had to find out who residents were, and explain to residents who we were. We did a door-to-door survey to introduce ourselves.

Not everyone welcomed us. One survey was returned ripped to shreds because he believed we were an arm of management.

Others indicated they supported AMRA in principle but felt conflicted because of their friendship with Rob and Danelle. I explained that our frustration toward Rob and Danelle was because they were our only connection to management. By talking directly to management, AMRA got them off the hook.

We Release the Survey

But 242 households took the time and devoted the attention to complete all twenty questions. The results, which we released in the February 1993 issue of *The R.A.P.*, became major agenda items for our next meeting with management.

THUMBS UP

- The biggest concern, hardly a surprise, was the increasingly high rents, which were seen as a major problem by 175 residents and a minor problem by another 40. Residents wanted to understand why the rents were increasing at a rate far higher than expenses. At our next meeting, Hoekstra kicked the discussion upstairs to his bosses. When we moved out of Arbor Meadows, we were still waiting for answers.

- Other issues, though, we were able to resolve. Through the survey, we were able to identify the lot numbers that had major or minor levels of flooding under their homes or on their lots, as we had promised at our first meeting.

Meanwhile, we brought in associates of Washtenaw County Drain Commissioner Janis Bobrin to answer questions about the lack of drainage under and around homes and on the streets. They offered cost-effective ideas to discuss with management and suggested other government branches that might be helpful.

- Hoekstra had suggested previously that owners of outdoor pets would object if we took away the fee for indoor-pet owners. I changed the base: "Are you saying if they don't object, you would get rid of them?" He encouraged me to ask them, the survey did, and the overwhelming majority favored eliminating the indoor-pet fee, 169 to 37.

I challenged him to eliminate the fee before the meeting adjourned. He didn't. But it was officially eliminated on May 1, 1993.

- And cars speeding through the park! Arbor Meadows had recently been visited by a hit-and-run driver. What could be done about speeders? Rob agreed to post more speed limit signs throughout the park, along with three signs warning of bicyclists.

Speed bumps, grating, and security all were presented as possible solutions, all were debated, none were enacted. But the Pittsfield Township police agreed to extend their route into the park and ticket any offenders. They also provided tips on how residents could track down speeders.

> • Complaints were made over the seemingly arbitrary way in which violation notices were dispensed. We suggested that a management-association tribunal be established to handle grievances arising between management and one or more residents.

> • We noted that the office was often unattended during work hours because the managers were out showing houses. Rob agreed to add hours and make himself available by appointment.

No action was taken on the monthly family-size penalty or in setting up a grievance tribunal.

Occasional revelations from the survey had nothing to do with management and more to do with how we treated each other as neighbors. We learned, for instance, that some dog owners weren't cleaning up after their dogs or were allowing their dogs to be on leashes that extended into neighbors' yards.

In a sign of our support, a voluntary ten-dollar annual tax found support from 158 households.

THUMBS UP

A Dynamic Period for AMRA

In coming weeks, I felt a sense of community for the first time. This was a dynamic period for AMRA. Communication was generally open between us and management. Some issues were resolved. Others remained in discussion.

Management added a third playground for the kids.

At least thirty-five driveways were repaired.

Almost fifty percent of survey respondents said they would take the AATA bus if the route was extended to Arbor Meadows. I didn't need Hoekstra to take care of that. I just called Ann Arbor Transit Authority (AATA) and arranged with them to add a stop by our mailboxes so senior citizens who didn't drive could get into town at least once a week.

Attorney Steve Reed successfully secured AMRA's nonprofit status. In *The R.A.P.*, he shared what other states were doing to address concerns of manufactured home owners, especially Florida, which was seen as a cutting-edge state.

We gave residents tips on selling homes.

With help from Richie Coleman of the Pittsfield Township Police Department, we started a Neighborhood Watch program. Neighborhood Watch programs rise or fall on the strength of block captains who represent different areas. We already had block reps for every street so we had the infrastructure already in place.

The urgency for such a program was stressed in the April 1993 issue of *The R.A.P.*, which reported on an escapee from the nearby prison who had been spotted at the Mayflower Motel—just across the street from us! The article also noted instances of vandalism, auto theft, break-ins, and personal property stolen in the park.

The Building and Grounds Committee sought feedback from the community about what issues mattered to them in the pool area, the clubhouse and recreation facilities, the basketball court, the playground, and other common areas. Then they proposed a set of rules and regulations to define and regulate standards of conduct, for community approval.

Seen on the Electoral Scene

This was a period when elected officials and electoral candidates were just coming to see manufactured home owners as an emerging constituency. In advance of the August 4 primary election for Pittsfield Township board of trustees, AMRA hosted a debate for the only two contested seats out of seven races, for treasurer and supervisor. Lynn Rivers debated Terrence Bertram for 53rd district state representative to succeed Perry Bullard.

Legislators passed bills that improved our lives and we lobbied for them. The Rent Committee was a strong supporter of two bills in particular:

> • The Gire Bill to create a vehicle to help management and manufactured home owners resolve disputes through mediation and arbitration; and
> • Senate Bill 584, which required manufactured housing owners to supply a Master TV Antenna Tower for residents as an alternative to cable.

Emily and I spoke in favor of the Gire Bill in Lansing at a Summer 1993 hearing before the Housing and Urban Affairs Committee with about a dozen other residents from around the state and one

THUMBS UP

representative of the park owners' and builders' association. As the first person to testify, Emily was grilled heatedly by committee opponents, on the intricacies of the bill and how it differed from what the Mobile Home Commission already provided.

Then, members began roaming the halls, going to the bathroom or heading out to other committee meetings. But before they disbursed, Emily managed to receive a positive answer from Rep. Sandra Hill, the committee co-chair: Yes, manufactured home owners had the same rights as apartment renters to set up escrow accounts without being penalized or threatened with bad credit ratings. Subsequent witnesses received fewer and fewer questions.

What Emily remembers most about the adventure are all the lobbyists trying to schmooze with us.

We Leave Arbor Meadows

In December 1994, I received a $5,000 advance from New York publishing company Facts On File to edit their four-volume Banned Books Series. That money combined with whatever we netted from selling our house plus whatever money we had put away enabled us to buy our house on Pine Valley Blvd. in Ann Arbor.

I remained AMRA president until we left Arbor Meadows. I had visions of our becoming a force for statewide change. We met with residents from Saline Meadows, Westland Meadows, Scio Farms, and other parks as far west as Battle Creek who had heard about our successes and wanted to learn how they could emulate us. We began laying the groundwork for a conference to create a statewide network of associations to lobby Lansing for favorable legislation and to help other parks organize their own associations.

Unfortunately, I wasn't president long enough to assure continuity when I left. I recruited who I thought was one of our most dynamic members to succeed me but I lost track of AMRA after we left. I don't know how long it lasted. I hope for a long time. It was a fleeting vision of what an organized residents' community could be.

As an organization, we were fierce advocates for our fellow residents. Some issues we resolved while I was president. We got rid of the hated pet fee for indoor pets; saw to it that the flooding under homes and on properties was drained; and revised the rules in the common areas to fit our needs rather than management's.

Other issues were still ongoing when Emily and I moved out. We never got far on the rent issue beyond making management feel uncomfortable whenever they saw us, and rent control never happened.

Our success highlighted the value of organizing and one-on-one communication to benefit both resident renters and management. Our ongoing dialogue would be a main reason why Arbor Meadows was one of the most desired parks in the state.

The issues that provoked and inspired residents to rise up and organize themselves were of a new world to me. The issues were no longer about sexism, racism, and militarism. They were about drainage, rent, pet fees, sign sizes. I took them all seriously.

We were moving a mountain, not tossing a pebble.

At least that's how I remember it. My information comes primarily from my memory and surviving issues of *The R.A.P.*, which we published between October 1991 and January 1994. Those issues are the sole known record of what we accomplished.

CHAPTER 21
EMKEN ARISES AGAIN

In moving to Ann Arbor from Lansing, we agreed we would get out of catering.

One evening, I mentioned matter-of-factly to my students at Eastern Michigan University that I had been a caterer in Lansing. After class, one student told me she was getting married soon and she and her fiancé had been unable to find a caterer that suited their needs. She begged Emily and me to take the job.

Emily and I talked about the idea that night. We decided if we were going to do it again, we had to do it right, which meant finding a legal kitchen.

With those vibes in the air, we catered her wedding. The guests loved it. One guest happened to reveal that he belonged to the Ann Arbor Masons, who I knew had a legal kitchen. He agreed to introduce me to the chapter president and from our meeting came the agreement that we would pay them ten percent of our net for every job we did out of their kitchen but nothing if we didn't have a job.

It was free money for them, no risk for us, and we left the kitchen cleaner than when we found it.

We catered in Ann Arbor for twelve years. We began it there as a hobby, something we could do together to earn a few bucks while we were getting some other areas of our lives together. Then word-of-mouth prompted us into a full-time career as "caterers."

Ken Wachsberger

But what people liked most about us (or hated about us, depending on the stability of their marriages) was that we were a husband-and-wife team and we worked together so well. Our skills complemented each other. I was out front hustling jobs and setting up the banquet room; Emily was in the kitchen creating magic. We yelled and screamed and bitched at each other when we were tense during jobs but we never made lifetime decisions during busy season.

I didn't always enjoy catering. My reliance on it for income was proof to me that I wasn't "making it" as a writer. But I loved working with Emily. We brought up David and Carrie in the business and today they are both experts in the kitchen. Grocery shopping is still a family adventure.

Sadly, we heard the lie that husbands and wives can't work together. To those who believe it we partially dedicate this chapter.

I learned a valuable lesson during my career as a caterer, and I have learned to apply it to all areas of my life: You can promise the world once. After that, you have to produce. If you produce, you'll have gained a customer forever. If you blow it—well, as a caterer, I can't speak from experience on that one. Sorry.

PART 6
THE UNDERGROUND PRESS
GOES DIGITAL

CHAPTER 22
BRAINSTORMING WITH ED WALL

In my first weeks in Ann Arbor, I began making the rounds among local publishers looking for full-time or freelance work. Full-time work was nonexistent to me but I made inroads as a freelancer and met good friends.

Ed Wall, Visionary

One was Ed Wall. Ed was the first person I ever knew who had an entire desktop publishing operation. He was a visionary former head librarian at University of Michigan-Dearborn who was now the publisher, at his Pierian Press, of books and in-trade journals to help librarians understand the changing technology in the different library departments. He had one quarterly journal for reference librarians (*Reference Services Review*), one for serials librarians (*Serials Review*), and one for the techies who were inventing the future of libraries (*Library Hi Tech*).

But he didn't have any job openings—though by the end of the year I would be managing editor of all three journals and a quarterly.

However, his lawyer had recently written a book that he wanted Ed to edit. Ed was perplexed. He didn't want to offend his lawyer but the book's topic clearly did not fit Ed's catalog.

He asked me to edit it: "I can't pay you what you're worth but, if you edit it, I'll let you use my computers for anything you want."

Ken Wachsberger

I had no idea what I was worth. I said, "Even to publish a book?"

He said, "I'll teach you how to do it."

And that was how I founded Azenphony Press and published my first book, *Beercans on the Side of the Road: The Story of Henry the Hitchhiker*.

I Show Ed My History

We were in the waning years of the Reagan eighties now. One day, I was brainstorming with Ed. He was thinking of ways to help young serials librarians to understand the Vietnam era. He said, "Wouldn't it be wonderful to meet someone who worked on an underground newspaper?"

He said he thought it would be fascinating to publish an article by someone who had actually been on an underground newspaper, which was technically a serial. "What I'd like him to write about is what it was like. What kind of police harassment was there? How was the paper financed? How were decisions made?"

I told him about the series of articles I had written for the *Lansing Star* in 1976 that told the history of the Lansing-area underground press.

I showed them to him. And he read them. He said he wanted to publish them as one piece.

I got excited because I had always believed it was important that future generations hear our story and I didn't think anybody even cared.

THUMBS UP

Ed Makes Me Special Issue Editor

So, next thing I knew, he had made me special issue editor for one issue of *Serials Review* on the underground press. He gave me access to his telephone to call people I used to know all over the country whom I hadn't talked to in twenty years, people I admired but whom I had never met, people I had never heard of until someone said, "Hey, I know someone you should call." Leads came to me from out of nowhere:

- A staff member at Pierian Press connected me to Bob Hippler, who would write the history of Detroit's Fifth Estate, the longest-running underground paper in history.

- Ed Weber, head librarian at University of Michigan's anarchist Labadie Collection, connected me to Charley Shively, a founder of Fag Rag, from Boston, one of the many gay papers that came out after the Stonewall Rebellion.

- Charley, in turn, connected me to Michael Kindman, who had founded the legendary The Paper, from East Lansing, one of the first five members of Underground Press Syndicate, and then later worked on Avatar, which turned out to be a personality cult under the control of one man.

- A fellow member of National Writers Union, Martha Roth, connected me to Harvey Wasserman, the premier radical historian of my generation and author of the legendary Harvey Wasserman's History of the United States. Harvey wrote about his experience as a collective member of Liberation News Service, the AP-UPI of the underground press.

- I met John Woodford, editor of *Michigan Today*, the University of Michigan alumni magazine, when I was interviewing with him to do freelance work for the magazine. When I told him about the series I was compiling, he said he had been the editor of Muhammad Speaks, the Black Muslims' paper, right after Malcolm X was assassinated. His history became the opening story in volume 1 of the four-volume Michigan State University Press collection.

I wrote to them individually and enclosed my history. "Here's what I did for my paper. Can you do the same for your paper?" I said I wanted them to write everything: the anecdotes, the dialogue, the personality descriptions, their analyses. "You're going to die," I told them bluntly. "If you don't write your own story, someone else will, and it won't be the story you remember. Only you can write your own story."

I Discover a Quiet Network

What I discovered was a quiet network of political commitment and artistic accomplishment, folks most of whom I never knew personally, who had all experienced this incredible period in U.S. history as underground press writers and political organizers.

The responses were passionate, more than could fill one issue. When they were ready, I would run them one or two at a time in each of the next six quarterly issues.

But more often than not they held back their words. We were coming out of the Reagan years. There was fear in the air if you admitted that you had been antiwar, especially if you were having kids and looking for career jobs. No one remembered that we had organized the largest antiwar movement in the history of our country. No one knew there had been an underground press. Certainly, no one had asked any of us to share our memories.

THUMBS UP

I Awaken a Sleeping Giant

So, I edited every piece. With Track Changes turned on, I corrected mechanics, grammar, and spelling as necessary. But, most of all, I raised questions. I inserted queries right in the middle of the articles: What do you mean by that? Who was this person? What happened next?

The answers to those questions became content in the articles, not puff, so the articles grew longer.

The result was the most in-depth, analytical, and anecdotal insider history of the underground press that has even been told. Individual histories—of *Fag Rag* and *off our backs* and *Great Speckled Bird* and *The Oracle* and *Palante* and *The Black Panther* and Liberation News Service and others—describe vividly the gay, lesbian, feminist, Southern consciousness (thanks to Sally Gabb, in her history of Atlanta's *Great Speckled Bird*), countercultural, new age, student, Puerto Rican, Black, military, prisoner, and other alternative voices of the Vietnam era.

I awakened a sleeping giant.

Ed Freaks

I received more manuscripts than I could publish in the quarterlies. Two were so long, each filled more than 96 pages, which was the number of pages in a standard issue of *Serials Review,* including front matter and back matter.

I started calling it a book as soon as I read the first article. I visualized. Soon, Ed caught on. He even advertised it in a later catalog as an upcoming book. So, I went all out to recruit stories. I helped the authors expand them through my queries, and the manuscript grew.

Ken Wachsberger

We laid out the book using the same 8½ x 11, 2-column format used by *Serials Review* and the other quarterlies. The completed manuscript was over six hundred pages, the equivalent of a 1,500-page book in the traditional 6 x 9 format, literally the equivalent of four books. A 130-page resource guide accompanied the anthology.

Ed freaked, but not because of the size.

He freaked when he read the stories. And he learned about the government raids on the newspaper offices, and the harassment of newspaper distributors and sellers and printers, and the government's focused campaign to destroy the underground press by infiltrating our staffs and intimidating our advertisers and attacking us through the entire alphabet of government agencies: FBI, CIA, BIA, IRS....

Ed's Worry

Ed began to worry that he would be sued for libel. Being a small publisher who had already gone nearly bankrupt twice to win two previous libel lawsuits, he was scared he wouldn't survive another one, even if he won, despite the great publicity I told him he would get. His worst image was of a guy who had been a flaming SDS'er (member of Students for a Democratic Society) twenty years ago and was now a bigwig in the Republican party suing us for ruining his reputation.

"If it's a documented fact, you can't lose," I said. "It's not libel."

But Ed froze. He would have published it if I had demanded because he had committed to it and he was an honorable man, a Quaker. But his heart wouldn't have been into it.

THUMBS UP

I Find an Agent

I knew I needed to find an agent because publishing a book that big was beyond my present capability and I knew it demanded more respect and care than I could give it without help.

I had no problem finding one of the best in the business. He embraced the manuscript and even made it clear that he would want to get a piece of performance rights. He was sure the publishing world would love it as well.

And they did. But they were hands off.

One publisher apologized for taking so long to return the manuscript to my agent. "I was busy reading it—it's a wonderful, authoritative, and much needed collection," he wrote.

Another wrote: "… couldn't put it down … extraordinary book … rave rejection…."

What I now knew for sure was that for me to be able to tell the story of the underground press, I would need to create my own underground press all over again.

All I needed was $18,000.

CHAPTER 23

"HE'LL COVER THE UNDERGROUND PRESS"

I didn't always believe in predestination but then I began working on *Voices from the Underground*. Suddenly everything underground press began coming my way. I think somewhere between Day 6 and Day 7, God looked down at me and said, "He'll cover the underground press."

As I was coming to realize I would have to publish the book myself, I was working with Joe Grant, the founder and publisher of *Penal* [later *Prisoners'*] *Digest International*, the most important prisoners' rights underground paper of the seventies.

I Get Picked Up in Iowa City

I met Joe—indirectly—in May 1972 during the period when I was living in Madison. My all-time oldest friend, Ken Baker, was going to school at University of Colorado at the time. Boulder was less than a thousand miles away—like next door, I thought. So, I decided to visit him.

I traveled by my usual mode of transportation, my thumb. On this particular afternoon, I was hitching west on I-80 from Madison to Boulder and I got let off in Iowa City. Before I had time to recharge my thumb, a car pulled up alongside me. Two guys sat in the front seat. The guy sitting shotgun said, "Where ya headed?"

Ken Wachsberger

I said Boulder.

"Hungry?" he asked.

I was, although I didn't pay much attention to hunger in those days. I fed off the exhilaration of being on the road, going whichever way the wind blew, waving the shopping bag that revealed my destination so seductively—while always giving direct eye contact—that drivers had no choice but to either stop and offer me a lift or, well, pass me anyhow. But if they passed me up, they knew that I knew that they knew that I was standing there and so they felt guilty, and in the world of hitchhikers, that's known as a consolation prize.

If all that didn't satisfy my hunger, I always had a bag of raisins in my backpack—they were inexpensive, they lasted forever, they never went bad, and you could squeeze them into any open bubble of space, like socks in a suitcase.

The guy sitting shotgun opened the back door, I hopped in, and they drove me to 505 South Lucas, their office and home.

Born Under a Hash Pipe Haze

On the way to 505, as they called it, they explained to me that they were ex-cons and that they worked on a paper called *Penal Digest International*, or PDI.

I had never heard of *Penal Digest International* because it wasn't a member of Underground Press Syndicate, the first nationwide network of underground papers, including *Joint Issue,* the paper I worked on in Lansing. But I was intrigued by the idea of a paper that was published by ex-cons, and whose reporters were all prisoners covering their respective "beats" in Folsom, Leavenworth, Soledad, Attica, and other prisons all over the country.

THUMBS UP

The two guys spoke excitedly about the paper but they became even more passionate as they described the birth of the newest member of their collective, a girl who had been born less than a month before in an in-home ceremony that featured music in the background and a hash pipe being passed around the room in the foreground.

I Am Welcomed at 505

I was greeted warmly by everyone at 505 and I shared a delicious vegetarian dinner.

While I was waiting for the meal to begin, I noticed a light table in the back room. I figured that was the newspaper office so I went over to take a look. A partially laid-out page was on the table so I started to read it to get a preview of the upcoming issue.

Wouldn't you know it, I discovered a typographical error. Well, being the compulsive anal retentive that I was—and still am—I had no choice but to correct it. I saw a desk next to the light table, and a typewriter on the desk, and a piece of paper in the typewriter, so I typed the word correctly. I cut it out with a scissors, leaving as little white space around the word as possible. Then I picked up the correctly spelled word with a tweezers, lightly daubed the back of it with Glue Stick, and carefully positioned it over the incorrectly spelled word, using the light that shined through the page from the light table to line it up correctly with the other words on the line. That was it, but I felt a lot better.

I can't remember if I spent the night at 505 or had them take me back to the highway right away. What I do remember is that the visit left a major impression on me. I sent a letter back to the folks at *Joint Issue* that they published.

Ken Wachsberger

Don't Call Us

Sixteen years later, when I was conceptualizing what would become the first edition of *Voices from the Underground,* I knew I wanted PDI to be included. I was fortunate that the Special Collections library at Michigan State University had copies of PDI, and the general library upstairs had an impressive phone book collection that included Iowa City.

I perused the staff boxes and compiled a list of complete names—not just first names, nicknames, or pseudonyms. I looked them up in the Iowa City phone book hoping to find a match. I did. So, I called her and asked her if she had written for *Penal Digest International* in the early seventies.

When she said she had, I described my project, and said I was looking for an insider to write a comprehensive history of the paper. Then, to burnish my PDI credentials, I told her about hitching west on I-80 and the two ex-cons and the baby being born and the hash pipe celebration.

Unfortunately, she said, she was not the right person to write an authoritative history of the paper. I asked who I had to talk to. She said Joe Grant. I said, "Can I have his phone number?" She said no.

But, she added, "If you give me your phone number, I'll tell him to call you." So, I mustered up all the enthusiasm I could muster up and said, "Great," and I gave her my phone number. But as I hung up the phone, I said to myself, "Well, you can kiss that one goodbye"—because, honestly, how many people, when they say they'll call you back, actually call you back?

No Task Too Small

Two weeks later, Joe called me back! As it turns out, he had been out of town the day I visited the paper. But apparently, I had made such

THUMBS UP

a memorable impression on those who were there that they told him about me when he returned. "Ken," he said, "a lot of people stopped by 505 in those days. They drank our booze, ate our food, smoked our dope, partied with us, and slept with us. But you were the only person, ever, to work on the paper, voluntarily, without being asked."

He said many writers and scholars over the years had asked him to tell his story but he had always said no. To me, he said yes. All because I had corrected a typo.

So there's a lesson for you anal retentives out there: Put that on your resume. There's a job waiting for you.

Over the next year and a half, Joe and I formed a precious bond and a close friendship as he dove into writing his story and I dove into editing it. By the time we were finished, it was one of the two longest stories in the first edition.

Joe's Story

And what a story Joe tells! Joe had a few years on the rest of us who contributed to the Voices from the Underground Series. The rest of us were coming of age during the Vietnam era. Joe's story begins in 1953 when many of us were in pre-school and Joe was in pre-Revolutionary Cuba serving in the US Navy and he met and befriended a group of revolutionaries. It takes us through his years as publisher of a rank-and-file newspaper, then into Leavenworth where he did time in the mid-sixties for counterfeiting.

Prisons in those days were hell holes—but there was a spirit of rebellion and reformation in the air. Prisoners were catching the spirit of rebellion that was happening in the streets and becoming politically aware. They were overcoming differences that separated

Ken Wachsberger

them from each other by race and religion and uniting around common causes, including with inmates from other prisons.

It was in this atmosphere that Joe's idea began to take shape for *Penal Digest International*, a newspaper with two purposes: to provide prisoners with a voice that prison authorities could not silence and to establish lines of communication between prisoners and people in the free world.

And now, because I had corrected a spelling error, he was telling his story for the first time to me for my upcoming book.

If Anyone Can Do It

Because of his success with PDI, I was certain that, if anyone could raise $18,000 to fund a book about the underground press, it was Joe. My gift was in getting Joe to think the idea was his.

Sure enough, Joe found investors to enable him to print 2,000 copies of volume one and 2,000 of volume two. We typeset it and laid it out ourselves on WordPerfect 5.1. We had a collective dedication page, with names added by all my contributors.

We had pre-publication quotes of famous people saying nice things about us.

The forewords were contributed by Abe Peck, editor of Chicago's legendary *Seed* during the police riot of Summer '68; and William Kunstler, legendary attorney for the Chicago 7, who I met thanks to Joe, who had met Bill outside Attica during the riots in 1971.

Our logo was a white rose, in memory of a group of students in Nazi Germany named the White Rose who opposed Hitler and were killed for their convictions. In this way, we linked our generation of independent poets and writers to an earlier generation of independent poets and writers.

THUMBS UP

We called the company Mica Press after the gentle and legendary Mica—which is what Michael changed his name to in the eighties—Kindman, who died of AIDS soon after completing his story for me. Our copyright date was January 29, 1993, to commemorate the 156th birthday of Thomas Paine.

The book came out to great acclaim. Gerald Nicosia, the biographer of Jack Kerouac, writing for the *Los Angeles Times,* said it captured the sights and feel and texture of the period better than any book out there. The reviewer for *In These Times* called it the most important book on American journalism published in his lifetime. *Choice* magazine named it one of the top five books in the field of communication for 1993.

Words of praise came in from Ben Bagdikian, David Du Bois, Barbara Tischler, Bill Ayers, Country Joe McDonald, Noam Chomsky, Charlotte Bunch, Barbara Grier, Erwin Knoll, and many others.

But with the exception of the *Los Angeles Times*, none of the over two hundred dailies that requested and received copies reviewed it. The Pulitzer Prize committee that year did not give out a prize in history. So overall sales through the mail were modest. Most went to public and academic libraries around the world. We were beginning to build our own distribution network. The money I sent back to Joe was absorbed in promotional costs.

Ripped Off from Storage

Then Joe's remaining inventory of books were confiscated from storage by the man whose mother gave Joe the money to print *Voices*. He claimed Joe ripped off his mother and demanded all the money back immediately.

After the man confiscated the books, his lawyer told Joe that all the books would be returned to him if he would sign a promissory note stating that he had received the money from the son and not the mother. However, since the son was a coke freak, drug dealer, and informer who was doing time now for selling cocaine, Joe believed that signing such a note would implicate him and everything connected with *Voices*. All his computers and his business could be seized by the government.

In a letter to me, the son acknowledged he made a mistake but insisted that he was really a good person who would love to share his ideas with me on how to market *Voices*.

Joe said bullshit. "He wore a government wire when he sold his drugs to unsuspecting users. That's general knowledge. He's in prison because he was running a drug business on the side that the government only discovered when he sold drugs, with his wire turned off, to another informant, who had his wire turned on."

Joe believed the government was after him—Joe, not the son—for past political activity and when they couldn't get him they settled for the books. Nothing of their business arrangement was ever put down on paper.

Our arrangement, however, was. As publisher, he agreed that if Mica Press went out of business, I, as editor, would automatically inherit all outstanding copies. Those were the books that were confiscated.

Depression Knocks Me Down

Where was I then? I owned all the books but had possession of none. I might have gotten the books back with a lawyer, but lawyer and court costs would have drowned any potential profits from sales of the book.

THUMBS UP

I did outreach to publishing companies I thought might be interested in picking it back up, including Michigan State University Press, but they all treated it like it was dirty because it had been touched by another publisher.

Meanwhile, reviews dried up and so did public appearances.

I went into a major depression, but I couldn't hit the road like I did back when. I was married now, with a son, David, and a daughter, Carrie, both of whom I adored. I had to just sit on my feelings.

Those were not my best years as a parent. I was impatient. I had suicidal thoughts, though none that I would have acted upon—that was just how I expressed resignation and hopelessness, and I was haunted by them both, while I was trying to be a good father and husband. I lost my temper often, always angrier at myself than at anything that was happening around me. I yelled more loudly than necessary to get a disciplinary point across. Most of all, I was despondent, certain I was destined to burn out while failing to get *Voices from the Underground* back in print.

I've had an overall magical life, but I'm haunted by those years.

I Reconnect with My Contributors

And then, twenty years after my books were taken from me, something snapped in me. No magic "straw broke the camel's back." I just changed my mind. Or maybe the evolution was complete. I began thinking "when" and "how" instead of "if." I went into a whole new mindset, from hopeless and despair to my time has come and nothing is going to stop me.

I reconnected with all living contributors and told them I was putting out a second edition. I worked with all of them to update their pieces.

Ken Wachsberger

Well, almost all. Victoria Smith wrote the history of *Space City!*, an underground newspaper from Houston. What a story she tells, about how social movement organizations become victims of organizational failure, using *Space City!* as her example. Hers was easily the most analytical story in the series. We worked mostly by email, as she sent me her updated article and I returned it to her with questions.

We went back and forth a few times and then she stopped responding. I still had two or three minor questions I needed her to answer. I called her office numerous times and left messages always. I couldn't figure out where she went.

But I continued to call periodically. One day, I called her office and someone answered. It wasn't Victoria. It was her replacement. Victoria had just been elected assistant director of the School of Communication and had recently finished a history of the school when she died of heart failure on June 13, 2008.

Then, call it *b'shert*, I received a call from Thorne Dreyer, who had worked on *Space City!* with Victoria and was curious about whether or not *Voices from the Underground* was going to be coming back out any time in the near future. I told him I didn't know what to do about Victoria's piece. He said, "We didn't always agree but I think I can answer the questions the way I think she would have answered them."

Thanks to Thorne, I was able to finish Victoria's piece.

Welcomed by MSU Press

Still, I had no idea how I would finance *Voices* or publish it. I was driven by The Force. Or maybe I was hallucinating.

I ran into Bill Castanier, an old Lansing journalism friend, at the Kerrytown BookFest in Ann Arbor where I was displaying my

THUMBS UP

books. I told him what I was doing. He told me to check out MSU Press. I said I already had and they had rejected me. He said, "They have a new board now. I'm on it!"

So I did, and they did. I worked with Martha Bates, a former member of SDS (Students for a Democratic Society), as my MSU Press editor, and publisher Gabe Dotto.

They asked me for a representative table of contents for a book that would consist of some of the histories. I said the collection could not be split up. They conceded.

We divided the entire collection into the four volumes it should have been the first time. Mica and Joe's stories, the two longest, became their own monographs. The others formed two anthologies.

With four volumes, I needed more foreword writers. I used Abe Peck and William Kunstler's forewords again for volume 1. In an historic third foreword, Markos Moulitsas, founder of the Daily Kos blog, connected yesterday's underground press generation with today's blogger generation. I was honored to add new forewords in the other three volumes as well from Paul Krassner, Tommi Avicolli Mecca, Susan Brownmiller, and Mumia Abu-Jamal, and an afterword by Paul Wright.

Finding Mumia

I could think of no one better to shine a light on the most important prisoners' rights underground paper of the seventies than Mumia Abu-Jamal.

No Plan B

Mumia is an award-winning journalist and former member of the Black Panther Party, as well as a founding member of the

Ken Wachsberger

Philadelphia chapter of BPP. He is a brilliant philosopher and historian whose words often read like poetry, but whose message can only be terrifying to the white and nonwhite power structure.

I might add that he is an honorary member of the National Writers Union, in part due to my yes vote while I was a member of the National Executive Board. (If my memory is correct, the vote was unanimous.)

He is also the most famous political prisoner in the world and, when I finally succeeded in reaching him, he was the most famous death-row inmate in the world.

He was the only one I considered to write the foreword to Joe's book. I put out the call to the universe because I didn't have a Plan B.

Connecting to Death Row

Connecting to anyone on death row is a logistical challenge because of the barriers that are set in place to prevent communication. After obtaining his mailing address from my friend, fellow National Writers Union member Susan Davis, I sent him volume 1 of the Voices from the Underground Series and a cover letter of introduction. It was returned.

A second attempt yielded the same result and led me to discover that a book to a prisoner on death row can only come from the publisher. My friends at Michigan State University Press complied with my request to send a book from their inventory. Meanwhile, I sent my cover letter for the third time, this time without the book.

I Connect to Mumia—at Panera!

While still trying to get through to Mumia, I read his book, *Jailhouse Lawyers*. One day I was at Panera in Farmington Hills, Michigan,

THUMBS UP

doing my e-mail. The book was lying on the inside corner of the table along with my notebook and appointment book. A regular member of the morning Panera crowd, whom I recognized but had never talked to, stopped by the table and inquired about my interest in Mumia.

I was surprised that anyone there even knew of Mumia, let alone would stop and introduce himself. I explained my interest, as well as my failed attempts thus far to reach him.

The man introduced himself as Michael Fox, director of the Japan Innocence and Death Penalty Information Center. He said he knew Mumia, had met him before, and was the very next week going to be visiting him again. He invited me to email him the cover letter that I had written for Mumia so he could relay my request personally!

I did it that evening. When I next heard from Michael, it was in the form of an e-mail: "I had a good meeting with Mumia yesterday. We talked for close to three hours. Unfortunately, he didn't seem to know anything about your project. A weird thing indeed."

In *Jailhouse Lawyers*, Mumia mentions a prison paper called *Prison Legal News*, which was founded in 1990 by Paul Wright when he was a prisoner in a Washington state prison, and which Paul continued to publish after his release in 2003. By the time Michael introduced himself to me, Paul had already accepted my invitation to write an afterword to Joe's story.

When I told him about my failed attempts to reach Mumia, he told me that he was in regular contact with him and promised to pass along my cover letter and get an update. The next time I spoke to Paul, he told me that he had spoken to Heidi Boghosian, executive director of the National Lawyers Guild, and had given her the letter. Further, she was going to be meeting with Mumia that very day and had promised to report back to us.

Ken Wachsberger

When she did, she explained that she had spoken to Mumia and mailed him my cover letter. She promised to get back to us again when she heard back.

Five days later she wrote to Paul and me again:

> Good news: I received a letter from Mumia today with the enclosed note to Ken. "Dear Ken W.: I have rec'd Vol. I of the Underground Press series. As you know, your other books, etc., were returned for some reason. This very day, Prof. Fox (the American fellow whom you met in a coffee shop . . .) mentioned your name to me, and while I wasn't sure, I told him it sounded like the guy who edited a book I was riffling through this morning on the Underground Press. I won't make this long, but I look forward to reading your MSS., and hopefully contributing to this project. We have both had the honorable pleasure of having our work awarded the Choice award (mine for *We Want Freedom: A Life in the Black Panther Party*). As you now know, I heard from Heidi this evening on your behalf. I look forward to hearing from you— Alla best— Mumia"

Convergence Brings Conversion

So, after all that time, after approaching him from so many directions, three separate routes—the book, Michael Fox, and Heidi Boghosian—all converged on the same day. Vibes, karma, *b'shert*. I'm a believer.

In his foreword, Mumia wrote: ""Don't [read Joe's story] because I say so. Do it because it's a great story. Do it because it's great first-person history. Do it because the dreams of yesterday must once again take wing, to bring new days to live in the vast prison house that we all inhabit today."

THUMBS UP

Mumia's Death Sentence Overturned

On October 11, 2011, the United States Supreme Court rejected a request from Mumia's prosecutors to reinstitute the death sentence that the federal appeals court had declared unconstitutional.

What was a death sentence now became life in prison without the possibility of parole, unless the district attorney elected to seek another death sentence from a new jury, which has not been done.

I don't know for a fact if Mumia is innocent or guilty of pulling the trigger, or what the circumstances were that led up to the officer's death. What I do know is that Philadelphia's city government, including its police force, under Police Commissioner and Mayor Frank Rizzo in the 1970s and beyond, was known universally as an incredibly racist, cruel institution that itself should be standing trial for crimes against humanity.

It isn't. Therefore, Mumia shouldn't be.

My invitation to Mumia to write the foreword for this volume was my declaration to Free Mumia! I am deeply honored that he accepted.

Mumia Enters General Prison

The ruling from the Supreme Court meant that Mumia should have been released to the general prison population for the first time since his arrest in 1981.

However, in violation of the court order, prison authorities moved Mumia, on December 7, 2011, into administrative custody (a.k.a., "the hole," or solitary confinement), where, according to his attorneys, his living conditions were more restrictive than when he was on death row. Only seven weeks later, on January 27, 2012, was Mumia officially transferred to the general prison population.

Three New Stories

We added three stories to volumes 1 and 3 that do not appear in the Mica Press edition.

It Aint Me Babe

Not long after the inventory of *Voices* was ripped off and it went out of print, I received a phone call from Susan Brownmiller, the legendary feminist author who put rape on the map as a feminist issue through her book, *Against Our Will: Men, Women, and Rape*. At the time of her call, she was writing a history of the feminist movement and wanted a copy of my book so she could read the *off our backs* and *Furies* entries. I didn't have one—fortunately, she found one on her own—but the experience stayed with me.

Years later, when I was working on the second edition, I contacted her for a testimonial quote, which she gladly gave to me. On my next trip to New York, I met her for the first time at her apartment. Okay, I admit it, I was in groupie mode: I thought she would greet me with a hug and say what a great job I was doing. I was prepared to feign modesty.

Instead, the first words I remember her saying were, "You don't have enough of the women's papers." I don't even remember her saying hello, though I'm sure she did. I became defensive. I tried to explain to her that *Voices from the Underground* was representative of papers from the period; it wasn't all-inclusive. But she insisted. She said the women's papers were everywhere, and that, if you wanted to understand the history of the women's movement, you had to study their papers. Then she said, "You've got to have *It Aint Me Babe*."

THUMBS UP

It Aint Me Babe was the first feminist paper to emerge on the west coast. It actually came out a few weeks before *off our backs* so it gets credit for being the first national feminist underground paper.

But to Susan it had another level of significance. During one meeting of her consciousness-raising group with New York Radical Women in the early seventies, they discussed an interview that had appeared in the paper with a woman, a staff member, in fact, who had been raped on her way home from a meeting. Her husband's response had been less than sensitive—he had tried to make a joke out of it. Susan became inspired to write the book that made her famous.

The person who conducted the interview and wrote the article was Laura X.

Laura embraced my invitation and signed on immediately. She co-wrote the history of *It Aint Me Babe* with founder Bonnie Eisenberg, cartoonist Trina Robbins, Starr Goode, and poet Alta. Working together on their history, I was told, enabled members to heal old wounds that were left over from the period.

Akwesasne Notes

I was already a fan of *Akwesasne Notes* when I was working on the first edition of *Voices*.

Akwesasne Notes, the most influential Native-American newspaper of the twentieth century, was born into the Mohawk community in 1968. It was the word of record for the most significant events of Native history, including the takeover of Alcatraz Prison, the FBI massacre at Wounded Knee, and the imprisonment of Leonard Peltier, who was the longest-serving political prisoner in U.S. history until Biden granted him clemency as one of his last acts as president.

Ken Wachsberger

As fellow members of Underground Press Syndicate, we exchanged issues with each other. I read every issue cover to cover and my awareness expanded.

Unfortunately, at the time that I was recruiting contributors, editor Doug George was facing a murder charge. Fortunately, he beat it. So, when I invited him again for the second edition, he signed on. His story fills a major gap from the first edition.

New Age

I'm the eternal optimist. I keep the vision no matter how bleak the future appears to be. So, when my inventory of *Voices* was ripped off by the coke freak, my prospects of republishing it seemed to evaporate, and I was seeing life from the bleakest perspective, I wrote on my website that *Voices* was "temporarily out of print."

Paul Krehbiel ran across my site one day. At the next Labor Notes conference in Detroit, I was selling books at a display table and he was an attendee. He stopped by my table, noted my website, and said, "Does that mean you're going to be back in print, and would you be interested in a story about an underground paper put out by rank-and-file union workers?"

As it was, his timing was impeccable because by this time I was already conceptualizing the second edition even though I didn't know how I would publish it. I said I would be interested, but I wasn't going to take just any story. "It has to be up to the level of the stories in the first edition."

Paul rose to the challenge.

He recalls: "When I walked into the factory [in South Buffalo] I was assaulted by loud crashing and banging sounds. Black and green pipes and hoses crisscrossed everywhere, hissing like coiled cobras.

THUMBS UP

The once-white walls looked like old teeth, coated in a yellowish-brown film after years of smoking. My nostrils sucked in the stink of sickening smells. A grey mist hung in the air, like fog in a Hollywood movie. But it wasn't romantic or intriguing. The mist was deadly. It had ground-up glass in it. After four hours in the foggy room, I felt like someone had rubbed sandpaper over my throat."

This was not a torture chamber. It was one room in the auto parts factory where he worked, eight hours a day, five days a week. It was also his first step on the way to becoming a founder of the progressive rank-and-file workers' newspaper, *New Age*.

His history fills another gap in the first edition.

The Me-You-Us Theory

One final note before I conclude this chapter. The period when I was editing the four-volume Voices from the Underground Series was one of the most difficult periods of my long, happy life with Emily. I was obsessed with the need to get the underground press story back in print before it was forgotten, and also to undo a wrong that had been committed against me. The two drives overlapped but always travelled in the same general direction.

"I remember there were many times when that was all you thought about," Emily told me. "You struggled between being in a relationship, having a family and other obligations. It was difficult for you to balance all of that."

Tell me about it. While I was working on Voices, I had a full-time job, also as an editor. I drove a long way on several connecting freeways from Ann Arbor into Farmington Hills, a suburb on the northwest side of Detroit, to be underpaid and disrespected. I had to psych myself up every day to get through the day.

Ken Wachsberger

Every day, I arrived in Farmington Hills two hours early and edited at the Panera down the road from the company. At the end of my work day, I'd return to Ann Arbor and stop at the Panera that was on the route to my home to edit until closing.

By the time I got home most nights, Emily was in bed and about to turn off the lights. I'd kiss her. We'd share about five minutes of our respective adventures for the day. Then she'd go to sleep and I'd grab a late dinner.

I put in as many hours as I could on weekends.

Our relationship was saved only by the Me-You-Us Theory, a brainstorm that came to me in a flash and that I introduced to Emily as soon as I realized she was going to be a major part of the rest of my life if I didn't screw up. It states that a successful relationship includes three partners: the Me, the You, and the Us; and each has to be fed regularly to keep them all healthy.

A corollary states that at any one time, one may dominate and the others will have to adjust. I was in my Me.

If you're an author, there will probably come a time in your relationship with your book when it becomes possessive and demanding of your time. Tell your family members you love them and you'll be back. They'll understand. If they're like Emily, they'll take advantage of that time to pursue their own personal and professional growth.

On my part, I was always aware that Emily was missing me. I was missing her, too. So, I worked harder to support the You when we were together, which had the desired effect of making the Us stronger. I saw whatever movies she wanted to see, ate at the restaurants of her choosing, or stayed in and watched TV if that was her mood for the evening.

THUMBS UP

Mostly we went out with each other but no one else, to reconnect. When we socialized, Emily often spoke for me because, even though I was present in the physical plane, my mind was elsewhere. I can shut down my laptop but I can't always shut down my mind, even for small talk.

Emily was my hero during that time because she gave me the space I needed to do what I had to do to finish four books at the same time and she trusted that I would come back

To my credit, I prepared her early.

Who Can Ask for More?

One gap I was unable to fill in the series: the Chicano community. I put too much of my effort into a futile effort to recruit someone from the United Farmworkers to write about their paper, *El Malcriado*, and ignored local Chicano newspapers.

But *Voices* was out again! The four volumes appeared in four consecutive MSUP quarterly catalogs in 2011 and 2012.

As it made its rounds, now with distribution help from MSU Press, I was grateful that I had had two major career highs related to the underground press. Through all my depression, I had kept the vision. I had fallen and gotten back up. I had put it out to the universe and the universe rewarded me.

As Emily noted, "I know from my world you mellowed out quite a bit and you were able to focus more on 'us' and our life."
Who could ask for more?

CHAPTER 24
THE UNDERGROUND PRESS
DIGITAL COLLECTION

I got more.

In the late sixties, during the heyday of Underground Press Syndicate, Tom Forcade, UPS publisher, negotiated a deal with the microphoto division of Bell & Howell—when it was still an independent company and microfilm was still a cutting-edge technology—to create a microfilm collection of underground newspapers.

According to the deal they negotiated, UPS members would send copies of every issue to Bell & Howell, and the company would microfilm them. By the time it was completed, the collection consisted of 476 microfilm reels with underground papers published from 1963 to 1985.

A Call from the Underground

One morning, in the final days of Summer 2009, I received a phone call from Jeff Moyer, the co-owner of a company in nearby Saline just south of Ann Arbor called Reveal Digital. Jeff was the former head of the digitizing department at ProQuest. With a partner, he had bought the microfilming operation and master copies of microfilmed periodicals and started Image Data Conversion.

Jeff also started Reveal Digital because he had a vision for an economic model that would create wondrous keyword-searchable digital collections in a way that was friendly to library budgets and would end up with the collections going into open access.

When Jeff bought the digitizing department, he inherited all the assets that went along with it. In the mid-1980s, Xerox sold University Microfilms International (UMI) to Bell & Howell, which changed the name of UMI several times before settling on ProQuest. ProQuest became a mega-academic publisher. Their collection included the underground press collection.

Now Jeff owned it.

He had a brilliant idea for his first digital collection, to digitize groups of underground papers, but he knew nothing about the underground press.

So, he made a visit to the Eastern Michigan University library. Since I used to teach at Eastern and I was friends with the librarians, they had purchased all my books, including the original two-volume *Voices from the Underground*.

I Sign On

Jeff read it. He realized he had to get in touch with the editor: me. Then he saw I was local. *B'shert.*

We met at my favorite Panera, where Jeff explained his vision and asked for my help. He bought me coffee.

I signed on.

His vision was to create a series of digital collections, each focusing on a different type of underground paper. Each collection would consist of keyword-searchable digital reproductions of the originals. He needed me, he said, to help him figure out which papers to include and how to get permission to include them.

THUMBS UP

Financing the Digital Collection

I was attracted to the project because I knew that surviving underground newspapers could mostly be found in the dark, misty shelves of special collections libraries. They were yellowing with age, getting frayed around the edges, and starting to crumble. Meanwhile, students and young activists did the majority of their research online. For many of them, if it wasn't online, it didn't exist.

What attracted me also, besides the opportunity to explore the underground press again from a digital angle, was Jeff's economic model, which he called "cost recovery = open access." Briefly, he explained, we would market and promote upcoming collections to libraries through our crowdsourcing website (revealdigital.com), where we would describe each collection, list the expenses, and invite libraries to commit to purchasing it.

When we had enough commitments to recover the costs for any collection, sales would stop and we would go into full production, including rights gathering, sourcing from libraries, and scanning and digitizing.

Tiered Payment Structure

Libraries would pay according to a tiered structure, but it would amount to, he explained, about twenty percent of what they would pay one of the larger digital publishing companies for a comparable project. Those that supported us would receive immediate access for their patrons even while the product was in development. Once it was completed and after a certain period of exclusivity for our supporters, it would go into open access where even those libraries that didn't support it had access to it.

In other words, some libraries paid; every library and their patrons benefited. We counted on the goodwill of librarians, especially from the large consortia, to support our vision of open access. By the time we were done, California Digital Library and Big Ten Academic Alliance had come on board as two of the biggest, but the list included about a hundred other supporters.

"Open access" was a huge selling point.

My Role

He hired me to be the official consultant. My job was to come up with the list of papers to include in each collection, then figure out who the rightsholders were—because in the underground press days, when we were writing for the cause and to get the word out as widely as possible, no one thought about copyright.

Then I had to locate them and obtain permission to scan and digitize their papers.

The idea was to do a collection at a time: feminist papers, campus papers, minority papers, GI papers. I would get a cut of sales for each collection as it was completed and introduced to the purchasing public.

My day job at this time, since the turn of the millennium, was as an editor of multivolume encyclopedias at a major academic publisher on the outskirts of Detroit. During my tenure there, I oversaw the writing and publishing of numerous award-winning titles, including *Encyclopedia of Public Health* (4 volumes), *New Encyclopedia of Africa* (5 volumes), and *Tobacco in History and Culture* (2 volumes).

But the company had recently been taken over by a private equity firm. Private equity firms, we at the company all knew, were known to take over companies, drain the companies of their assets, and make money for the owners at the expense of the workers. This

THUMBS UP

time was no different. The company went through a series of mass layoffs. I made it until the third round and then got the call.

But I didn't know that yet. Since I still had my paycheck, future royalties sounded fine.

We Begin with Feminist/Lesbian Collection

We began with papers from the women's movement, which included feminist and lesbian titles. As our own awareness grew, we realized the two collections needed to be separate. In Independent Voices, they are. Because it was our first collection, we went into production before we had reached our goal just to give us a model to show libraries.

The first paper I brought on board was *It Aint Me Babe,* the first nationally distributed feminist newspaper. That one was easy because I had only recently worked with them to write their history for *Voices.*

So were *off our backs*, the first nationally distributed feminist paper to emerge on the east coast; and *The Furies*, a paper published by a group of revolutionary lesbian feminists from DC that appeared briefly during the Watergate era but left a long-lasting legacy. Both also had histories in *Voices.*

Others came easily as I expanded my network, shared my vision, and found overwhelming support.

I mentioned my project to fellow members of the National Writers Union—founded in 1981 as the first labor union for freelance writers and whose founding members were underground press veterans—and discovered that they had edited feminist papers, which they gave me permission to include: *Lavender Vision* (Sue Katz), *Battle Acts* and *New Directions for Women* (Susan Davis), and *Voices of the Women's Liberation Movement* (Jo Freeman).

Ken Wachsberger

Barbara Grier, publisher of *The Ladder*, the best-known lesbian paper from the fifties, joined the project only months before she died.

I was honored to connect, also in her final days, with a frail Edythe Eyde, known in underground press circles as Lisa Ben. Lisa Ben, whose letters, rearranged, define her audience, published the first gay/lesbian publication, *Vice Versa,* in 1947, on a mimeograph machine, I received permission from her caregiver to digitize the complete collection. *Vice Versa* is the earliest paper in the collection. The others all were published from the fifties to the eighties.

I read Barbara Love's *Feminists Who Changed America, 1963–1975*, then contacted every woman whose bio said she was associated with a newspaper if I didn't already have it on board. Barbara's *Matriarchist* joined the collection.

When *Branching Out* signed on, Canada's first national feminist newspaper became the first feminist newspaper from Canada to join the collection.

Other titles whose rightsholders came on board: *Aegis; Ain't I a Woman* (Iowa City); *Amazon; Amazon Quarterly: A Lesbian Feminist Arts Journal; And Aint I a Woman (Seattle); Aphra; B.A.D. (Big Apple Dyke) News; Big Mama Rag; Black Belt Woman: The Magazine for Women in the Martial Arts and Self Defense; Black Maria; Black Woman's Voice; Bread & Roses; Common Lives/Lesbian Lives; Conditions; Country Women; CWLU News: Newsletter of the Chicago Women's Liberation Union* (and three papers associated with CWLU: *Womankind, Blazing Star, and Secret Storm); Dandelion; Dyke, A Quarterly; Dykes & Gorgons; Everywoman;* Female Studies Series; *Feminary; Feminist Alliance Against Rape; Feminist Bookstore News; Heresies: A Feminist Journal on Arts and Politics; Her-self; KNOW; Lavender Woman; Lesbian Connection; Lesbian News; Lesbian Tide; Lilith;* Marin Women's News Journal; The Matriarchist; *Media Report to Women;*

THUMBS UP

Meeting Ground; Motive (lesbian issue); New Women's Times; New York Radical Feminists Newsletter; Newsreport; No More Fun and Games: A Journal of Female Liberation; Notes from the [First/ Second/ Third]Year; On Our Backs; Quest/a feminist quarterly; Radical Chick; Second Wave: A Magazine for the New Feminism; Sinister Wisdom; SPAZM; The Spokeswoman; Tell-a-Woman; Tooth and Nail; Tribad; Triple Jeopardy; WomaNews; Woman's World; WomanSpirit; Women: A Journal of Liberation; Women and Art; Women Organizing; and *The Women's Page.*

They represented the Redstockings, New York Radical Women, Daughters of Bilitis, Chicago Women's Liberation Union, The Furies, and other of the most important women's voices of the time.

As a bonus, we included one non-serial, "a kind of memo" (later published in *Liberation* as "Sex and Caste"), the article that is often credited with giving the feminist movement its jumpstart. Permission was given by co-authors Casey Hayden and Mary King.

Abortion, rape, unequal pay, women in the service, child care, women's self-help, pornography, gender roles, and every other major issue of the period were extensively covered in the pages of the feminist and lesbian underground press.

A quick perusal of the titles in the collection on the JSTOR website shows that seventy-six of the feminist titles were actually digitized for the collection. Though the others were left out because funding for the project ran out, it is a goldmine of historical information for anyone wanting to understand women's history from the fifties to the eighties. Lesbian titles were combined into the LGBT collection.

Jeff's Imagination Explodes

Jeff, as the financial backer and technological visionary behind the project, was loving what he saw and what he was hearing from satisfied librarians. His imagination exploded. No longer thinking of individual smaller collections, he now wanted to create one keyword-searchable digital collection of one million pages of exact reproductions of underground papers that would be available 24 x 7 anywhere in the world, any time of day, on any search device.

I Get Laid Off but Keep the Vision

Meanwhile, I got laid off.

My ADHD self was prepared to flourish with Jeff's new vision. But, I said, "Jeff, I can't do this anymore for a promise of future payments. This has become a full-time job. I need income now."

He knew I was right but he was still growing into the company. Fortunately, my company had given me a separation agreement that included two weeks' pay for every year worked and I had worked there for eleven years. I watched the calendar and periodically asked Jeff for updates.

Then my agreement ran out.

The next week, Jeff hired me.

Timing is everything. And I kept the vision.

Working at Reveal

I started working at Reveal in 2010 but I don't believe I went on salary until 2012. It was by far the best job I ever had. Emily remembers me as being less stressed, more fun loving. I travelled the country promoting Independent Voices and obtaining permissions.

I attended and spoke at conferences: *Berkeley Barb* and *Fifth Estate* 50th-anniversary reunions; Boston Women's Liberation Conference;

THUMBS UP

two Left Forums; Michigan State University's Digital Scholarship and Radicalism Studies symposium; University of Michigan's "50th Anniversary of First Anti-war Teach-in" symposium; Bryn Mawr College's "Women's History in the Digital World 2015" conference; and others.

I caught up with old friends and vastly expanded my network while preserving our history in a new format.

James Lewes and the GI Underground Press

I met James Lewes after I read his book, *Protest and Survive: Underground GI Newspapers during the Vietnam War,* and realized he was the worldwide expert on the Vietnam era GI underground press.

The antiwar movement during the Vietnam era was the broadest, most diverse antiwar movement in the history of the United States. The most powerful segment of the antiwar movement was led by members of the military. The GI underground press was their voice and there were over 900 of them. They could be found on military bases and in movement coffeehouses and organizations in the United States and around the world in every branch of the military.

In his book, he argues that opposition among servicemen was the primary motivation for the United States to withdraw from Vietnam. I agreed. A highpoint in my educational and political growth in those days was meeting members of Vietnam Veterans Against the War. I marched with the Gainesville 8 in Miami Beach. To me, they were the heroes of the Vietnam War.

"By 1970, antiwar periodicals for GIs were available near most military bases in the US and at bases in Europe and Asia, especially in West Germany and Japan," he wrote. "Some were newspaper tabloids with substantial circulations; others were turned out on mimeograph machines. Many were short-lived, partly because of steps that military or local authorities took to suppress them."

Through the GI underground press, GIs could anonymously question the logic and criticize the actions of their commanders without fear of retribution. Among the major issues these papers covered regularly were military indoctrination, mindless and unnecessary rules and regulations, racism, sexism, the bounds of power and authority, legitimacy of U.S. involvement in Southeast Asia, the military as an institution, and exactly who was the enemy. Formats included news, editorial, fiction, poetry, cartoons, letters to the editor, and more.

At the time I was reading his book, James was traveling the globe on a mission to find obscure collections of GI underground newspapers and digitize all of them.

He was thrilled to accept our financial and technical help. I envisioned us including all nine hundred titles he had in his collection. Unfortunately, our declining budget limited the number we could include to just over four hundred of them.

Minority Papers

"Chicano" is a term that you don't hear often nowadays. Members of the Mexican community in this country are more often known by the terms "Hispanic" and "Latinx," both of which seem to be either softer terms coming from the communal desire of Mexican immigrants to be accepted in this country with a path toward citizenship; or else the desire of the corporate press and mainstream political establishment to blunt Mexican-American progressive activism.

"Chicano," on the other hand, was the self-identifying term used by members of the politically radical community from the sixties and seventies as they demanded equal justice in the fruit and vegetable fields and by educators in Arizona and other states as they demanded Chicano Studies programs on campuses.

Cesar Chavez, president of the United Farm Workers (UFW), who I interviewed for *Joint Issue;* members of Mexican American Youth Organization (MAYO) and their political party, Raza Unida Party; and writers and editors of the many underground and alternative newspapers that originated in that community during that period were Chicanos, not Hispanics or Latinos.

When I was compiling stories for the first edition of *Voices from the Underground*, I put all my effort into getting the history of *El Malcriado*, the newspaper of the United Farm Workers. I invited Dolores Huerta, a co-founder of the United Farm Workers with Cesar Chavez, to write a history. She was unable to accept my invitation. That was it for my effort to include a Chicano paper.

Fortunately, my knowledge expanded as I researched.

For Independent Voices, I signed up the following; *El Alacran, Basta Ya!, Bronce, Carta Editorial, La Causa, CCR Newsletter, Comisión Femenil Mexicana Nacional, Con Safos, El Corno Emplumado, La Cucaracha, El Diario, El Gallo, El Grito del Norte, La Guardia, La Hormiga, In Fact or Fiction, Inferno, Inside Eastside, Luz del Sol, El Machete* (Los Angeles), *El Machete* (San Jose), *Maguey,* (MAYO) *El Azteca,* (MAYO) *El Deguello,* (MAYO) *El Despertador,* (MAYO) *El Golpe Avisa,* (MAYO) *Hoy,* (MAYO) *MAYO Times,* (MAYO) *La Revolución, Nuestra Lucha* (Homestead, FL), *Nuestra Lucha* (Toledo, Ohio), *El Paisano, Palante, Pamoja Venceremos, Prensa Popular, El Pueblo Obrero, The RAG, Regeneración, El Renacimiento, El Servidor, Sol de Aztlan, Third World, El Tiempo Chicano, Triple Jeopardy, Venceremos, ¡LA VERDAD!, La Vida Nueva, La Voz de Los Llanos, Voz Fronteriza, La Voz Hispana de Colorado,* and *Ya Mero!*.

Ken Wachsberger

I read the book *The Making of a Chicano Militant: Lessons from Cristal*, by José Ángel Gutiérrez, then was honored to communicate with José personally over email. José was a co-founder of MAYO and one of the key Chicano organizers of the sixties and seventies. He personally gave me permission to include nine of the above newspapers in this collection, mostly those associated with MAYO.

His book is informative and inspirational, but it ends sadly. "Our children are not well versed in Chicano politics; some don't even speak Spanish or like Tejano music. It seems then that we have lost another biological generation to the white world. Like dinosaurs, those of us who called ourselves Chicanos and led the fight for our self-determination are on the verge of extinction."

Independent Voices is an essential tool to reverse that negative flow.

A few examples of minority papers that signed on to be digitized:

- *Freedom* (forerunner of the Civil Rights movement, published by actor Paul Robeson and other black activists in the early fifties)
- *Akwesasne Notes* (official publication of the Mohawk Nation in upstate New York, possibly the most influential Native American alternative newspaper of the seventies)
- *Quilt, Y'Bird,* and *Yardbird Reader* (literary magazines edited by poet Ishmael Reed)
- *Gidra* (voice of the Asian-American community in the greater UCLA community, from 1969 to 1974)
- *El Azteca, El Deguello, El Despertador, El Golpe Avisa, Hoy, In Fact or Fiction, La Revolución, MAYO Times,* and *The RAG* (newspapers of Mexican American Youth Organization (MAYO), pioneering organization from San Antonio, Texas, that, with its Raza Unida Party, fought for Mexican-American rights in the late sixties)

THUMBS UP

- *Lakota Times* (the first independently owned Native American newspaper in the United States)
- *Palante* (the voice of the Young Lords, the most important Puerto Rican-American nationalist organization of the sixties and seventies, primarily from Chicago and New York)
- *Survival News* (edited by Janet McCloud, considered the Rosa Parks of the American Indian movement)
- *Bronce* (published in Oakland, CA, by Mexican American Liberation Art Front (MALA-F), the first Chicano nationalist political arts collective)
- *Muhammad Speaks* (newspaper of the Black Muslim community)
- *The Student Voice* (published by Student Nonviolent Coordinating Committee, SNCC, the premier voice of the Civil Rights movement at the start of the sixties)
- *El Grito del Norte* (one of the first Chicano papers to discuss welfare, prisoners, historical Mexican feminism, birth control, and male-oriented consumerism)
- *Indian Times* (edited by Charles Trimble, founder of the American Indian Press Association)
- *El Paisano* (newspaper for the United Farm Workers Organizing Committee)

Local and national radical groups represented by these papers included El Movimiento Estudiantil Chicano de Aztlán (MECHA; *El Machete*), Northwest Indian Women's Circle (*Moccasin Line*), National Congress of American Indians (*The Sentinel*),Los Siete de La Raza (*Basta Ya!*), Committee on Chicano Rights (*CCR Newsletter* and *El Tiempo Chicano),* Dodge Revolutionary Union Movement *(DRUM Newsletter)*, Oakland Latinos United for Justice (*La Hormiga*), Mexican Liberation Party (*Regeneración*), Black Allied Student Association (*The Faith*), Survival of American Indian Association (*The Renegade*), United Native Americans Liberation News Service (*The Warpath*), and many others.

Ken Wachsberger

Police brutality, poverty, Civil Rights, racism, sickle cell anemia and other health issues, political prisoners, government spying, international liberation movements, urban renewal, fishing rights, and community survival programs, as well as music, art, and poetry, were among the major issues that were covered regularly and with more depth and understanding on the pages of these papers than could be found in any other media.

Not every one of the above titles made the collection, of course, because of tightening finances, but over one hundred did, representing the Black (7), Native American (17), Chicano (33), and other minority communities.

Gay and Lesbian Papers

In 1948, at a time when homosexuals were considered degenerates and they had no organized community, a gay visionary named Harry Hay proclaimed that homosexuals were a "cultural minority" and could organize themselves to demand dignity. That call is credited with inspiring the creation of lesbian, gay, bisexual, and transgender communities on every continent.

In 1950, he organized the Mattachine Society, considered the first sustained gay activist group in America. Through the Mattachine Society, he founded *ONE*, the first gay magazine in the United States. In the 1970s, he co-founded the gay spiritual men's group the Radical Faeries.

To celebrate the one hundredth anniversary of his birth, the Harry Hay Centennial Committee and the Center for Lesbian and Gay Studies at the City University of New York presented a four-day conference in September 2012 in New York City. I was honored to be one of the speakers. My topic was the life of underground press legend Mica Kindman, who had been a member of Radical Faeries and whose story was all of volume 2 in the Voices from the Underground Series.

THUMBS UP

Throughout the four days, I networked heavily, introduced the project to everyone, and came away with a long list of contacts, many of which never panned out but some of which did. I also came away from the conference with four new titles:

- *Lavender* U: thanks to Murray Feldman
- *Come Out!*: thanks to Perry Brass, and
- *Gay Alternative* and *OUT/LOOK*: thanks to Jeffrey Escoffier

By the time I was done, these papers had signed on as well: *Ain't It Da Truth, Au Courant, Bay Area Reporter, Chicago Gay Pride 1971, The Effeminist, Fag Rag, Faggots on Faggotry, Gay Flames, Gay Liberator, Gay Post, Homophile Action League Newsletter, Janus Society Newsletter, Mattachine Society Newsletter* (Philadelphia), *Motive* (gay issue), *New Gay Life, ONE Confidential, OUT/LOOK, The Paper* (Chicago, IL), *Philadelphia Gay News, Philadelphia Weekly Gayzette, The Phoenix, Tangents,* and *Vector.*

In the end, unfortunately, only a handful of them made the final cut. JSTOR shows thirty-four titles in its LGBT collection.

Budget starvation.

Campus-Based Papers

Underground newspapers sprung up on campuses and surrounding communities all over the country to capture the local voices of dissent and to build a new society. Independent Voices received permission to digitize over three hundred of them.

Ken Wachsberger

A few examples:

- The first five members of Underground Press Syndicate: Berkeley Barb, East Village Other, Los Angeles Free Press, The Paper, and Fifth Estate
- *Great Speckled Bird* and *Kudzu* (from Atlanta, GA, and Jackson, MS, two of the premier underground papers from the Deep South)
- *Ann Arbor Sun* (published by John Sinclair and the White Panthers/ Rainbow People's Party)
- *Other Scenes* (newspaper of underground press pioneer John Wilcock)
- *Quicksilver Times* (underground paper of record in the nation's capital)
- *Prisoners' Digest International* (from Iowa City, the most important prisoners' rights newspaper of the seventies)
- *The Buddhist 3rd Class Junkmail* Oracle (published by legendary Cleveland poet d.a. levy)
- *The Rag* (Austin's mighty underground paper that lives today in the electronic world as *Rag Blog*)
- *The Ghost* (dissident news sheet published anonymously in Richmond, Virginia, by civil rights pioneer Edward Peeples)
- *Chicago Seed* (leading antiwar newspaper during the police riots in Chicago outside the 1968 Democratic Presidential Nominating Convention)

Local and national radical groups represented by these papers included the Weather Underground (*Osawatomie*), Students for a Democratic Society (SDS; *New Left Notes*), Southern Student Organizing Committee (SSOC; *New South Student*), Yippies (*Overthrow*), Diggers (*Kaliflower*), Free Speech Movement (*Wooden Shoe*), and many others.

The Civil Rights Movement, the war in Vietnam, music, art, poetry, the drug wars, government spying on citizens, the emerging gender, minority, ecology, and other liberation movements, and every other major issue of the period were covered extensively in the pages of the campus underground press.

Eighty of them made it into the collection.

Rich Liberals and Rock Stars

As I've been noting, the company was not able to sustain the economic model that relied on larger libraries to pay for a service that would eventually be free to all libraries, whether they contributed or not. It relied on the spirit of cooperation and giving that is so much a part of library culture, as far as I could see with this project.

But library budgets have trended downward in recent decades, and libraries were our biggest source of income.

For a brief period, Jeff and I talked about approaching rich liberals and rock stars and asking for donations to fill the gap our library campaign was unable to fill. Many rock stars of the period, I still believe, owe their success in part to the publicity they received in the underground press. The Woodstock Festival itself only advertised in the underground press. They are an untapped resource if the project ever is going to grow, and I hope it will.

That strategy, unfortunately, was not aggressively pursued. I was laid off—my last paycheck came in the middle of January 2018.

By this time, we had already digitized over a half million pages from over eight hundred papers. Independent Voices is the most extensive digital collection of underground, alternative, and literary newspapers and magazines from the fifties through the eighties that has ever been conceptualized and created.

Ken Wachsberger

It can be even better with the necessary funding.

Papers represent the gay, lesbian, feminist, black, Native American, Chicano, Puerto Rican, Asian-American, military, campus, community, new age, Southern consciousness, prisoners' rights, and other alternative voices of the political left during that period, like the mosaic I created with the Voices from the Underground Series but digital and expanded.

It even has four "underground papers" published by the FBI to sow dissension in the Movement and eight papers from right-wing groups.

Permission was given personally by the pioneers who brought the papers to life (except for the FBI papers). In most cases, contributors understood the historic nature of the collection and were grateful to be part of it.

A few were suspicious and hostile. One lesbian editor rejected my invitation because she misunderstood copyright law and ignored my explanation. The rightsholder from one Black paper accused Whitey of ripping off Black culture.

Every time I obtained a permission, Jeff had to find a library whose underground press collection included that title. We sourced from more than two dozen libraries and many individuals who sent us original papers from their collections that we scanned and digitized and then returned safely to them along with keyword-searchable digital files and metadata of the papers that we scanned.

Large contributions were made by Duke University, Northwestern University and the GI Press Project, University of Wisconsin, University at Buffalo, Michigan State University, University of Michigan, University of Texas, New York University, University of Kansas, Bowling Green State University, University of Arkansas Little Rock, and others.

THUMBS UP

Most Comprehensive *Barb* Collection Anywhere

In other instances, individuals loaned us their personal collections. I worked with Raquel Scherr, who, as daughter of Max Scherr, founder of the legendary *Berkeley Barb,* was the designated rightsholder.

I became aware of the *Barb* before Kent State, which is when I became radicalized. I remember the day. I was visiting my brother, Don, in Manhattan Beach, California. I was listening to Johnny Rivers sing "Going Back to Big Sur" and I realized that Big Sur was only about four hundred miles north on Highway 1.

So, the next morning, I filled my laundry bag with two days' worth of clothing and camping gear, slung it over my left shoulder, and rode my right thumb up Highway 1. I know it was 1969 because that was my first of what would turn out to be a decade of hitchhiking adventures and it was the year, I learned later, that Jack Kerouac died. Naturally, I drew a karmic connection between the two of us, two generations of hitchhikers.

Three short rides brought me out of the Los Angeles area, and then I got picked up by four long-haired hippies, two male and two female, in—cliché alert—a VW microbus with multi-colored swirls and shooting stars on the sides. So much smoke was coming out of the car, I was high before I sat down. Sometime before I passed out with a big grin on my face, they introduced me to the latest copy of the *Barb*. I'm pretty sure that was why I had a grin.

For a kid from the eastside suburbs of Cleveland who wasn't ready yet for the politics, the *Barb* was outrageous with its cartoons, graphics, and layout that told me there was something different out there that I couldn't ignore. Later, when I came of age at Michigan State and realized that *The Paper,* East Lansing's underground newspaper, was one of the first five members of Underground Press Syndicate, I discovered that the *Barb* had been another. Berkeley was the epicenter of the counterculture. The *Barb* was the voice of Berkeley.

When I began working with Raquel, no comprehensive print collection of the *Barb* existed anywhere. We did outreach to former *Barb* staff members and inspired them to search their archives for any issues they could find there.

This was 2015. Fifty years before, the *Barb* had been founded, so Raquel and former staff members were in the process of organizing a fiftieth-anniversary celebration. I was honored to be invited to give a major presentation. I talked about the project and put out the word.

We promoted it on the *Barb* Facebook page.

Our final collection still isn't comprehensive but it is the most nearly comprehensive collection anywhere, and it's digital!

Obtaining Permission by Consensus

Knowing who to ask for permission was easy with the *Barb*. It wasn't always that easy. For many papers, ownership had never been a topic of conversation. Was there even one person only? Maybe it was a group.

In cases like that, I looked for consensus.

That's how I got *East Village Other* on board. I sent my invitation to a list of every EVO veteran I could find, and even some folks peripheral to EVO who weren't in a position to give permission but who might have opinions. No one claimed rights. Suggestions were shared but no name emerged as the true one rightsholder. Finally, everyone agreed to disavow any personal claim to the paper but be okay with it being digitized and we called that consensus.

THUMBS UP

A paper that came on board at the same time was *Gothic Blimp Works*, owned by EVO and billed as "the first Sunday underground comic paper." Unfortunately, it only had a brief run of eight issues in 1969.

Full Weight of History

In other cases, the copyright holder was clearly known, and obtaining permission was still a challenge. I felt the full weight of our history when I tried to bring the legendary *Los Angeles Free Press* on board.

Founder Art Kunkin was now almost to the end of his time on this plane. He went in and out of good days.

But he was passionate about Independent Voices. Every time I talked to him on the phone, he was fully on board. He would sign the agreement as soon as we hung up and send it right to me, he promised every time.

But every time, as soon as he hung up the phone, he forgot what he was going to do.

Finally, one time, he remembered and sent me the agreement. Shortly after that, he died.

A New Adventure Begins

When I was laid off, rights gathering continued for a short while. Reveal struggled to hang on but it never went out of business, and, in fact, in 2018 they finished raising the $1.8 million in funding they needed to reach the cost-recovery goal they established for Independent Voices.

Ken Wachsberger

In April 2018, they suspended fundraising and digitization operations when Image Data Conversion, the mother company that provided office space and backend support for Reveal Digital, was, according to Peggy Glahn, "evicted from their office space and their assets repossessed. Reveal Digital's few physical assets, backup servers and hard drives, were lost to that process. However, most of our assets were digital and we retained control over them, including our published collections on the Veridian platform, our email and business files, and our Customer Relationship Management (CRM) system."

It was acquired by ITHAKA in 2019 and became a sister organization to JSTOR, ITHAKA S&R, and Portico. The underground press collection, now called Independent Voices, became available on the JSTOR platform but as a separate entity from JSTOR.

According to Peggy, who was associate director at Reveal when we worked together, and who survived the move to ITHAKA, "Reveal Digital had strong support from academic libraries, and we were self-sustaining. While we could have continued as an independent entity, we felt that it was critical to our long-term success that we join a larger organization that could provide the technical and business support that would enable us to grow much more quickly than we could on our own."

She noted that they have completed two new collections that are open to everyone, American Prison Newspapers and Student Activism. They have also started three new collections, which are open access even as they are being built: Black Periodicals: From the Great Migration through Black Power; HIV, AIDS, & the Arts; and Behind the Scenes of the Civil Rights Movements.

As my final contribution, I sent them the contracts from the papers that gave permission but were never digitized. In poker, that's called money on the table. I was pleased to hear from Peggy that "Black

THUMBS UP

Periodicals: From the Great Migration through Black Power will build on the work you did to acquire rights for the Black Periodicals series in Independent Voices. There are around eight periodicals we had targeted for Independent Voices and for which you obtained copyright agreements that were never digitized. We are planning to include those eight in the Black Periodicals collection plus more that we have added onto the target title list."

Looking to the future, she adds, "Having a pool of titles where the copyright agreements are already in place represents a tremendous opportunity for adding onto Independent Voices. Although we do not have defined plans for doing so beyond Black Periodicals, we remain open to opportunities that may arise with special funding contributions in the future."

In any case, it is still open access and the best digital source on the underground press that has ever been created. It can be found at bit.ly/3Wl6psT

The Underground Press Today

The underground press was the voice of the largest, most diverse antiwar movement in the history of our country. It changed society's understanding of our unholy war in Vietnam and forced it to an embarrassing halt. At the same time, it created a peace community around the many issues of the period that it embraced. No wonder corporate historians and political leaders wanted to write it out of history or just let it be forgotten.

Independent Voices is one step in preserving that history. Many papers I was unable to reach before we ran out of money. Others, I did reach and even obtained permission to include, but we lacked the financial resources to digitize them. May the work continue.

And may it be an inspiration to young activist scholars to embrace their own independent, noncorporate media. The timing has never been better.

The reactionary forces won the 2024 election not because they had a better message or because progressive forces have to move to the right to win, the line we are being fed, but because the reactionary corporate press shed any pretense of independence and totally crumbled. Jeff Bezos censored the *Washington Post*'s endorsement of Harris and went with no endorsement. The *Los Angeles Times* did the same and ruled that any anti-Trump article must have a corresponding pro-Trump article. Fox News lies as a matter of practice.

All the money in the world would not have helped the voices of the people to penetrate that wall.

It's time to make the media the issue; and to listen again to the poets and visionaries of the independent, noncorporate press.

PART 7
ON THE ROAD AGAIN

CHAPTER 25
EMU LECTURERS MAKE HISTORY WITH FIRST-EVER BARGAINING UNIT

For over forty years, I taught writing at a string of colleges and institutions including Michigan State University; Lansing Community College and its Jackson State Prison branch; Washtenaw Community College; and my own School for Compulsive Communicators. I could always count on getting a job because I had a Master's degree but it was never a tenure-track position because I didn't have a doctorate, even though I was far more widely published than most other faculty members.

In 1987, I began teaching Freshman Composition at Eastern Michigan University.

Five years into my non-tenure-track tenure at EMU, in March 1992, I responded to an invitation I found in my mailbox to meet with other lecturers and Rollie Hopgood, field organizer with and future president of Michigan Federation of Teachers and School Related Personnel (MFT&SRP), for drinks, light hors d'oeuvres, and to explore the idea of creating a bargaining unit for adjunct faculty.

That's Outrageous!

It was an outrageous idea. No such animal had ever existed in the entire state of Michigan: a bargaining unit for both full-time and part-time adjunct faculty, as lecturers are also known.

Ken Wachsberger

Oh, there were faculty unions for the tenure-track faculty. Sometimes adjuncts were allowed to belong, but they were secondary members in those unions. They didn't have their own union.

And it showed. Adjuncts received few or no benefits besides free parking and a library card. They worked extra classes on multiple campuses to earn more money to pay for the benefits they weren't paid because they were part time (as they were generically called; in reality, they often taught the equivalent of more than full time, on multiple campuses).

But the timing was right. These were the years when, nationwide and industrywide, in all white- and blue-collar industries, full-timers were being fired or retired and replaced with part-timers, in the name of budget cutting and saving taxes.

In academia, schools stopped hiring tenure-track experts who would be paid livable wages; and replaced them with non-tenure-track part-timers, also experts, whose salaries were way lower and whose number of credits taught always fell under the number needed to earn benefits and qualify for union membership.

At EMU, one lecturer earned approximately $1,800 per three-credit course. If you taught four classes, or 12 credits, for two terms, the equivalent in some departments of a full-time load, the university would pay you $14,400 with no days off, even for funerals.

To receive a salary equivalent to that of the average professor, which was $47,700 and included full benefits equal almost to the lecturer's salary, a lecturer would have to teach approximately eight three-credit classes per term over two terms. But if the university gave you that many classes. they would have to reclassify you as full-time and make you eligible for the same benefits as the full-timers.

THUMBS UP

So, you were forced to pick up classes at other colleges in the Ypsilanti, Ann Arbor, Toledo, and Detroit area communities. It was not unusual for part-timers to actually teach eight classes divided among the colleges in those four communities.

We found ourselves on the cutting edge of labor organizing in this country.

Martha Kransdorf

So, I showed up to meet Rollie, along with Martha Kransdorf and a handful of full- and part-time lecturers representing mostly the liberal arts majors and less the business and technical majors.

Martha, the sender of the meeting invitation, was a lifelong union family member. Her father had belonged to the rail workers' union; her grandmother was in the furriers' union. She grew up listening to Pete Seeger and considered Pete and his wife, Toshi, to be personal friends. "I was lucky to have them as friends. They were a huge influence."

She was also a full-time lecturer in the education department. She was inspired to meet with Rollie when her summer workload was cut below full time and she lost her insurance.

Her first visit actually had been with the AAUP, who already represented the tenure-track faculty. They seemed an obvious part of our community of interest.

But, "They said we were too transient. I called MFT. Rollie came out the next day."

MFT attorney Mark Cousens offered to go to court for her but the best offer he could get for her was full time if she taught a Saturday class. Martha, who is an observant Jew, could not accept.

Ken Wachsberger

EMULOC Is Born

As a result of the meeting with Rollie, a small group of lecturers, including Martha and me, both full time and part time, working with Michigan Federation of Teachers (MFT), began an official campaign to determine if there was a "show of interest" among lecturers in the idea of unionizing. EMULOC (EMU Lecturers Organizing Committee) was born that afternoon.

Workers "show interest" in unionizing when they sign a certain card authorizing and designating a union to represent them in collective bargaining. In order to be allowed an official election approved by Michigan Employee Relations Commission, or MERC, which is Michigan's National Labor Relations Board, any group must show that at least thirty percent of its members have signed those cards. MERC then conducts an election among all the workers; a majority of those who vote determines the outcome.

The contract of EMU's tenure-track faculty union, EMU-AAUP (American Association of University Professors), required the administration to give them a list of lecturers at the end of each term. The number of lecturers regularly hovered around the 400 mark so we used 120 as the number that would give us thirty percent and then shot higher, at MFT's recommendation, to ensure a margin of safety, as insurance against invalid cards and administration tricks.

Card Campaign Ends in Disaster

We did two initial card campaigns. In the first, lecturers were encouraged to sign the cards and mail them in. Then disaster struck. The cards were all lost by our MFT contact person and we had to start over.

THUMBS UP

We Regroup

We regrouped. We resolved to start all over but this time we would hang onto the cards until we had all the signatures and then deliver them all at once.

We found one pro-union lecturer in every department and empowered them to collect cards from their fellow adjuncts. They met with them in their offices and in their homes, and answered their questions.

I was the card collector. All cards were handed over to me. I kept track of who had signed and not signed in each department and made sure those who had not been reached were reached.

Meanwhile, a small group of us met regularly in meetings that were open to all lecturers. We organized rallies and marches and workshops. We sponsored a showing of the labor movie, *Salt of the Earth*, about Latino miners in the Southwest and their struggle for basic justice and union recognition. We fed lecturers streams of information through news releases and our newsletter, *Lecturers' Link*.

We began unofficially representing members in their labor disputes with the administration and dared them to dismiss us. Lecturer Sue Bullen wrote in *Lecturers' Link* about her experience meeting twice with Barry Fish, dean of the College of Arts and Sciences, and a union rep (who happened at least once to be me), including once with her department head: "The union organizing committee representatives were helpful in clarifying these issues for administration and also in giving me the 'moral support' I needed to air my concerns."

We Reach Our Safety Margin

When we reached 120 plus our safety margin in the opening days of winter term 1993, I contacted the MFT office and reported that I had the cards. I was happy to hand them over to our MFT contact person, Leonard Field, for him to present to MERC so they could see that the signatures were all there and grant us our election.

Len had only recently joined our struggle after we made clear to Hugh Jarvis, president of MFT, our displeasure with the previous contact person who they had assigned to us. Call it a difference in style but kudos to Hugh for listening to us. Len met with us right away to find out where we were and how he could best work with us.

EMU's Bad Faith

The rest should have been merely procedural. Unfortunately, William Shelton, president of EMU since 1989, made clear, with the support of his rubberstamp board of regents, that the university was going to use deceptive legal practices and high-priced lawyers in a bad-faith campaign to defeat us, because they knew we had the numbers.

They hired a well-known, much-despised union buster attorney, James P. Greene, from Dykema & Gosset, to delay us to death.

As Jon Curtiss, who I'll introduce shortly, wrote in what he referred to as "an (unfinished) essay" on his involvement with EMULOC: "Like the model anti-union lawyer in Martin Levitt's *Confessions of a Union-Buster*, Greene 'understood that management would almost always win a war of attrition'" by employing one main strategy: "pile up obstacle after obstacle, insisting that every challenge and obstacle be given the scrutiny of a lengthy labor board hearing—and then appeal the rulings that don't go his way."

Foreshadowing: He didn't know who he was dealing with—but we're not there yet.

At the first MERC hearing, during winter term 1993, they submitted a list with 1,460 names on it, going back three years. Some of the lecturers were reportedly dead. They called that their "pool of lecturers from which to pull."

At the next hearing, held Friday February 18, 1994, in Detroit, their list had increased to 1,850 names going back four years. "Employed," according to the U's definition, meant "has taught at least one course during at least one term going back 4 years." Again, no longer being alive was not an automatic disqualifier.

The hearing woke up the EMU employee community. MFT charged that the list was "fraudulent" and requested a hearing. AAUP filed a grievance against the university. MEA (Michigan Education Association), who had competed for EMULOC's loyalty but lost out to MFT, agreed to consider a precedent-setting collaboration approach with MFT to fight the university's chicanery.

We charged, in support of AAUP's grievance, that if that number was correct, the university had been lying to AAUP all this time. They lied to MERC, too, hence our lawsuit.

The Shelton Gang dragged their feet and erected roadblocks at every opportunity. Greene called in sick one time. They refused to release the information we requested and that we needed to refute their absurd charge that we were casual laborers.

Words of Hope from Marge

On Thursday March 24, 1994, in a telephone interview, Marge Paquet, the state employee from MERC whose job it was to verify signatures, told *Lecturers' Link* that she had just received the list of lecturers from Fall 1993, the term when we filed. MFT's Joe Crowell had sent it to her after receiving it from AAUP Executive Director Cheryll Conklin, who had received the list, as per their contract, from EMU. The list contained 389 names. Paquet promised to review it soon and then set a date for the hearing. She warned us to expect EMU to appeal.

Ken Wachsberger

In the June 1994 hearing, Paquet revealed she used the shorter list presented by MFT. But we still fell short of the number needed to "show interest"!

What! Why was that?

According to Paquet, only cards signed by lecturers currently teaching when the cards were submitted counted. We had spent a year collecting signatures. A significant number of lecturers who were teaching when they signed were not teaching when we submitted the cards.

Her decision informed our strategy going forward. Instead of challenging their decision, we withdrew our petition and started over. But we began our campaign at the start of the Fall 1994 semester and submitted the cards during finals week.

"Casual Laborers"

The university called us "casual laborers" because casual laborers are denied the right to collectively organize. This was the same argument used by lettuce and grape growers against the migrant farmworkers.

But nothing about their lifestyle was casual. As they bounced from school to school, prepping in the car, grading between classes, and meeting with students when they could fit them into their schedules, they were tired and discouraged.

Our unionizing gave them hope, and so did the support of the other unions on campus. The tenure-track faculty union, AAUP, provided us their list of lecturer names because the university refused to release it to us, and also their mailing list so we could send our newspapers to elected officials, media, and university administrators and trustees. The union of technical and office professionals provided technical support for the EMULOC film series. The secretaries' union provided us with names of lecturers in all departments and helped us distribute our newspaper.

THUMBS UP

The Issue Is Dignity

The issue to us was dignity. Teachers never enter the profession with visions of gold in their eyes. They just don't. The saying, "They're only in it for the money," never is applied to teachers. Their goal is to teach your children, to do good for society. They are community people. They are taxpayers also. They want to be appreciated.

At least one EMU lecturer was half-time in two different departments during the same term. Together she would obviously seem to be full-time. But, because she wasn't full-time in either department, she was denied benefits.

Another lecturer told me at the end of one summer that, two weeks before classes were to begin, her department head still had not told her which class she would be teaching fall term. Only two classes remained to be assigned. Her options, therefore, were to either wait until he told her and then prep in a shorter amount of time or prep two classes, one of which she would then not teach. It would not have cost the university a penny to have treated her with dignity.

One friend, a published author with a Ph.D. in teaching, and a full-time lecturer with minimal insurance, was not docked for her eleven-day hospital stay one semester only out of the goodness of her department head's heart. Dignity.

Another was denied her insurance coverage one year because her department mistakenly labeled her as being full-time one term at a time for two consecutive terms instead of full-time for the year even though two consecutive terms is considered a year. Dignity.

Some of us didn't have phones in our offices. Our names didn't appear in the campus phone book or in the schedule book. The university hired over 400 of us a term. We taught an estimated one-third to one-half of the classes that were offered on campus—all while the university tried to pretend that we didn't exist or were simply casual labor.

Without a Union, we had no vehicle through which to express our grievances.

So We Organized

So, we organized against a recalcitrant administration.

They hoped we would go away. But we had nowhere to go. Their delay tactics inspired us rather than discouraging us. The principles of Zen at work.

They forced us to create the organization that would become our local when we won our election. Our newspaper, *Lecturers' Link*, which I co-founded and we began publishing when our effort began in 1992, continued to improve. In the February 1995 issue, we announced that we were now taking ads from community stores as a way of showing that we had community support.

Our organizing committee was invited to join EMU's All-Union Council. All six member unions placed ads of support in *Lecturers' Link*. I spoke at the annual conference of the faculty union, EMU-AAUP (American Association of University Professors). We participated in an informational picket at an EMU football game. We supported other unions in their struggles.

Meanwhile, we began outreach to other part-timers' unions. At the first National Adjunct Faculty Guild conference, held on December 18, 1994, in Ann Arbor, members of 11 institutions nationwide formed the Adjunct Faculty Union Network of America (AFUNA) to help adjuncts overcome the stifling isolation that comes from thinking you are operating in a vacuum, like we used to feel.

THUMBS UP

We envisioned AFUNA as a vehicle through which we could exchange newsletters and share successes, failures, and ideas with like groups around the country. We saw ourselves as a resource for adjunct faculty at colleges and universities that were in the early stages of unionizing; and part of a growing network of part-timers' unions in all professions.

Attorney Mark Cousens

EMU lecturers were fortunate to have the legal counsel of MFT lawyer Mark Cousens. We worked closely with him as we devised a strategy to achieve our goals.

First, he helped us define "largest convenient unit" (LCU).

Working with MERC always was a guessing game because the members were appointed by far-right governor John Engler. Our challenge was to define our unit as broadly as we could that MERC would accept, according to their definition, which we didn't know in advance.

In our definition, it meant all lecturers except the continuing education lecturers, who we felt were a different entity. During our card-gathering campaign, we hadn't even approached them. Using our figures, we comfortably exceeded our goal. But the list MERC used to count lecturers included continuing ed. So, we fell short.

On September 21, 1994, after consulting with EMULOC, Cousens submitted to MERC an amended petition restricting the main unit to campus only, but including on-campus continuing ed folks.

In a letter to EMU Attorney Greene five days later, Cousens requested names, dates of appointment, salaries, and other relevant information on all lecturers who had taught at the U since July 1, 1990.

Ken Wachsberger

Lecturers Finally Get MERC Hearing

On February 16, 1995, EMU lecturers finally got our hearing at MERC. We were represented by Len Field and Mark Cousens. Our community of interest, as per Cousens' advice, included all regular lecturers plus the continuing education lecturers who taught on campus. Based on the AAUP lecturers list for Fall 1994, we had safely exceeded that number during our three-month campaign that began and ended that semester.

But, as Cousens had anticipated, the U countered that our numbers fell short because they didn't include administrators who taught; employees who were called lecturers but only did research; and all continuing ed lecturers throughout the state. And, of course, cards were irrelevant anyhow; we were all just "casual labor."

Marge Paquet, the MERC employee whose job it was to verify signatures, gave the U two months—until April 1995—to submit a formal list of who they considered to be lecturers based on our description of our bargaining unit. In other words, off-campus continuing ed lecturers would not be included, nor would administrators who also taught courses. Another victory for us.

A Serious Review

Paquet agreed to review the list. If she ruled against us, Cousens warned, we would have to gather signatures all over again.

Further, filing the various briefs could take six to eight weeks. Then the judge could take another three to six months to rule—which meant that at best the election could be a year away. Or, one side could appeal and then the case would go to the three-member MERC board for yet another hearing and another delay.

We were learning patience.

THUMBS UP

Shoved by VP Goon, but MERC Rules for Us

On June 13, 1995, MERC ruled that lecturers had signed enough cards to earn the right to hold a union election. They still wouldn't tell us how many of us we were but we had the numbers.

Based on advice from Cousens, we expanded our definition to include on-campus continuing ed lecturers because 1) we thought MERC might rule that they were in our community of interest anyhow; and 2) we had the numbers.

We anticipated EMU's two objections: 1) that every continuing ed lecturer from anywhere in the state be included; and, of course, 2) we were "casual laborers."

We solicited volunteer lecturers to share their stories in front of MERC. We helped Cousens gather statistics to prove our stability. We asked for information from the U's public information files, and subpoenaed President William Shelton when they refused. I was one who delivered the subpoena and was shoved by a vice president goon in the process. The irony was, his brother was a fellow lecturer and a member of EMULOC.

At the October hearing, Cousens argued that the off-campus continuing ed lecturers were not in our "community of interest" because they wouldn't be able to attend meetings, they likely wouldn't come to social functions, and they would have no natural reasons to choose to bond with us.

Then he drew his favorite analogy of the ten-year-old kid who lives next door who you pay $10 to shovel your snow all winter whenever it needs it. "This is a casual laborer, not a lecturer."

But, no, Greene objected, we were casual because we all had "definite term appointments ... never in excess of one or two terms."

Ken Wachsberger

Judge Kurtz, playing a cautious defense, naturally couldn't make a ruling without the statistics that EMU had been withholding from us all along, which is what the U wanted. But, he ruled, the university must come up with that information by a definite date, December 11—a victory for us!

As Cousens concluded: "There's no doubt they're dragging their feet and stalling. They bought thirty days. But we got the stuff we wanted for two years."

Lecturers Receive the Data

We thought.

On November 2, 1995, Greene sent Cousens the withheld employment data that we hoped would prove that we were not "casual laborers." Unfortunately, it was provided only in the form of reams of unsorted papers going back to 1990 and including employee rosters, and lists of classes taught and by whom divided by department.

This was the best they could do? Really? How could there not be a simple roster for lecturers and grad assistants? It was up to us to sift through the papers and compile the definitive list of lecturer names—by December 11.

Alas, even for a group of dedicated lecturer volunteers, the job was too mammoth.

So, at the hearing, Cousens tried, and failed, to get the judge to accept the list we had gotten from AAUP. But the judge gave the U a deadline to come to an agreement with us on the list. It was another step forward, a partial victory for us.

Greene promptly tried to have the hearing adjourned until we finished organizing the data. He succeeded in a poetic justice sort of way: Judge Kurtz ruled that both sides had to wade through their copies of the data and come up with their respective definitive lists by February 21, 1996.

Thus, during January and most of February, lawyers from both sides met several times to come up with a mutually agreed-upon list.

That obviously didn't happen.

Meanwhile, in the September 1996 issue, *Lecturers' Link* announced that EMU Lecturers Organizing Committee was now EMU Lecturers Organizing Congress for two reasons: to reflect the strong support we had from lecturers all across campus, based on our recent phone survey; and because "Committee" sounded too exclusive.

We Confront Union-Hostile Times

In early 1997, a brief thaw suggested that Greene was being authorized to acknowledge our obvious existence, help us get the issue out of MERC, and communicate with us face to face. Lawyers for both sides arrived at a definition of who would be eligible for union membership.

Unfortunately, it excluded three-quarters of us. Briefly, it said anyone who taught five or more credits a term for two terms would be eligible the third term. It would have guaranteed us an unstable membership because any member could lose eligibility regardless of longevity at EMU and have to wait the obligatory three terms to get back in for falling behind in any one term. It was not nearly how we envisioned the union to be.

But, accepting the premise that we lived in union-hostile times, this was the best deal we were going to get for now, and later we could expand it, we agreed to support the compromise definition with the understanding that Greene would take the definition to Shelton, and he did.

Liberated from the Yoke

Shelton then dropped the leadership decision onto the laps of the board of regents, who systematically omitted it from their monthly agendas. After finally agreeing with us that the university was acting in bad faith, MFT returned the matter to MERC.

Our collective fate was placed in the hands of three Engler appointees. Could they put aside their political ties and look at the facts, or would they simply find their own facts to fit their politics?

Alas, in a decision handed down in June 1997 that lecturer Chuck Bonney called, in the November *Lecturers' Link,* "remarkable for its tortured logic and complete distortion of fact," they disregarded the stipulations of the compromise definition; lumped those of us whom we had agreed to exclude (including me) because we taught so few credits with those 102 lecturers who received COBRA (Consolidated Omnibus Budget Reorganization Act) benefits because they taught so many; and labeled us all casual laborers.

Chuck, a veteran of twenty-five years as a lecturer in the sociology department, was our showcase witness when it came to disproving the ludicrousness of their argument.

But all was not lost. We were now liberated from the yoke of that confusing, unstable definition of membership eligibility.

We Consider Alternatives, Then Buy In

After MERC's decision, EMULOC provided MFT with a detailed analysis they could have used to demand that MERC reconsider its decision. Unfortunately, following Cousens' advice, they allowed MERC's decision to stand. Their proposed alternative strategy: a third card campaign, this time with just the 102 full-timers who were receiving COBRA benefits. They believed going this route would at least get us a union whose membership we could begin to expand when Michigan elected a more employee-friendly governor.

Members of EMULOC were frustrated. For a brief moment, we considered alternatives. AAUP suddenly was interested in reopening the issue of our eligibility for membership with them. But the frustration lacked wings. We found validity with MFT's approach and embraced it.

We filed a Freedom of Information Act (FOIA) request that revealed statistics proving that EMU was employing 102 full-time lecturers. The evidence, of course, had been available all along but our attempts to obtain it had always been restricted or ignored.

We conducted a third card campaign, but this time only with full-time lecturers.

Enter Jon Curtiss

Up until now, EMULOC energy was strictly volunteer-fueled. In March 1998, MFT finally sent us a full-time on-staff organizer, Jon Curtiss, to carry us over the finish line. Jon was the wunderkind organizer for MFT, a recently hired staffer but long known and well respected for his time as president of the University of Michigan Graduate Employees Organization, AFT Local 3550, the union of U of M teaching assistants.

I was happy to pass along my data and information to Jon, who I considered a friend from our times supporting each other's struggles. I was confident he would lead us through the final stretch to our ultimate victory.

Jon recalled meeting with the committee in my backyard to strategize: "I don't think we even had 60% of the full-timers signed up. The Administration could have dropped its objection to the petition, run a mild anti-union campaign, and we would have lost the election. We needed to build our strength: recruit more members, get the membership active, and bring more people onto the Organizing Committee."

And we needed a Plan B: "What if we didn't win the hearing at MERC? Our only option then would be to force the Administration to recognize us, and that would mean a strike."

But we weren't strong enough.

His strategy: "I had the organizing committee meet weekly and implement a systematic plan to contact every FT lecturer in person, either in their office or at home."

We filed with MERC in April 1998. We had about sixty percent signatures.

A Subtle Shift

On August 31, 1998, six EMULOC members traveled to Detroit to attend a consent hearing with EMU's attorney Jim Greene—who at the time was also helping Wayne State University to block their graduate students from organizing—and Robert Strassberg, MERC's elections officer.

The hearing was our most encouraging to date. First and foremost, Strassberg set October 20, 1998, as the date for the MERC hearing to determine our electoral fate. Greene tried to stall by proposing more meetings before going to the full MERC board, but Strassberg—recognizing the urgency of the matter—insisted on setting the date before Greene left the building.

THUMBS UP

And then history made a subtle shift. Greene contended that the university's definition of "full-time" was 15 credit hours, a bar so high it would have greatly reduced our proposed bargaining unit. We made it clear that the university itself used different definitions of full-time; some departments considered 12 credit hours to be full-time.

We presented our list, which came from the university's own Office of Human Resources, of nearly 100 lecturers working at 100%, about twice the number Greene had posited. Greene said he was unfamiliar with our list and wanted the opportunity to study it.

But here was the subtle shift, despite no resolution having been reached: The university was discussing what constituted a full-time position. In earlier hearings, they had simply called us "casual laborers" and closed the book. We six who attended the hearing believed our presence sent a message to MERC and the university that we were still here, we were not giving up, and we were organized.

Justice Delayed Again: The October 20 Hearing

The October 20 hearing began an hour late so lawyers for both sides could meet privately with Judge Kurtz, hopefully to find a common path forward with the election for what now numbered 108 lecturers. Not surprisingly, no common ground was found.

The University presented its usual attempt to label us as casual laborers.

We conceded, again, that we were hired for limited periods. But, in fact and practice, we argued, again, lecturers were hired back term after term, and were statistically as stable a unit as the tenure-track faculty.

Ken Wachsberger

Lecturer witnesses Tom Figurski and Julie Frentrup illustrated this argument with compelling evidence, presented convincingly and resolutely. Tom was in his fifth year as a full-time lecturer in the psychology department. Julie was in her fifteenth year of teaching in the chemistry department, eleven of them as a full-timer.

Both Tom and Julie taught a range of courses in their respective departments. They gave assignments, progress reports, and grades, including failing grades, that became part of the students' transcripts. They were hired a year at a time and for their efforts each received a salary, which included health and retirement benefits. They were eligible for COBRA benefits during the spring and summer terms when they were not employed. They no longer required yearly evaluations. Their yearly rehire was just a routine act of signing the new contract.

Tom was considered full time with a 12-credit-per-term workload; Julie had to teach 15 hours for the same status. The message from lecturers: "There is no consistency among departments."

This message was important because the University was already limping in their ability to sustain the casual laborer argument. Now they were arguing that a key issue should be how many credits the employee taught. Lecturers argued that the University already had its own method for determining full-time status, which, though mysterious and inconsistent, had determined that Tom and Julie both were full time.

During the brief cross-examination, Greene asked the witnesses if they were paid by the General Fund or Continuing Ed.; whether they taught on or off campus; and whether or not they had regular interaction with off-campus teachers. Assumedly, his goal was to show that on-campus and off-campus teachers were not a "community of interest," the same argument that was used to prevent lecturers from joining the AAUP in 1974. Overall, he appeared disinterested in the proceedings.

THUMBS UP

A much more passionate Judge Kurtz asked Tom and Julie questions about faculty sizes, ratio of faculty to lecturers, and ratio of full-time lecturers to part-time lecturers.

According to Tom, the psych department employed approximately 20 regular faculty and 20 lecturers, 4 of whom were full time. However, when faculty left, the full-timers were not considered to replace them.

> Kurtz: "I'm wondering why the full-timers are not considered to be part of the regular staff."
>
> Figurski: "I'm wondering the same thing."

The judge concluded: "So, you're basically just like the tenure-track faculty except you get paid a third as much?"

According to Julie, the chemistry department employed 22 faculty plus 11 lecturers, 4 of whom were full time. As far as turnover, she estimated the lecturers were "more stable than the faculty."

Ten-year veterans were not unusual in either department.

Greene Requests Adjournment

After Cousens rested his case, Greene pleaded that he had received no notice of who would be testifying and now needed time to line up witnesses to rebut Tom and Julie's testimony.

Cousens, in his most impassioned counter plea to date, argued that the process already had been "unnecessarily prolonged" by expensive University stall tactics; the University could have called him any time to learn the witnesses' names but never did; and they had six months to prepare their case.

Judge Kurtz, playing defensive, determined that not allowing the delay would prevent Greene from making "a complete record." He set the next round of hearings for Friday November 20 and Friday December 4.

As Jon noted, "The MERC process is just slow-moving." Another hearing date was scheduled for February 10, 1999. Attorneys submitted briefs on June 2, 1999. "Then the ALJ took six months to issue the ruling. We continued to organize and hold actions and rallies."

Victory

We had to wait until December 1999 to finally get a decision from MERC but the wait was worthwhile. A press release from EMULOC, dated January 5, 2000, quotes from MERC's ruling: "Our decision herein will give lecturers who have been employed for many years, some close to 20 years, and who have a continuing interest in their employment relationship, the benefits of collective bargaining."

> The MERC decision rejects the administration's argument, finding that full-time lecturers "certainly have more than a casual or temporary interest in their wages, hours, and working conditions, in view of their full-time employment with, and dependence upon, the University."

> The decision also concludes that "lectures receiving the equivalent of a full-time employment have a reasonable expectation of continued employment from year to year" and that "there should not be a great degree of fluctuation in the unit from year to year," dismissing the Administration's contention that a union of lecturers would be too "unstable" to negotiate with.

THUMBS UP

As Jon noted, "We were in great shape."

Indeed. EMU lecturers won their eight-year struggle to form a collective bargaining unit in the last week of March 2000 in a landslide vote of 91-2 with eighty percent of the 115 eligible voters submitting ballots. EMULOC became EMUFT Local 9102. Rollie Hopgood, who became MFT president on February 1, 1996, was on hand as an observer.

A year later, they negotiated their first contract. With the protection of a union contract, full-timers' lives improved dramatically immediately.

As Sonya Alvarado recalled, "The biggest improvement was year-round healthcare for FT non-tenure and longer than 1 year appointment potential. There were other benefits like retirement contributions and year-round library access that felt more respectful." Sonya has been the AFT Michigan Field Representative for the local since 2016. Prior to that, she was the president from Spring 2012 to Winter 2015, and treasurer or trustee going back to 2002.

EMULOC Shows President the Door

We wore down the administration. We smashed Attorney Jim Greene in his own "war of attrition." We outlasted the unpopular president, William Shelton, who resigned his position in 2000, on the cusp of our victory. We kept the vision.

We won because I had a strong cadre of leaders working with me—Martha; Marjorie Lynn, JoAnn Riley, and Karen Ehrlich, my colleagues in the English department; Mary Gray, in foreign languages; and others—who met regularly, marched often, welcomed everybody, and believed in the cause. But there were times when depression cast a pall on the collective energy level of the whole effort and even the hardcore started to express doubts.

Ken Wachsberger

I won't speak for how the other leaders felt at those times. Everyone treated despair in their own way. I know that too often I faltered in my efforts for any number of reasons: burnout, despair, cynicism, sadness, anger at an overpaid upper-level administration that gloried in the new buildings it built but attacked the employees who made the buildings run.

But I always radiated optimism. The optimism was real. The cause gave me energy. "We're having fun now," I would say. I would remember Stew Albert, from the Yippies, who told me in Miami Beach in 1972, "We can't lose. We're having too much fun."

They weren't going to beat us because I was obsessed. I was angry. My ADHD was my super power. I was unbeatable. When others said, "We can't do it," I said, "We're just getting started."

The Compromise, Then the Vision

Our victory came with a big compromise: Only full-time lecturers were allowed to join the union Our goal from the start had been one union for all lecturers. With the compromise, we sacrificed 285 part-time lecturers for the sake of 115 full-time lecturers.

In supporting the compromise, I was voting myself out of the union because I was a part-timer. I reasoned that we had just won an historic victory and should savor it. Going from 0 to 1 can be harder than going from 1 to 100. We made it to 1. No one had ever done that before.

So I, and the others, accepted the logic of Cousens, who argued that Judge Kurtz would never accept a definition of our bargaining unit that included three credits as a minimum teaching load. It was Judge Kurtz, Cousens reasoned, who had ruled against lecturers in 1974 in the decision that prohibited lecturers from becoming members of AAUP, the tenure-track faculty bargaining unit, and their definition included a six credit-per-term minimum.

THUMBS UP

Cousens believed we had the data to successfully argue that not every lecturer was automatically a casual laborer. He was confident he could convince Judge Kurtz to accept a minimum teaching requirement of five credits per semester.

But three? Cousens insisted the judge wouldn't buy it. "If he doesn't, we lose. It's non-negotiable."

So we went for five.

Commitment to Those Left Behind

At the same time, I obtained commitments from the new leadership of the full-timers union that they would continue to prioritize bringing part-timers into the union.

To their credit, they succeeded, although it took a long time.

In 2010, part-timers, for the first time, became eligible for union membership. They negotiated their first contract in 2011. Only in 2022, thirty years after the struggle began, did lecturers all merge into one unit as we had visualized at that first meeting with Rollie Hopgood. I was no longer teaching there. They signed their first contract with EMU in September 2023. Perks included a 16.5 percent raise for all members over the next five years, a professional development fund, limitations on unpaid work, and a stable system of promotions for full-time lecturers.

Why did it take so long to have one union for all lecturers? "EMU fought unionization for years plus the number of part-time employees grew to around 500 to 600 in the 2008-2015 time period," wrote Sonya.

> It was very hard to get a majority of cards for the election. There were two major attempts by AFTMI before we finally hit the majority. Then President Sue Martin

insisted that the part-time faculty would have to be in a separate unit. The organizing committee voted to go with a separate unit and create another constitutional mandate to merge the units which finally happened last year."

She concluded:

> The union has shone a light on the fact that non-tenure workers do most of the teaching at EMU with only a fraction of the pay. Students know who the lecturers are and that they are just as credentialed and professional as those with tenure. This respect is priceless. The fact that the union was able to work with and get first a second unit for the part-time lecturers and then win a merger vote for one contract has finally righted the wrongs done by MERC and EMU. There is now much better job security and pay for all lecturers.

It was Sonya who, as the AFTMI field rep for the local, signed the paperwork to request the MERC merger election. "I cried because I was in the position to be the one to put in motion the mandate to have one full- and part-time union of lecturers at EMU. I wear my EMUFT colors proudly."

According to Jon, "Without a doubt, the lesson of the EMULOC campaign is a lesson in perseverance."

Martha looks back proudly at the legacy of EMULOC and concludes: "We made an important contribution to underpaid, overworked lecturers. Even in a hostile environment, it helps to not give up. Victory is possible."

We fell often but we always got back up. We kept the vision and never let go.

CHAPTER 26
WRITING FOR HEALING AND TO PRESERVE YOUR LEGACY

I noted in the last chapter that I began teaching Freshman Composition at Eastern Michigan University in 1987. Freshman Comp., as it was affectionately known, was the class that every student hated and every major required. To pass, students had to write a twenty-page research paper on a news topic of little or no interest to any of them. By the end of the semester, they hated writing. I hated teaching it. Then the next semester began.

One year, on the Friday before a new semester was to begin, a colleague gave me a book, *Searching Writing*, by Ken Macrorie. I read it over the weekend. In his book, Macrorie introduces his idea of the I-Search paper, a research paper that is laid out more as a narrative than a formal research paper.

If you want to learn more about the I-Search paper, I refer you to my book, *Transforming Lives: A Socially Responsible Guide to the Magic of Writing and Researching*, the first textbook ever written for the I-Search paper. Here, I want to just emphasize his main point: that students will write better if they care about their topic.

I Have a Vision

Once you see the truth, you can't unsee it. That Sunday night, in the middle of the night, I had a vision and in the vision a voice said to me, "Are you nuts?" The next day, I passed out one hundred copies of the syllabus that I had laboriously typed and printed on the English Department's mimeograph machine in the two weeks leading up to this day and said, "We won't be using this."

Then I said, "You know that twenty-page paper you were expecting to write? Forget it." Before their disbelief could transition to relief, I added, "It can be as long as you want it to be. As long as"—this was my one stipulation—"the topic matters to you. It has to have an I-Factor."

This was a tough concept to grasp: writing because it mattered. Some took longer than others to embrace the opportunity. Others got it right away.

Alcoholic Father

One student wrote about alcoholism. That sounds like a fairly typical academic topic. What was her I-Factor? Her father's alcoholism had led to the breakup of her family. Her goal was to help him stop drinking and bring the family back together. She read books and articles. She interviewed the most important experts on the topic: her brother, her sister, her mother, and her father.

In the end, she failed her original goal miserably. Her father was still an alcoholic. The family was not back together.

But she realized there was nothing she could do to help her father if he didn't want to change. She stopped blaming herself and transformed her life by reclaiming it. Can you imagine how she felt interviewing her father and coming to her sad conclusion?

Feminist Art

Another student was about my age. We came of age in the sixties and seventies, but while I was living in the streets and organizing

THUMBS UP

against the war in Vietnam, she was starting a family. Years later, she went to college and I was her teacher.

She wanted to be an artist but she got turned down by the art department. They said her artwork "doesn't have balls." That's what they told her. She was devastated. How could she ballify her artwork to get herself into the art school?

During her research, she interviewed owners of a feminist art gallery. She wrote, "I didn't even know there was such a thing as feminist art." Her paper's conclusion: The art department is sexist. She found her inner feminist artist.

Campus Safety

I used to meet with every student one at a time at the beginning of the semester to discuss their topics and help them focus.

One student, a shy girl, insisted she couldn't think of a topic. She was from a wealthy family so she had no material needs, like her less well-off classmates who often did research before purchasing big-ticket items.

She was firm in her choice of major, another popular research topic.

The third type of topic my students often selected related to personal growth. By the time kids get to college, they're carrying eighteen years of baggage from their childhoods. The personal growth paper was their release, like my student with the alcoholic father. But I never pushed them to do personal topics. It could be too dangerous if they flipped out in any way and I wasn't trained to handle them.

So, she said, "Well, I could write about campus safety."

"That could work," I said encouragingly. Then I asked the question I always asked: "Why? Why is that topic important to you?"

Ken Wachsberger

She looked down at the floor and stared for an uncomfortably long time. Then she looked up at me and said slowly, "Well, I was raped last year."

Maybe if you're a woman reading this, you're thinking, "Well, of course, that's what she said," but I didn't see it coming.

She had never told anyone, not her parents, not her roommates. It just all came out in a brief student-teacher conference in Freshman Composition.

But, an essential part of my class was peer grouping. Students read their assignments out loud to their group, self-evaluated them, and then opened the floor for discussion. Now she was afraid of men, who comprised half the class. I said I couldn't force her to do that topic but, if she did, I could promise her she could always be in an all-female group. That was all the assurance she needed.

The next week, they read their first assignments. She was sitting in the front row to my left. As she stood, I saw the chains that surrounded her, like Jacob Marley, hanging from every appendage. But as she spoke, the chains broke and fell to the ground without a sound. I watched that happen. The second time she read, she was just looking for help with mechanics, grammar, and spelling.

But she was free. She had reclaimed her humanity, her womanhood, her dignity.

She was a spring semester student. I didn't teach over the summer. I ran into her at the beginning of fall semester. She told me she organized a women's shelter over the summer. From victim to advocate to organizer in two seasons!

Papers were always well over twenty pages.

THUMBS UP

"I Am Now Ready to See My Ancestors"

Outside the classroom, I had the honor of helping a Holocaust survivor write his memoir.

Bernard Mednicki was a Belgian Jew who took his family to southern France in 1940 when the Nazis invaded, posed as a Christian, and, through a series of street-smart moves, found his way into the Maquis, the French Resistance.

Bernard Searches for His Horrendous Act

While there, he committed an act so horrendous, he blocked it from his memory. He never spoke about it, even to his wife. Somewhere along the way, he forgot about it. Years later, he spoke one day to a group of college students about his life in the Resistance. That night, bits and pieces of the memory awakened and began to seep out from behind the wall that protected him. They haunted him.

He began having nightmares. He cried out. Unfortunately, he had his nightmares in French and his second wife, Minnie, didn't understand French. "Bernard," she would tell him, "you were talking in French and I didn't understand."

He began speaking in public more frequently, hoping speaking would help him remember. He spoke to all age groups—children, public school, college, senior citizen communities—but the format was always the same: forty minutes of surface stories, twenty minutes of QA.

I Discover the Resistance

I met him at a Holocaust conference in Millersville University. I had grown up believing the Jews went "like lambs to the slaughter." I was embarrassed by the passivity but it was taught to me as fact so I believed it.

But years later, when I had returned to college and was now getting a Master's degree in Creative Writing, I took a class on "Literature of the Holocaust." For my research, I looked to see if any Jews had resisted.

What I discovered was not only a huge resistance but a growing body of literature about the resistance. Now I was going to an annual Holocaust conference and the theme was the Resistance.

So, like a good academic, I submitted my paper and it was accepted. While there, I met Bernard, who was there to talk about his experience.

I was so excited to meet an actual member of the Resistance at the night-before reception for contributors, I followed him around all night, like a puppy dog. When I confessed my interest, he invited me to visit him any time in Philadelphia, where he lived. The next summer, on my way to New York with Emily and our son, David, to visit Emily's family, we stopped in Philadelphia to visit Bernard and Minnie. While we were there, he asked me to write his story.

Writing Bernard's Story

To write the book, Bernard and Minnie came to Ann Arbor for a series of twelve ninety-minute interview sessions on my cassette recorder. Working with Bernard, I asked follow-up questions to his answers that enabled him to go deeper than his usual format allowed.

By tape eleven, he was tired. His own resistance was lowering. I asked him a question about what he did that night after he slit a young Nazi's throat. "I don't remember!" he asserted immediately. I was taken aback but I respected his silence and let him keep thinking, in deference to the journalistic mantra: "Don't step on the silence."

The Wall Breaks!

Suddenly, the wall that was holding back his repressed memory crumbled and he exclaimed, "I remember!" He broke down over the kitchen table, sobbing as the memories burst forth, in bits and pieces at first, and then a steady stream. When he was done, he said, "I am now ready to see my ancestors."

We cut that session short, the only session to not run the entire ninety minutes. That night, he fell asleep without his sleeping pills for the first time since we had begun. The next morning, for the first time, he was still sleeping when I woke up.

We had one more session to wrap up and they returned to Philadelphia. Six weeks later, I sent him the final draft. He photocopied it a dozen time and shared it with family members. He had preserved his legacy as a fighter, not a lamb, and he had found the healing he so craved.

Not long after that, his family moved him to an assisted living facility. He died shortly after that. He never saw the published version of his story, which we co-authored and I published as *Never Be Afraid: A Belgian Jew in the French Resistance*, but he didn't care. He died at peace with himself. He was ready to see his ancestors.

In chapter 19, "Like Blood out of the Aorta of a Pig," Bernard shares his revelation.

The Power of Writing

These experiences, at EMU, with Bernard, and others, showed me the power of writing and my own ability to help others write more and better.

Ken Wachsberger

So, when I lost my job with Reveal, my transition to Ken the Book Coach was natural. I find purpose in helping others to write and publish the books they need to preserve their legacy, find healing, and—especially as a member of National Speakers Association—advance their careers through writing. I wrote *You've Got the Time: How to Write and Publish That Book in You* for them but it's for anyone who has a book in them.

CHAPTER 27
TEMPLE BETH EMETH JOINS THE SANCTUARY MOVEMENT

At the next stop light to the left off Pine Valley, a half mile from our home, is Temple Beth Emeth, the Reform Jewish congregation where we are members.

TBE Is a Fit

TBE is the first congregation that had us as members whose politics we fully supported. Among the policies that mattered most to us, they were pro-women and pro-LGBTQ; they supported Israel but not its treatment of the Palestinians; they favored the two-state solution; and, through its Back Door Food Pantry, they distributed groceries and hygiene products to anyone who asked without ever asking for ID or proof of need.

TBE is special for another reason as well. It is the first Jewish congregation in the country to share ownership and maintenance of their place of worship with a church, in this case St. Clare's Episcopal Church. Standing next to each other on the front lawn are a giant Jewish star and a cross.

The relationship that came together to formally seal the relationship is known as Genesis. Members of both congregations serve on the Genesis board. Together, they maintain the building, hire and fire staff, and care for grounds upkeep. Together, they run the Back Door Food Pantry.
Emily and I were passive members of TBE while the kids were

growing up. They received their b'nai mitzvot there in the sanctuary and we catered the two events in the ballroom. We catered many of their friends' as well. When Emily was fifty-two, she celebrated the Bat Mitzvah she was denied as a child.

We attended High Holiday Services and then a handful of services the rest of the year. We liked the people. On Yom Kippur, Emily led the kitchen crew in preparing and serving the break-the-fast dinner.

Obama and Trump Inspire Second Sanctuary Movement

Then President Obama began deporting undocumented immigrants. By the time he was done, he had deported over three million, the most of any U.S. president in history.

And then Trump became president. He scapegoated immigrants and blamed them for all the ills of society, whether real or made up. He promised wholesale deportation.

Through his actions and under the mechanism of ICE (Immigration and Customs Enforcement), he and his regime broke up families at the border and separated children from their parents. They harassed community folks who had arrived legally and were struggling to work their way through the complex citizenship application process. They threatened DACA (Deferred Action for Childhood Arrivals) residents, who had been brought to this country as infants by parents who were both undocumented.

These actions woke up the sanctuary movement, a nonpartisan immigrant rights movement that was born in the 1980s to provide safe housing for refugees from Central America. It was a call to religious congregations to declare that they would work to change unjust immigration laws and practices; and at the same time willingly house immigrant families—or support congregations that did—who were being unjustly pursued until just policies could be put in their place.

Sanctuary II's mandate, like Sanctuary I's, was to provide safe housing for refugees, including long-time residents, facing deportation back to the same Central American dictatorships, which we supported with our tax dollars. The failure to create a simpler asylum process is a sorry feature of both Sanctuaries.

Using sanctuary as an act of civil disobedience to house refugees within "places of worship, such as churches, synagogues, mosques, and temples," only worked as a strategy if the government honored what was only an unofficial policy of avoiding these "sensitive locations." In 2011, the Department of Homeland Security had ordered ICE to not raid them. But it wasn't a law so uncertainty was always present.

Would it hold up under Trump? No one knew, but the sanctuary movement wasn't taking chances. Sanctuary congregations within religious institutions arose around the country that invited refugees facing deportation to stay with them as temporary but long-term guests.

Introducing Washtenaw Congregational Sanctuary

In Ann Arbor, the sanctuary movement was led by Washtenaw Congregational Sanctuary, a multifaith coalition formed in February 2017 that included the Interfaith Council for Peace & Justice (ICPJ) and the Washtenaw Interfaith Coalition for Immigrant Rights (WICIR).

One goal of WCS was to recruit congregations in Washtenaw County to declare themselves to be sanctuary congregations. You could become a sanctuary congregation at one of three levels of commitment. Most strongly committed to the cause were Level

1's, who were willing to provide food and shelter to families facing deportation and advocate for them. If that was more than a congregation was able to commit, they could be a Level 2 and offer support to Level 1's in the form of volunteers and donations. Level 3's were just learning about sanctuary and eager to learn more. Every level counted.

This is the story about how Temple Beth Emeth became partners in an historic sanctuary congregation and helped to save a life.

TBE Hires a New Rabbi

At TBE, President Carol "Ketl" Freedman-Doan asked Abbie Egherman, vice president of TBE's Social Action Committee, "What is SAC doing about sanctuary?"

Then Rabbi Josh Whinston, only recently hired but not afraid to take a stand, said to Abbie, "We need someone to write TBE's Declaration of Support for Becoming a Sanctuary Congregation."

Abbie looked at a list of TBE members who had attended meetings about Jewish Sanctuary in Ann Arbor and saw my name. At a meeting at Panera on March 4, 2017, she asked me to write it and to represent TBE in the whole sanctuary movement. "The last two Bar Mitzvah sermons were about sanctuary," she said. "Rabbi Whinston is on board. We're already moving in that direction."

We talked about what it would mean to be a Level 1 congregation, including construction limitations. One requirement before hosting a guest: You had to provide a shower. Oops. We'll have to work on that.

She asked me again to take on the issue.

THUMBS UP

Emily and I had both supported the first sanctuary movement that came out of the eighties when we lived in Lansing. Emily had used her Spanish fluency to translate for refugees who didn't speak English. She also taught children of migrant workers through both the Lansing and Eaton Rapids school districts.

I had worked with many religious organizations and leaders in my political organizing over the year, but I had never belonged to a Jewish congregation that was leading the way in any social cause other than Israel. I agreed to write it.

My Mission

My mission was two-part: to introduce the resolution to the board that would declare TBE a sanctuary congregation; and to get St. Clare on board.

To succeed in the first, I needed grassroots support from the congregation, led by activist members of the Social Action Committee (SAC), and a majority vote from the board. SAC director Shoshana Mandel was my most passionate supporter in SAC and she became my partner.

I was told which board members would likely support the idea right off, which would lean negative, and which could go either way.

I Meet with Rabbi Josh

Nine days after my meeting with Abbie, I met with Rabbi Josh. We talked about what it meant to be a sanctuary community. We agreed that Obama's policies, as bad as they were, had been benign compared to Trump's, which represented pure hatred.

"Obama was deporting violent criminals and also at least verbalizing the need for a solution," said Josh. "Trump is looking for people with parking tickets and has no desire to find a solution beyond getting rid of Mexicans and Muslims."

He revealed that he had already talked to the board and they were interested. Only one member of the congregation, not from the board, had expressed hesitation and it was over the issue of liability, not principle. "Most of her issues were no different than if anyone else stayed in the building, like we're doing with our rotating shelter: What if someone gets hurt or hurts someone else?"

Nevertheless, we agreed that we needed to recruit a lawyer from TBE to provide pro bono services in part because we didn't have any legal protection from the law. "What stops the police from invading sanctuaries now when they have no legal standing?" he asked. "All that protects us is they need a warrant first and they don't want to be seen as entering a religious institution."

"As Jews, we have a moral obligation," he added. "I could be wrong; I usually am. But I don't feel anyone who is against it has a strong argument."

He wasn't sure which specific individuals we needed to convince but he believed that, first, I needed to write the Declaration. He noted that he had already talked with his counterpart at St. Clare, James Rhodenhiser. James agreed on the need for a joint statement but hadn't yet taken any action. We needed to reach out to sanctuary supporters from St. Clare and start working together.

"We are a symbol to the undocumented community that we support, but what are our parameters of support? Do we take care of whoever we take in forever? What about housing a known felon? Do we help just women and children? These are among the questions that need to be defined."

THUMBS UP

He noted that some people think it would be enough to support other congregations that are doing sanctuary work, be a Level 2 supporter; but we agreed that level of commitment was too narrow.

We also agreed that one part of being a sanctuary congregation should be our mandate to educate the community about all aspects of the sanctuary movement. I promised to recruit someone from the community to gather and provide links to educational materials including summaries of suggested readings, links to what other sanctuary congregations were doing, how the government was acting toward sanctuary congregations, and more.

Finally, we agreed that refitting our facilities to provide the necessary shower was a surmountable obstacle. Our downstairs restrooms were already set up to have showers even though they didn't actually have them. Surely someone in the congregation possessed the skills and the willingness to donate the necessary labor, I thought.

"Later we can deal with logistics," he concluded. "We can set up a living space in a current downstairs classroom and convert the downstairs bathrooms to showers for a few thousand dollars. We would have access to food through the Food Pantry."

He was confident the final decision on TBE's level of commitment should be made not by the larger TBE community but by the board: "Members voted for the board. We should trust them." Nevertheless, we both wanted to get as much community buy-in as possible. He suggested that he and I introduce the statement to the board along with the SAC motion of support and that we recruit members of the community to attend the board meeting where the vote is taken.

Declaration Adopted by SAC

But first I needed to write the Declaration. It came easily. I didn't know when I accepted the assignment how passionate I felt about the emerging sanctuary movement, how angry I was at the hatred that passes for political statesmanship over the issue of immigration, how despondent I felt living under this darkened aura of divisiveness, how much money was being wasted, how damaged our international reputation was becoming, how many individuals and families were being deliberately harmed because cruelty and revenge had replaced problem solving and love on the political agenda.

What I wrote came to me as a channeled message while I was driving to Panera one morning. I wrote the first draft in the parking lot. I wrote it while in a hallucinatory trance. I was Allen Ginsberg reading "Howl" for the first time at the Six Gallery in San Francisco. The words emerged from my fingertips; I barely wrote them.

What it said was that sanctuary wasn't a permanent solution but it was necessary to protect the most vulnerable at this time. And it spelled out, one at a time, four major reasons why I believed Jews had no choice but to embrace the movement:

> 1. The prophetic mission of Reform Judaism is not only to pray for justice but to work for it, and to stand up to injustice when it gets in the way, "for you were strangers in the land of Egypt."
>
> 2. With the exception of any Jews of Color who may have come to America as slaves, we are all within four generations from that same immigrant experience.
>
> 3. We can never forget our working-class roots.
>
> 4. Even if we are breaking a law, outdated practices may be changed only when good people follow their consciences and even commit civil disobedience regardless of the consequences.

THUMBS UP

Was the sanctuary movement dangerous? I knew it could be. People get crazy when they're angry, and people were angry. Was it legal? It depended on who you talked to.

But, I concluded, we are compelled by our Jewish history to act decisively, to face fear and do what is right anyhow, to stand with the weak, to protect the stranger among us.

The Declaration, which appears in full in the appendix, was embraced by everyone who read it, including Shoshana, Abbie, Ketl, and Rabbi Josh. SAC adopted sanctuary as its first major activist campaign in many years. They voted unanimously to present a motion to the board to approve the Declaration as TBE's vision for why we needed to declare ourselves a sanctuary congregation.

The Board Votes

At its May 3, 2017, meeting, board members expressed no disagreement with the overall message or the stated reasons why our Jewish history compelled us to support it. A few were already yes votes to our motion.

But the phrase "even house immigrants, refugees, and others" at the beginning of the Declaration raised the fiduciary eyebrows of the two lawyers on the board who feared they would be violating their fiduciary duty to safeguard the TBE community if they failed to act cautiously, as they were required to do. Others raised questions about the legality of giving sanctuary, board members' individual liability, and what it would do to our nonprofit status. Who was Washtenaw Congregational Sanctuary, some members wanted to know? Do they have a website or some current literature? And before we could make any moves, we had to bring St. Clare on board.

They weren't saying no. They just wanted more information.

So, no formal vote on the Declaration was taken. Instead, the Social Action Committee was empowered, with the board's unanimous blessing, 20-0-0, to educate the congregation, through sermons, speakers, bulletin articles, and planned events, on what sanctuary meant, including dangers, costs, practicalities, effects on our liability and insurance, and why Jewish history makes our support of sanctuary obvious and inevitable.

SAC was charged with creating a nondiscrimination statement and participating in Washtenaw Congregational Sanctuary meetings as representatives of TBE.

The board also said, "How much of what we are able to do is dependent on what St. Clare is willing to do? What other congregations are involved in WCS and the sanctuary movement? What are its goals? How will we work together to attain them?"

All were important questions that needed to be answered. But the main takeaway? They were persuadable.

We Explode onto the Scene

At the next Friday evening service, Rabbi Josh gave a passionate sermon, which he distributed to the congregation through his weekly email announcement. He noted: "Something has changed in our country. The Department of Homeland Security, through Immigration and Customs Enforcement (ICE), has taken a new tack. ICE no longer seeks only criminals and dangerous people. Any undocumented person who is present in our country is now being sought by ICE."

Ketl wrote passionately about sanctuary in her President's Post.

One member emailed me about the board's vote: "I know how frustrating that can be for those of us who are passionate about getting things done. Yet, it is the way of the world and it is the duty of Board members to protect the institution they serve. It is up to us to keep pushing them to find a way to do the right thing while executing their duties. Passion lights the fire, and persistence prevails. I often come back to the saying a friend shared with me during a trying time: *Non carborundum illegitimi* (Don't let the bastards wear you down)."

In the coming days, Barry Shapiro signed on to write the nondiscrimination statement. By this time, many members of TBE were already attending meetings of Ann Arbor Jewish Sanctuary, the network of affiliated and unaffiliated Jewish sanctuary supporters throughout Washtenaw County, which was led organically by Ruth Kraut, from Beth Israel.

Member Jerry Lax offered his legal services for any zoning issues, his specialty area.

Abbie and I began to represent TBE at Washtenaw Congregational Sanctuary meetings but, as per the board motion, TBE was not officially a member of WCS. When I told steering committee member Jane Pacheco their credibility hinged in part on whether or not they had a website, she pointed to the "big lift" that would be required to keep it updated given that they were all volunteers. They already had a Facebook page, though, she assured me.

Joy Enser, a member of the TBE board as well as the Genesis Bridge Committee, volunteered to be education coordinator and compile a list of sources on Sanctuary to share with the community. Her FAQ sheet was an informed, powerful voice as she anticipated the questions members would be having and then answered them:

- What is the Jewish meaning of "Sanctuary"?
- What is the history of the Sanctuary movement?
- What does it mean to be a Sanctuary congregation?

- How have other congregations and groups engaged this issue?
- Are houses of worship legally protected in Sanctuary activities?
- What does our Reform movement recommend?
- What is TBE's response to the RAC (Religious Action Center) Resolution on Protecting Individuals at Risk of Deportation from the United States?

And I addressed the concern that had been raised at the board meeting about my use of the term "even house immigrants, refugees, and others" at the beginning of my Declaration. I was urged to put it, "as much as possible," at the end to soften the blow without changing the message, which I did.

I also wrote a revised version of the Declaration to focus on one individual at a time rather than the whole congregation. It didn't speak to our partnership with St. Clare or the readiness of our physical environment. It said only that I, as an individual, understood the issues around sanctuary, was aware of its danger, and was nevertheless compelled by the urgency of the times and our own history to support TBE's becoming a sanctuary congregation to the fullest extent necessary and possible.

I distributed copies at the information table at our events as a way to build visible support one congregant at a time.

TBE Signs RAC Brit Olam

TBE was an early signer of the Religious Action Coalition's Brit Olam.

On Friday June 30, Ketl wrote in her monthly newsletter column:

> Brit Olam means, "A covenant with our world".... Following direction from the Religious Action Coalition

THUMBS UP

(the Social Action division of the URJ [Union for Reform Judaism]), TBE has signed a Brit Olam, joining Reform congregations across the country in committing ourselves to "moral leadership through congregational and community-based action." This is the first step in our congregation declaring ourselves a welcoming community for all.

By signing onto the RAC Brit Olam, we became leaders in the national sanctuary community. It was a proud moment for TBE.

What Did Other Congregations Do?

Meanwhile, I realized I needed to educate the members and win over the skeptics. How did other congregations handle the trigger issues of legality, liability, cost, fear of harassment, and others? I interviewed leaders of two congregations that had adopted sanctuary policies and wrote an article that I submitted to *Washtenaw Jewish News*.

Birmingham Temple Congregation for Humanistic Judaism

The Birmingham Temple Congregation for Humanistic Judaism in Farmington Hills made news in February 2017 when the board of trustees voted to make them the first Jewish congregation in Michigan to declare themselves a sanctuary congregation.

It was no surprise that they would be at the forefront of the sanctuary movement. The congregation was founded in 1963 and led until he died in 2007 by Rabbi Sherwin T. Wine, whose leadership and philosophy gave birth to Humanistic Judaism.

They showed no concern for fiduciary fears or ICE invasions, unless one of the residents was a criminal. As Rabbi Jeffrey Falick noted, "How could we not support this? We do not make our ethical and moral decisions with our eyes on the budget. As it happens, we gained members."

However, because of physical limitations in the building, they never had the infrastructure to actually house a guest, so they became a Level 2 congregation. They provided financial and material support for Freedom House, an immigrant rights organization that had its roots in the sanctuary movement of the eighties.

"The one member who left said if it's illegal we shouldn't do it. We categorically reject that argument. All social justice movements engage in nonviolent 'illegal' civil disobedience. The nonprofit status issue was not a real issue. No 'religious' organization has ever lost its nonprofit status for something like this. Very few have ever lost it at all."

Temple Sinai, in Washington, DC

In DC, Temple Sinai was a liberal congregation with a rich social justice history. Members worked in the federal government, in Congress, in local government, and on behalf of organizations involved with public policy issues.

According to Gary Friend, president of the temple's board of trustees, administering sanctuary was relatively easy and start-up costs were minimal because the building already had logistical resources; and its infrastructure included a shower, bathroom, full kitchen, and room that could be converted to a living space.

They were advised that their insurance probably would not rise. Discussion got more intense around the subject of who would be eligible to be a sanctuary family. "We narrowed eligibility to an individual or a family with a material connection to a member or employee of the temple, not just anyone."

I asked questions concerning the financial and practical risks they confronted, the effect on their nonprofit status and liability, and the concern of parents for their children. None of these issues were

THUMBS UP

deemed more serious than the moral urgency of the moment of welcoming the stranger.

We Connect with St. Clare

We became partners easily with St. Clare because, in principle, both congregations already strongly supported sanctuary.

Would they take in a stranger? That was a different question and neither side had an answer. To find it, we needed to educate ourselves and the community first, but we both were coming at the issue from the same general direction.

By the time I came on board, the dynamics of a partnership already were in place. Rabbi Josh had already talked to St. Clair's Reverend James C. Rhodenhiser, and they agreed the two congregations needed to work together.

Rachid Hatem, a former senior warden, had stepped forth and volunteered to lead the sanctuary effort from St. Clare even though he didn't know at the time what that meant.

Neither did we. We were figuring it out as we went along, on a unique path. But our two congregations knew we had to do it together.

Rachid was a like soul. I met him for the first time in early July at Panera because I knew I would be missing the first meeting of what was about to become the TBE-STC Joint Sanctuary Committee (TBE-STC), which was scheduled for the following week, July 13. I asked what the mood was like at St. Clare and also if they could become a sanctuary congregation without approval from the church hierarchy. When the announcement was made at the end of services, he said, many volunteers came forth, an indication of their interest. He didn't know what limitations the bishop could impose.

Carolyn Sampselle emerged later as a co-leader with Rachid. The first time I met with her, she was immediately on board with the idea of sanctuary. "How else could we do it?" She was confident St. Clare would be on board also.

The First Meeting

That first meeting was the result of Josh's suggestion to Judith Erb, at the time senior warden at St. Clare. Attending from TBE were Abbie, Shoshana, Barry, and Wendy Lawrence.

From St. Clare were Rachid, Barb Scoville, Rob Stone, and Frankie Simonds. They were, they said, at the earliest stage of assessing congregational interest and feasibility. Our committee was their first step.

Abbie and Shoshana talked about the pros and cons of being a sanctuary congregation, along with the challenges. They shared what we had done so far including our upcoming showing of the film, *The Other Side of Activities*. Rachid suggested St. Clair become involved in the film event, making it our first Genesis Joint Events Committee event.

On August 16, St. Clare's vestry (similar to TBE's board) passed a motion similar to TBE's authorizing them to explore the issue of sanctuary in partnership with us and to participate in Washtenaw Congregational Sanctuary. In other words, to do what by this time we were already doing as the Joint Sanctuary Committee.

Our goal was to make Genesis a Level 1 sanctuary congregation, take Level 2 as a fallback, and, either way, declare ourselves the first-ever interfaith declaration of sanctuary in the country.

THUMBS UP

SAC Educates the Community

But first we had to get the two boards to declare our congregations Level 1's.

We were an ambitious group. We met weekly or bi-weekly and planned a series of educational events that made it hard for anyone to not be aware of our efforts.

We accepted donations to pay for refreshments and we signed up volunteers.

Board members always were encouraged to attend to get their questions answered.

SAC was superb at promoting our events through weekly announcements to the congregation; through the TBE listserv; and through the TBE newsletter. Events on the calendar after Rosh Hashanah SAC promoted in the High Holy Days insert. St. Clare did the same through their network.

Following are some of the events that came out of sanctuary activities through the work and inspiration of TBE-STC and Genesis beginning in August 2017:

Mary Anne Perrone Talks Sanctuary at Community Conversation

On Saturday, August 19 in the Adult Lounge after morning services, SAC held a Community Conversation with Mary Anne Perrone, a member of the leadership team of Washtenaw Interfaith Coalition for Immigrant Rights (WICIR) and co-founder of Washtenaw Congregational Sanctuary (WCS).

Guided by WCS's new Sanctuary 101 PowerPoint presentation, Mary Anne spoke about the roots of the sanctuary movement, why it was necessary today, its goal, what it meant to be a sanctuary congregation, and how to do sanctuary.

She noted that sanctuary began under the Obama administration. Although no congregation has been prosecuted in forty years, she continued, "Trump wants to take the shackles off DHS (Department of Homeland Security)." She pointed out three recent raids in Kalamazoo and six in Detroit, and three in Washtenaw County.

She reminded us that three members of the kitchen staff from Sava's Restaurant in downtown Ann Arbor had been detained by Immigration and Customs Enforcement (ICE) agents in May; Lourdes Salazar Bautista, a twenty-year resident of Ann Arbor and mother of three U.S. citizens, had been deported in August; and later that same month, Café Zola had refused to allow ICE agents to enter their kitchen. In July, Emily and I had joined four hundred sanctuary supporters, including three dozen from TBE, at a vigil and rally for Lourdes, whose stay of deportation had been denied in March.

She gave background, going back to the eighties, which inspired Betty Cotzin, from TBE, to recall the good work TBE did back then when we rescued immigrants from Guatemala.

Mary Anne named other congregations that were now sanctuary, explained levels of participation, and listed elements to consider.

Most of all, she emphasized that we were all in this together. "Sanctuary congregations will get help from others," she promised.

What method would we use to determine who stays with us? Mary Anne acknowledged that was a work in progress but it began with WICIR vetting the prospect through a series of "clearness meetings," a term WICIR borrowed from the Quakers. If a family was felt to be clear, they would be recommended to WCS, who would refer them

THUMBS UP

to us and we would then hold our own clearness meeting with the family.

Before accepting a family for sanctuary, she noted, WICIR encouraged the family to check their legal options and try them first. "Sanctuary is the last resort, a desperate move."

Seventeen people showed up to hear Mary Anne give her presentation, including Rabbi Josh and members of the board. They asked intelligent questions, always, I thought, with the idea that they wanted to come on board and just wanted to learn how. Two specifically said they supported the idea of allowing immigrant families to stay here if it were necessary.

Ellie Davidson, SAC's acclaimed hospitality expert, saw to it that refreshments were provided.

The Other Side of Immigration

On the evening of Monday August 28 in the Sanctuary, SAC showed the movie, *The Other Side of Immigration*, with help for the first time from St. Clare and the Genesis Events Committee, a partnership forged at the first TBE-STC meeting in July. Fifty congregation members and others attended the film showing.

The film is based on over seven hundred interviews in Mexican towns where about half the population has left to work in the United States. It asks why so many Mexicans come to the United States and what happens to the families and communities they leave behind. It is a vivid portrayal of life in the Mexican towns where half the population has left to work in the United States.

TBE's Annette Fisch, who was head of the Genesis Events Committee, led this activity, while Abbie moderated. As she introduced the film, Abbie declared, "No one wants to live in sanctuary. Our longer-term goal is to make it so people can pass between the two countries in a legal way so they aren't threatened by deportation."

Ellie coordinated an elegant food spread that included wine, cheese, candy, and pastries.

What about DACA?

On Saturday, September 9, SAC's Community Conversation presented Margo Schlanger, a law professor at the University of Michigan who led the U.S. Department of Homeland Security's Civil Rights office in the Obama Administration. Margo was part of one legal team fighting in federal court to stop the deportation of hundreds of members of Detroit's Chaldean community; and another challenging Trump's recent travel ban executive order.

Over two dozen people came to hear her talk. She came to answer questions about how sanctuary status would affect TBE's liability, legal issues, how our nonprofit status would be affected, and other specific questions raised by skeptical board members.

But, four days before her talk, on Tuesday September 5, Trump ended DACA, the program that allowed the Dreamers, undocumented immigrants who had been brought here as children, to remain in this country and work. It wasn't clear if Congress would be able to preserve their protections and the final opportunity for Dreamers to sign up for DACA was quickly approaching.

Even with gratis legal help, they faced a $495 filing fee that many of them could not afford. So, Margo made DACA a major topic of her discussion. She directed us to the Michigan Coalition for Immigrant and Refugee Rights, a 501(c)(3) organization that offered interest-free loans and easy repayment terms through its "fee bank."

THUMBS UP

She concluded her talk by appearing to advocate that DACA was a more important issue than Sanctuary.

We're in This Together

Fortunately, most of us didn't view the issue through an either/or lens.

Eight days after Margo's presentation, on Sunday afternoon, September 17 in the ballroom, SAC co-sponsored a DACA registration workshop with St. Clare and Michigan Immigrant Rights Center (MIRC), where a dozen law students volunteered their time to help Dreamers fill out paperwork.

As one volunteer noted, the process was not that difficult, but it was intimidating and had to be filled out completely. "You want to have outside eyes review it."

Shoshana and St. Clare's Judith Erb coordinated this event, which was directly inspired by Margo's talk. St. Clare brought beverages; TBE did food. Volunteers came from TBE, St. Clare, the University of Michigan law school, and the immigrant community,

Mary Anne Makes Repeat Performance

On Monday September 18, Mary Anne Perrone gave a repeat performance of her presentation, this time during the first half of the SAC board meeting.

She noted that WICIR had been founded nine years ago after a violent ICE raid in Ypsilanti; and that Sylvia Nolasco-Rivers, the owner of the popular downtown restaurant, Pilar's Tamales, had herself found sanctuary when she fled El Salvador in the middle of a civil war in the early 1980s, by escaping to Mexico and then the United States.

"Sanctuary is a public act by nature," she said. "It is against unjust laws and tearing families apart."

It is also a protection for the congregation from the "harboring" law. "Harboring means concealing. That's why we call a press conference to announce when someone goes into sanctuary."

No congregation had been prosecuted for providing sanctuary in forty years, she noted. She doubted Josh or the board would be liable either.

Meanwhile:

> • Rabbi Josh and Ketl continued to speak and write about Sanctuary.
> • My article, which revolved around answers by two Jewish Sanctuary congregations to the questions raised by reluctant board members, appeared in Washtenaw Jewish News on Sunday September 10, 2017.
> • We were by now leading members of the greater Washtenaw County sanctuary community through our active involvement in AAJS and WCS.

How persuasive were these activities in changing the minds of board members?

Ketl Shows Support

On Monday October 2, 2017, Ketl noted in her President's Post that SAC had fulfilled our mandate to educate the TBE community about the Sanctuary movement, to develop a nondiscrimination statement that would foster a welcoming and safe place of worship, and to represent TBE at the Washtenaw Congregation Sanctuary meetings.

THUMBS UP

She stated three issues that still needed to be addressed as next steps:

> 1. We needed to consult with our legal counsel and understand our insurance liability before offering sanctuary to an undocumented immigrant.
> 2. Too few congregants attended SAC's events to form a consensus.
> 3. We couldn't become a Level 1 without St. Clare being one with us.

It was a fair assessment. Where were we already with these issues?

> 1. It helped that Rich Friedman—an attorney, TBE member, and strong supporter of immigrant rights—had already accepted Ketl's invitation to meet with us. He became part of the committee.
> 2. I experienced a different level of enthusiasm. It could have been my ADHD but I felt an energy that was increasingly escalating. It came from members who I spoke with at services or ran into at Panera. I knew they would never come to every event but they exuded important energy and it was moving in the right direction.
> 3. We were already hard at work partnering with St. Clare's sanctuary committee.

The rest of her piece was an overview of what she noted was "a symbolic act of civil disobedience." She laid out what it was, the implications of giving sanctuary to a stranger, its nonpartisan-ness, and what life would look like for the person who declared sanctuary until our policies move beyond arrest and deport.

> [B]y declaring ourselves a Sanctuary congregation, we are saying publicly that such policies are antithetical to our religious tradition, and that we are mindful of our recent history when similar policies led to the destruction of our communities.

Ken Wachsberger

Support Sanctuary or Feed the Poor?

Then a new issue arose, a game changer, a conflict between two sources of good. On December 20, 2017, the two co-chairs of Back Door Food Pantry, Kathy Daly and Ellie Davidson, shared their concerns in a letter to the St. Clare Vestry, the TBE board, and the Genesis board:

> We are concerned that our Back Door Food Pantry clientele might be fearful of using our pantry if we were a highly publicized sanctuary space, and that the attention surrounding a public commitment to providing shelter for an undocumented person might cause immigration agents to take note of the myriad of people entering our pantry each week. Although we have no knowledge of the status of our patrons, we do know that a few copies of published immigration information that we make available are anonymously taken each week.

They recommended "a commitment to level 2 at this time, *support* of an active sanctuary facility," but added, "In the event that the sanctuary demand grows dire, we note that a level 2 commitment at this time does not preclude a future move to the deeper level of full sanctuary status."

Our conundrum: two popular causes apparently competing with each other. Must we compromise our support for one cause to help another? It was a "bigger picture" question that could not be ignored.

On the committee, we clearly wanted to be Level 1's but not at the expense of the Food Pantry.

But was there another solution? How much actual likelihood was an ICE raid? We asked around, interviewed members of other congregations. For the most part, the feeling was that the likelihood was low—but the possibility could never be denied.

Consensus Is Reached

In the end, consensus became that we seek Level 2's all the way around. The resolution submitted by the TBE-St. Clare Joint Sanctuary Committee to both boards in February 2018 asked that we "affiliate with the Washtenaw Congregation Sanctuary movement at what it calls Level 2." It concluded, "This resolution does not preclude later consideration of affiliation at Level 1."

At their February meeting, St. Clare's vestry passed our resolution, with the clear vibe, which they spelled out in a separate resolution, that, if a sanctuary seeker came forward and the urgency arose, they would reconsider becoming Level 1.

TBE approved the same resolution the next month, and with the same clear vibe to reconsider.

I had no doubt that both congregations would have risen to the occasion.

As Level 2's, both congregations committed to generous donations every year as long as the need was real.

Because we were no longer going to consider becoming a Level 1 congregation, we could put aside for now our concerns about liability, legal issues, and showers in downstairs restrooms. They were no longer relevant.

Although I had been a staunch advocate for becoming a Level 1, and I always had confidence that someone in one of our two congregations with construction skills would come forth and complete the plumbing to put in the shower, I still saw the decision as historic. We became, as far as I could tell, the first multifaith institution in the country to become a sanctuary congregation.

In her April 2, 2018, monthly President's Corner, Ketl proudly announced the board's decision while acknowledging the Food Pantry's misgivings as being the reason "we have decided to provide support rather than housing."

She was generous with praise:

> Thank you to Kathy Daly and Ellie Davidson, BDFP co-chairs, for highlighting this important issue. I also want to thank our SAC members, Shoshana Mandel-Warner, Richard Friedman, Abbie Egherman, and especially, Ken Wachsberger, who started this crusade for Sanctuary well over a year ago. You have brought us all on an important journey.

Genesis Leaders Sign Historic Joint Sanctuary Support Statement

Every sacred achievement deserves a celebration, and could we really be expected to let a good media moment pass quietly? In an historic joint act of civil disobedience that was proclaimed loudly in a public ceremony co-sponsored by Genesis and WCS, leaders of Temple Beth Emeth, St. Clare, and Genesis signed a shared document declaring their support for the growing sanctuary movement in this country. The event took place on Wednesday June 13, 2018, in, ironically, the Sanctuary.

The resolution read in part:

> St. Clare's Episcopal Congregation and Temple Beth Emeth, together with Genesis of Ann Arbor, resolve as follows:

THUMBS UP

- We proudly declare our affiliation with the Washtenaw Congregational Sanctuary movement.
- We commit ourselves to taking an active role in educating our members and the broader community about the needs of immigrants and refugees and the threats facing them, and to providing an ongoing forum for discussion of these issues.
- We pledge to provide support – financial, personal, and logistical – for congregations and other organizations that provide housing and other services for immigrants, including those facing the threat of deportation.

The signing was witnessed by over one hundred supporters from the two congregations and members of the greater sanctuary community.

Mary Anne Perrone, acting as emcee, thanked TBE and St. Clare for bringing to twelve the number of congregations in Washtenaw County that were now officially in support of the sanctuary movement.

Program speakers represented all three organizations:

- Rabbi Josh, from TBE, affirmed that the event was an act of civil disobedience. "Tonight, we declare … that the law is unjust, the treatment is unjust, the dehumanizing and political pawning is unjust.…" In his opening prayer, he offered "the knowledge to know in what type of civil disobedience we are engaged, to act for the good of the less powerful, to work for greater justice. May our actions communicate our values, and may we live up to the values we profess."

- Ketl Freedman–Doan, president of TBE, recalled how a Bat Mitzvah speech about sanctuary by Lottie, the daughter of a congregant, inspired her to promise Lottie that TBE would become a sanctuary congregation, despite legal limitations on what safety that declaration actually could provide. In her conclusion, she evoked Emma Lazarus: "This is a good day for us.... It is a promise to our community that as a nation we are the 'Mother of Exiles' and must be a 'beacon-hand [that] glows world-wide welcome.' And it is a promise to Lottie who represents our future and only asks that we make the world a place of comfort and safety to all who seek it."

• Murray Rosenthal, president of Genesis, shared three stories that opened his eyes to the immigrant experience and enabled him to grow personally: teaching English to a Russian immigrant while learning about his life of oppression as a Jewish engineer in Russia; bonding with a survivor of the Chernobyl power plant breakdown from Ukraine over the deaths of her parents from cancer and his mother's death from a car accident; and marveling at the bravery of a Kurdish translator from Iraq during the Iraq War. "Imagine if we had had a government that was xenophobic and did not allow those immigrants in our country."

• John Little, senior warden of St. Clare, recalled living with his wife in Virginia Beach in the early seventies when their church adopted a Vietnamese family: "There is no higher calling than to create a sense of peace and security and safety for a family." He expressed pride at how easily the call to sanctuary was introduced and passed at St. Clare, with "no dissension, only questions about what it meant." He was "humbled to be a part of an organization that honors the human spirit the way we do," even though "on the receiving end of that … unfortunately it's an insecure place to be."

• Rev. James C. Rhodenhiser, of St. Clare, warned that "we will be ultimately held responsible for how we treat the needy, particularly those we are most tempted to other-fy." He commended the two congregations for their commitment "to the process of humanizing the world, loving our

THUMBS UP

neighbor, and loving the stranger as our neighbor." In his closing prayer, he called out to the Holy One to "open the eyes of this country. Help us throw off the temptation to exalt ourselves at the expense of another, to feel more secure because someone else is less secure."

The three lay leaders signed the document after they spoke.

Music began and ended the program, with the TBE-St. Clare Joint Choir singing two songs on the front end and St. Clare's Judie Erb, playing piano, leading the congregation in singing "This Land Is Your Land" on the back end. A joyous reception, co-sponsored by both congregations, followed the program.

Carolyn Sampselle, from the Joint Sanctuary Committee, recalled the development of the resolution within our joint committee as being "a spiritual journey buoyed by the genuine love, respect, and trust that our two congregations share."

Shoshana added: "The experience of bearing witness to these injustices is a privilege and responsibility, a gesture of love and commitment, a journey that elevated us all, and reminded us of how much work there is yet to be done."

It was evident to everyone present, including the many visitors from neither of our two congregations, that this was a glorious day in the history of Washtenaw Congregational Sanctuary, Genesis, Temple Beth Emeth, and St. Clare. I kvelled—Yiddish for showed my pride—freely and didn't try to hide it.

I became a member of the WCS steering committee as the representative of Genesis.

Ken Wachsberger

Rabbi Josh's Foreshadowing Message

In Rabbi Josh's next "Thinking Torah" email blast to members, which he sent out the day after the public signing, he summarized and celebrated what we did the night before and concluded: "Regardless of what happens next, whether we ever actually provide support for a member of our community seeking sanctuary in a partner house of worship, tonight is an act of civil disobedience."

In the world of literature, this is known as foreshadowing. In every episode of *Law and Order*, this is the moment where the husband calls his wife to say, "I'm on my way home; see you in ten minutes," and you know he's not going to make it.

Quakers Become Level 1 Sanctuary Congregation

On Friday, November 2, 2018, at the Ann Arbor Friends Meeting House in Ann Arbor, the Quakers, or Friends, announced that they had just taken in the first person in Washtenaw County to seek refuge, in a place of worship, from the Trump administration's inhumane deportation policies.

Mohamed Soumah, a 44-year-old man from the West African former French colony of Guinea-Conakry, had lived and worked peacefully in Ann Arbor for fifteen years. He had a kidney condition that required him to receive dialysis treatments three times a week to stay alive. These treatments were not available in Guinea-Conakry, so deportation at the hands of ICE would have meant immediate death.

The Quakers were passionate in their support and protection of Mohamed. They saw to it that he had food and shelter. They arranged for his medical care, including getting him to his three

THUMBS UP

weekly dialysis treatments. Sheila Johnson itemized his expenses in regular updates on his progress to the WCS steering committee.

Raising money to help Quaker House pay those expenses became a primary mission of WCS. In addition, we recruited volunteers to lend invaluable support, including driving Mohamed to his appointments.

Members of the clergy often accompanied him. They wore full vestments so he would always be protected by religious symbolism outside Quaker House. They were prepared to declare their religious immunity if they were pulled over.

Mohamed Gets Partial Freedom

The Biden years brought the immediacy of ICE to a thaw. On Tuesday May 25, 2022, at the ICE office in Detroit, Mohamed was given an order of supervision that required him to check in virtually or on a periodic basis, but declared him at least temporarily off limits to the evicting eyes of ICE. For the first time since going into sanctuary, Mohamed could take walks through the neighborhood or go shopping without fear of immediate deportation and with no special conditions attached. The order was what Mohamed's lawyer wanted.

One week later, supporters arrived at Ann Arbor Friends Meeting House in cars, on foot, on bicycles, and on scooters to celebrate Mohamed's freedom—with all of us understanding the relativity of the term.

Mohamed was greeted with extended applause. He thanked the community and the press for treating him "like a human, for not forgetting me. All I can offer is thank you from the bottom of my heart. I will never forget."

Pastor Deborah Dean-Ware, WCS steering committee member from Church of the Good Shepherd/United Church of Christ, which had voted to become a Level 1 on Sunday July 23, 2017, praised the day as an example of what we can do when we come together. Pastor Deb, as she is known, organized Mohamed's team of three-times-a-week driving clergy whose religious vestments kept Mohamed protected outside Quaker House. She reminded us that sanctuary was "also a biblical statement to welcome the stranger, the immigrant, the widow. Abraham and Sarah, Moses, Jesus, they were all immigrants and refugees."

Rabbi Josh thanked WCS for challenging the community over three years. "Saving life takes precedence over any other law," he explained. "We couldn't say no. Our choice was, talk about or do. We cannot collaborate with injustice. When the law of the land is unjust, we must rise up against it."

Reverend Joe Summers, from the Episcopal Church of the Incarnation, noted that Christianity, Islam, and Judaism all claim Abraham as an early leader, and "he was an immigrant." Further, while the United States has accepted the Universal Declaration of Human Rights, we are, in fact, "the cause of the violence that we won't own but that is causing refugees to flee."

Mohamed Gets a New Kidney

In addition to giving him freedom to take walks at night, the order of supervision enabled Mohamed to be put on the kidney transplant list. On Sunday, September 4, 2022, he received a new kidney at Michigan Medicine.

Today, he lives on his own, is gainfully employed, and is a contributing member of our society.

THUMBS UP

Washtenaw Congregational Sanctuary was able to take a well-deserved step back. At the start of 2024, for the first time, WCS was able to announce to its supporting congregations that their generous annual donations were not being requested. At the same time, they asked that the congregations remain on alert.

Final Thoughts

I was successful at TBE and St. Clare because I immersed myself in the issue and I was passionate in my commitment.

At the same time, I belonged to one congregation and partnered with another who, to my great pleasure, were on board from the start with the moral arguments, possessed the volunteer power and committed leadership, and just had to learn the details and organize around them.

The sanctuary movement is one of the noblest causes in modern history. The failure of politicians to create a humane, informed solution to the immigration crisis that goes to the root cause of immigration instead of blaming immigrants is a stain on our history.

I began writing this book while Biden was president. By the time I finished it, Trump was president and the mood of the country had grown darker. The corporate press laid down their pens without a fight. We lost even the pretext of having them on our side.

But better the truth be told. We never had them, but when the anti-Trump movement was strongest, we were often in alignment. Then Trump won and the charade of an alliance was put to rest. It doesn't have to be this way.

We've been here before. We'll get through it if we learn from the past, keep the vision, read banned books, and laugh often. The next phase of the sanctuary movement has begun.

CHAPTER 28
ON THE ROAD AGAIN

We moved onto Pine Valley in December 1994. We bought the house from the mother of a school friend of David's and her second husband. They were going through a divorce, she had already moved out with her kids, and he had just realized he could no longer afford the house on his own. The first time we visited the house, David felt right at home.

Pine Valley

Pine Valley Boulevard is, despite its pretentious name, a quiet three-block tree-lined side street located off Packard between two main streets. Apartments line both sides of the street at the entrance off Packard before giving way to privately owned homes straight into the cul de sac where the street ends. Healthy turnover keeps the street and surrounding neighborhood vibrant and young.

And trick-or-treat-friendly. The annual trick-or-treating endurance race, one of our best memories of being here with the kids, began on Pine Valley. Friends of David and Carrie arrived with pillow cases in hand ready to cover as many houses as they could before the houselights went out. The kids wore costumes stitched together by Emily. We alternated each year between who went with the kids and who stayed home to give out candy.

Carrie and David grew up there. They attended the public school system, mostly on the alternative school track, all the way to graduation.

Ken Wachsberger

Carrie

Carrie was bright and insightful and caring, and she had the voice of an angel, but she was so unassuming about it.

When her fourth-grade class performed *West Side Story*, no one was surprised when this pretty blue-eyed, strawberry curly-haired girl got the role of Maria. She was the only one who could sing on key. She was wonderful.

On the Friday before Mother's Day 2000, we learned that Emily had breast cancer. The day of her surgery, Carrie starred twice as Little Buttercup in Gilbert and Sullivan's *H.M.S. Pinafore*. I spent all morning at the hospital with Emily, then drove to Carrie's school for the afternoon performance. Then I returned to the hospital, stayed until I got word that Emily's reconstructive surgery was going well, and returned to Carrie's school for the evening performance. My folks joined me at the hospital and at the school. After the play, I stood in the lobby and *kvelled* watching Carrie receive glowing praise from parents, grandparent, and students of all ages. Then Carrie went home with Grandma and Grandpa and I returned to the hospital to sit with Emily.

Community High School, the open school high school in Ann Arbor, had superb academic classes but their arts program was impacted by its small size. Pioneer High School, on the other hand, was one of the largest high schools in Michigan and they had a nationally recognized performing arts program, so Carrie took theatre and voice lessons there. She sang in an award-winning acapella group.

The same weekend that Emily was Bat Mitzvah'd, Carrie starred on stage at Pioneer in the first high school student production of Disney's *Beauty and the Beast* in the country. As Beauty and the Beast shared their first kiss under one spotlight, Carrie, playing Angela Lansbury's role of Mrs. Potts, sang the theme song under another.

THUMBS UP

In Carrie's senior year, Pioneer's music program won the Emmy for the best music program in the country. Bob Seger, a Pioneer graduate, presented the award. His song, "Main Street," is named after the street that runs from Pioneer past U of M Stadium to downtown Ann Arbor.

At Community, where she received her degree, Carrie was the lone soloist at her graduation ceremony.

Carrie expressed a fierce dedication to our Jewish roots. Her musical mentor was Cantor Annie Rose at Temple Beth Emeth. She sang in the choir until she graduated.

For her doctoral dissertation at University of Nevada-Las Vegas, in vocal performance, Carrie created a first-ever modality to sing opera in every variation of Yiddish. I edited Carrie's dissertation and her best friend's as well.

I cherish all of those memories.

Then she put aside her doctorate to explore other options. She was in school from two years before kindergarten all the way through her doctoral program with no time to think along the way. She's searching, while also being a paid soloist at one Las Vegas church.

David

David was born a businessman. He learned how to count by lining up all the pine cones that fell from the tree in our yard in Lansing and counting them.

He was in a chess club at Community and did well but he wasn't inclined to take part in many other extracurricular activities throughout school. He was too busy beginning his career as a chef. He got his first job at the local bowling alley, where he became the only fourteen-year-old allowed to run the cash register and, at sixteen, the youngest pizza chef they ever had.

We told him he could work as many hours as he wanted as long as he got all A's and B's. He never saw a C, and his paycheck bought him a robust collection of CD's. He especially enjoyed rap music; he introduced us to Eminem and wrote his own rap music.

David grew up in the catering business, of course, but I never realized what a love he had for the business until the time in high school when his friends organized a progressive dinner. The main course was prepared by David and served in our home. I was impressed, and so proud.

David was competitive also. He bowled. He played ping pong on the JCC Maccabee Team. He received his karate black belt when he was eleven.

We ran into a problem in his Jewish education when confirmation classes at Temple Beth Emeth conflicted with March Madness, which was closer to David's religion at the time. We decided if we forced him to go to classes, he would fully resent Judaism and that seemed like a failed outcome, so we let him stay home and watch. He came in fourth in that year's *Ann Arbor News* pool.

In David's first year at Michigan State University, he got into the Izzone, named after MSU basketball coach Tom Izzo, then became disenchanted with MSU. He called us to make an announcement: "I want to drop out, work for a few years, and then go to the Culinary Institute of America (CIA)." He was amazed when we supported his new vision. We could see that he was focused, so we had no doubt he would succeed, and he has. He completed his bachelor's degree from the CIA and has been in the food business ever since, including, as this is being written, as an executive chef.

THUMBS UP

Emily and Me

Emily retired in September 2023 after a storied career as an educator, a therapist, and a social worker. For over fourteen years, she was the statewide coordinator of the seventy-two local councils of the Children's Trust Fund (now called Children Trust Michigan).

It didn't take her long to attract board positions on the Washtenaw Area Council for Children, one of the seventy-two councils she led; and the Ann Arbor Comic Opera Guild, where she has performed since 2010. In addition, she is on a spiritual journey and is studying to become a practicing medium.

I've loved writing this memoir. It has transformed my life by enabling me to preserve significant slices of history that would otherwise have been neglected; and then let go of the past. My task was made easier because so many of the stories I share here I had already written up in journal or story form while they were happening; others were in my head. The memoir enabled me to put them together, rearrange them as made sense, and expand them. As an anal retentive who needs to fix disorder, I was compelled and now feel liberated.

Meanwhile, as my family genealogist, I have written narratives on all four sides of my family spreading from Eastern Europe into America and around the world. Before I move on to my next adventure, I'll want to publish my findings so others can build on them.

Emily and I still enjoy being together, traveling, and hanging out with friends. At home, we'll operate in our own worlds during the day, then come together for gardening or a walk before dinner.

We take the You-Me-Us Theory seriously.

Ken Wachsberger

Goodbye, Ann Arbor

We've loved living in Ann Arbor for nearly forty years and on Pine Valley for the past thirty years.

But, in the same way that Emily's and my story situated us in the Midwest, David and Carrie were drawn out west, David to Palm Desert, California, and Carrie to Las Vegas.

For us now, being close again to them, and now David's wife, Samantha, is too powerful a force to resist, and our lives are a lot more flexible than theirs.

So, as I write the final chapter in this book, Emily and I are getting ready to hit the road to California to begin a new adventure.

We're saying goodbye to the home where we raised the kids; and to our backyard Spirit Garden where Emily and I spent hours whenever the weather cooperated. We're giving away furniture and old clothes. I've donated my political files and papers to Walter Reuther Library at Wayne State University. Other files I've contributed to recycling. But what do I do with three hundred VHS videos and DVDs?

I'm as close as I'll ever be to living out of my backpack again.

I've gone with the flow. I've been blessed. All my life, I said, "It all comes together." It has.

But I still don't know what I want to be when I grow up.

APPENDIX

STORIES FROM THE UNDERGROUND AND ALTERNATIVE PRESS

Ken Wachsberger

My Waitress—I Think I'll Tip Her
(from *Joint Issue* 4:3, 2/12/1973)

In the wee hours of New Year 1973, after a long night of partying, I went out to eat with a small group of friends. When we got to the restaurant, I noticed through the window that the place was packed and the line was endless.

What a madhouse. The customers—flipped out, tripped out, strung out, drunk, or just moderately high—were all having a grand old time. Those already seated were eating or ordering; those still in line were waiting. Everyone had the luxury of setting their own pace. Everyone, that is, except the waitresses and busboys who were literally running themselves ragged trying to satisfy everybody.

I was sick. "We can't go in there. Look how busy they are." I wanted to leave. But we went in anyhow. Maybe it was a mystical attraction to find out why I had felt so strangely. Or maybe I just wanted coffee. We waited in line and then took our seats and ordered.

Once seated, I realized that it was even busier than I had first believed.

I watched the waitresses as they waited on their tables. Their moves were unnaturally automatic: smile, hold up pad and pencil, ask "Are you ready to order?" and say "Thank you." As they hurried to place their orders, the outline of their bones suddenly appeared from under the skin of their tensed-up fingers and their previously smooth foreheads showed signs of wrinkles.

I watched the busboys as they cleared tables: No sooner did they finish one table then another party got up to go. It seemed their tubs were always filled with dirty dishes.

THUMBS UP

I wanted to help them all somehow but I didn't know what to do. Should I eat quickly, leave my tip, and split so someone else could sit down, eat, leave their tip, split, etc. and thus help their tips increase? Or should I sit tight, relax, and thus give them one less table to worry about for a while? I chose the latter—money isn't everything, I figured.

A few days later, the waitress who had been working my section thanked me: "I didn't think I was gonna make it."

I confess, in the past I had always more or less taken restaurant workers for granted. When I heard talk about "workers' struggles," I usually thought first of factory workers.

But now things are different. Namely, I'm a dishwasher by trade. Two nights a week, Saturday and Monday, I have nightmares about pots and pans. New Year's Eve fell on a Sunday this year. One night either way and I would have been in the dishroom instead of at the booth. Their oppression became very real.

A typical comment by customers is, "If they don't like their job, why do they do it?" To me, such an attitude is not only ignorant but cruel and totally ignores the scarcity of jobs that we have here in the land of plenty. People just aren't able to find jobs that are personally fulfilling, so economic survival is the only motive for working.

The customer/waitress relationship is, unfortunately, much like the husband/wife relationship. If the waitress does the dishes, feeds the family, takes care of the kids, etc., the husband may buy her a mink coat. If the waitress takes the order, quickly brings the food, and refills the water and coffee enough times, she may get a nice tip. "My wife—I think I'll keep her"; "My waitress—I think I'll tip her." They're both put on a pedestal and then looked down upon.

Ken Wachsberger

Then there are the customers who feel that the restaurant is a rip-off. So they come in and take it out on the workers. How many times have you or someone you know turned a glass of water upside down on the table so, when the busboy picked up the glass, water spilled all over the table? And how often have you snapped at a waitress because your food wasn't prepared exactly to your liking?

In the development of any type of community based on sisterhood and brotherhood, customer/worker unity must be a reality. We should begin to slow our pace down when we go out to eat so that the workers can in turn slow their pace down to a more human rate. And we should realize that our waitress has other tables besides ours to take care of. People who take out their hatred of any store by making extra work for the workers display no more than a perverted sense of revenge.

THUMBS UP

A Fisherman's Tale: Part 1
(from *Lansing Star* 7:8, October-November 1975)

STAR roving reporter Ken Wachsberger recently returned home to Lansing after spending two months on a commercial fishing boat in the small town of Sebasco Estates, Maine. The following article, taken from excerpts of Ken's diary, is the first in a series of however many the staff will permit:

Thursday July 24, 1975

>The clouds are thick and grey
>As the night turns into day
>And we're 20 miles away
>　From the eastern shore
>
>I lie here on the stern
>With so much to learn
>And there's a yearning
>　In my heart for more
>
>>—Obscure young poet/
>>fantasy seeker who
>>thinks he's a fisherman
>>but who doesn't know
>>what the stern is

Somewhere along the eastern coast of Maine, about thirty miles north of Portland, carefully shielded from the nasty stings of this

Ken Wachsberger

world's Reality by nature's own blanket of unpolluted streams and plush green forests, is the small town of Sebasco.

Actually, Sebasco isn't legally big enough to be a town. Technically, it's merely one of countless sections that make up the town of Phippsburg, whose area is all of 105 square miles. But Sebasco has its own post office. Sebasco is so small, postal addresses require only name, city, and state.

Sebasco's official name is Sebasco Estates to distinguish it from Sebago, but Sebasco Road would be a name more befitting the hundred or so fishermen and women who comprise the greatest portion of the population. The present name, Sebasco Estates, suggests a bourgeois flavor that the local townsfolk simply cannot comprehend.

But who knows? Perhaps the name was chosen not to depict the present reality of the townsfolk but, rather, to predict the future dreams of the land speculators who come here to vacation in lovely Sebasco Lodge. Sebasco Lodge is a summer resort, hotel, cottage, recreation area that welcomes up to 250 guests at a time who want to return to nature but who don't want to get grass stains on their dress apparel. Its 500 acres of land cover property on both sides of Highway 217, all the way to West Point Beach, and include the lake by the Sebasco Post Office, plus mountains on both sides of the Lodge. Visitors play golf during the day and fantasize about shopping centers and parking lots at night. Sebasco is so small, one of the fairways on its only golf course, the one at the Lodge, crosses 217, one of the town's two main streets. The only payphone in Sebasco is at the Lodge.

Morningside Cemetery is the only town-owned cemetery in Phippsburg. But hundreds of family-owned cemeteries are maintained by the residents because they are tourist attractions—Phippsburg has more dead people than living.

THUMBS UP

Hidden in a cover situated two left turns off Highway 217 is the wharf, owned by Mickey and Marie Varian and two others. Mickey became our contact when Jerry and I picked him up hitching the day we drove to Wooster.

Mickey and Marie are both real honest community people. Marie was born and raised in Bath and is presently on the Phippsburg School Board. She was volunteer girls' basketball coach one year at Phippsburg High School, and this year she may teach a class in sewing. Mickey was born in Pennsylvania but his family moved here years ago. He currently serves on the local environmental board.

Both of them are respected community-wide—Jerry and I established credit at the local grocery store, Reid's Center Store, merely by saying we work for Mickey Varian.

We love them both not only because they're kind, hardworking, honest folks, but because they both are cooperative-oriented people like us. It was their cooperative spirit and our desire to work within the structure of a co-op as much as our fantasy of becoming fishermen that attracted us to Sebasco.

My vision of what the co-op would be like was a fishing collective of nine boatowners and the crewmembers on those nine boats, all of whom had equal voice in the decisions of the collective. Perhaps, I thought, they pooled their daily catches and sent them to market at better rates for all of them.

The reality shows six boats using the wharf: Three are lobster; two are gillnetters; one, now in Portland being repaired, is a dragger. Each one has a captain who runs his boat any way he wants. Several small dinghies with outboard motors and lobster hoists also utilize the services provided on the wharf.

Ken Wachsberger

The boatowners have nothing to do with the running of the co-op. Once they bring their fish in, their job ends and the co-op's begins. The members of the co-op are actually the Varian family and Junior, a 54-year-old lobster fisherman, who is also the co-op's only regular paid employee.

Mickey's dream envisions the co-op eventually moving the fish from the wharf directly to the retail outlets, thus eliminating all of the rip-off middlemen, and thereby creating at the same time greater profits for members of the co-op and cheaper prices for the public. Mickey hasn't been out to sea for two years because he's chosen to devote all his time to building the co-op. His dream is costing him personally $10,000 a year that he could be making on his boat, but I believe in Mickey because he believes in himself. That's another reason I love Mickey—because he's living his fantasy.

Once since I've been here, I saw a sheriff from the outlying town of Bath. He comes down to the wharf occasionally to warn Mickey that neighbors have been complaining about his noisy muffler. But he's the only pig I've seen around. According to Bobby, Mickey and Marie's son, there are no pigs in Sebasco, or, for that matter, all of Phippsburg: "There used to be two constables in Phippsburg but we run one of em outta town. The other was fuckin all the women, so we got rid of him, too."

The wharf itself is a conglomerate of buildings, additions on additions. Whiting used to be a big moneymaker here and the wharf has all the equipment to do a complete whiting processing business. But whiting is scarce now and the machinery, though in potentially good shape, has been inactive for years. The machine shop looks pretty extensive but it now is in a complete disarray.

However, here and there, hidden next to and under the junk is valuable woodworking equipment and a variety of parts and tools. All told, there are a dozen buildings, most of which are interconnected and

THUMBS UP

two of which are across the road. A few are used just for storage, so if the need or the desire appears we can clean one up and move in. There are numerous loading platforms and a number of special facilities, including two large drive-in freezers and several hundred feet of conveyor equipment.

Real estate developers would love to buy this 500-foot prime waterfront plot of land to rape and turn into condominiums. Mickey could make a bundle by selling out and then returning to his boat. But he won't. To me, he's a real man.

In the land area surrounding the wharf are the many homes that house a majority of the Sebasco community residents.

In the week that we've been here so far, we still haven't really gotten to know any of the residents, other than in the context of fishing talk. But that's our only down. Otherwise, our set-up couldn't be more ideal.

Our trailer sits on a small cliff overlooking the ocean and 100 yards from our boat, and we don't have to pay rent. There's a gas pump on the wharf and we get gas on credit. The electric outlet is hooked up to the wharf, so we get free electricity. A well two houses up the way gives spring water, so we get free water, and we can eat for free, except for lobster, which costs us $1.40 a pound. Since everything and everyone smells constantly from fish, we have little need to bother with laundry, so we save on that. And we're getting paid for doing something we wanted to do just to live out a fantasy.

We're in Heaven.

Ken Wachsberger

A Fisherman's Tale: Part 2
Yo Ho Ho—Ulp
(from *Lansing Star* 7:10, Winter 1975-76)

Hold onto your stomachs, Friends, as we take you back to the small fishing town of Sebasco, Maine, with our second installment from the summer diary of STAR roving anarcho-fantasy seeker, Ken Wachsberger.

Sunday July 27, 1975

The gods must have been with us when we set out this morning on the 160-degree course we take every day to reach our nets. The sea was still. No breeze was noticeable. There was not a sound save the buzzing of the miserable mosquitoes.

"Ah, to watch the sunrise from twenty miles out to sea."

Lying across the stern, I turned my attention from the stars above me to the bright orange ball appearing from behind the mountains to the east. Such a sight. Tis so profound, I, as a child, could not even conceive of such a feeling. It was beyond the realm of fantasy.

I looked forward to a healthy, invigorating day of work.

Five miles from the buoy, Captain Bobby startled us all: "Cocksucking mothafucking 'ho-a,' look at those clouds!"

Christ, he was right. The sky had changed so gradually we had failed to notice that the sky had turned a violent gray. The clouds looked bummed. And the waves seemed to be getting off on playing catch with Elaine Carroll III, our boat. No wonder I was no longer lying

THUMBS UP

on the stern. I had moved into the cabin miles back and hadn't even thought about why I got up.

"Lucky I'm not seasick," I thought. "It would be hell today. But I'm not, so, farout, this could be a lot of fun."

And it was.

The waves were wicked by the time we reached our nets. They must have been five-foot waves at least. That means five feet from trough to sea level and five feet from sea level to crest, ten feet altogether. Elaine Carroll was at their mercy as they thrashed against first her starboard side, then her port side. Then her starboard, then her port. Then her starboard, then her port.

Meanwhile, Jerry and I, our backs to our respective sides of the boat, had begun the flaking, the process of untangling the nets that consists of a random assortment of pulling, tugging, weaving, unweaving, and swearing until the nets look once more like nets instead of modern art: Sway to one side to receive the nets; sway to the other to coil it. Sway toward the bow to receive the net; sway to the stern to coil it. Sway to the bow, then the stern. The bow, then the stern. The bow, then the stern.

Our own movements plus those of the boat combined to produce a rapid circular path for our bodies to follow: from the bow to the port to the stern to the starboard back to the bow. Over and over.

"Yo ho ho and a bottle of rum," I bellowed, repeating a favorite chant that I first heard when I used to play pirates as a kid. All I needed was a patch, a peg leg, and a parrot, I fantasized. I was having the time of my life.

For four nets.

Ken Wachsberger

And then it caught up with me.

"Hey, Ken, ya don't look too good."

"Ulp!"

And just when I thought I was getting my sea legs.

My stomach was swirling, my head bobbed spastically, my mind went blank. For the next three hours, my bodily action fell into a pattern: flake, become nauseous, puke, feel better, flake some more, become nauseous again, puke again, feel better again.

Suddenly, Bobby leaned over his side, but not to puke.

"Jesus fucking Christ!" he screamed.

Jerry dropped his net and looked. "Holy shit!"

Ed threw down his picker, gashed his left thumb, cried "Fuck," and then forgot about his thumb as he saw what was happening down in the nets.

From my position in Sternport Corner, I tripped over nineteen nets to get to the starboard side, reversed my direction, slipped on two thousand pounds of dead fish on the port side, puked, then raced back to the starboard side to see what was causing the commotion.

It was a dead shark, a twenty-foot nurse shark, fifteen hundred pounds at least. Visions of Jonah, Pinocchio, and Ezekial, the legendary fisherman from Sebasco who hasn't missed a day in fifty-one years and has gotten seasick every time, raced through my head and my stomach.

THUMBS UP

For thirty-five minutes, we stabbed, we lunged, we grabbed, we plunged. We tried everything as the waves harassed our every organizational effort to get a rope around its tail and free this mass of dead weight from the nets.

What a sight we must have been. There was Jerry, jumping up and down screaming, "A shark, a shark. I've got dibs on the teeth!" And Bobby, leaning over the side trying to gaff it and yelling, "You cocksucking mothafucking hoa!" Ed was trying to contain himself, but I knew he was thrilled because he repeated "Pretty excited, eh?" to Jerry about a dozen times. And I was trying to put all I had into capturing the shark but I couldn't because—"Ehh, egh, ech, O Christ fuck"—I was so busy gagging and puking and running to the port side and slipping on dead fish.

But we did it. There it was, roped by the tail, being dragged through those same treacherous waters that she had in better days called home. Even in death, she had put up a valiant resistance. But she was no match for Captain Bobby and his proud crew.

"Fifteen hundred pounds!"—we were overawed. "How much does shark go for on the market?" we asked Bobby.

"Nurse sharks aren't marketable."

"What?!"

"Well, shit, I want at least to get the teeth before we cut it loose," said Jerry.

"Nurse sharks don't have teeth."

"No shit."

Ken Wachsberger

It was a disappointment to be sure. I had envisioned hundreds of tourists waiting on the wharf to greet us, pointing "Look, look" as we appeared on the horizon with our victim. And now we would have to cut it loose. It was worthless to us now. It had died in vain. It would never even make it as a fish fillet on the open market.

But there was a bright side. I had puked my guts out and now I felt better. A little lightheaded, to be sure. But better. That made the final four nets go quickly.

But then came the gutting: Bend over, pick up two hake, toss them on the table, grab a hake and a cod, onto the table, a pollock this time and another cod, now a monk fish—"Ahh, it's a heavy sucker; I need both hands." Up down up down for the next hour as the waves rocked us from side to side.

I was green when we pulled into the wharf.

The throngs weren't there to greet us, which was just as well today. But Mickey, the owner of the wharf and Bobby's father, was. "Hey, Jerry, what kinda fish ya got there?" he shouted down to us.

"Real funny, Mickey. You got an aspirin? Or a spare finger?"

And Gnossis, our dog, was there. He's always there to greet us, sure as the sun comes up. He lifted his leg and peed on me.

"Real funny, Gnossis."

I stepped onto dry land, but I could have sworn that I was still at sea.

"Tough day today, eh?" Jerry reminded me. "I could use a nice bath. How about you?"

"Real funny, Buddy. You got a Dramamine?"

THUMBS UP

"Story Time: A Fable"
By Henry the Hitchhiker
(from *Lecturers' Link*, September 1996)

I was reading Aesop's Fables the other day, as I do on those occasions when I am in need of wisdom reduced to a few paragraphs. I came upon the following fable (which I have renamed slightly for clarity):

The Fox, the Jackal, and the Stag: Management Version

The Fox, the Jackal, and the Stag went hunting one day with the Lion, and together they killed a Deer. When it came time to divide the Deer so that each could have his share, the Lion said to them, "My weak friends, the first part is mine because I am King of the forest; the second is mine because I am stronger than you are; the third is mine because I was the fastest of us all; and whoever touches the fourth part will be my enemy forever."

And so the Lion took for himself the entire Deer.

Moral: You may share the labors of the great, but you may not share the spoil.

* * *

Huh? According to legend, Aesop was a slave. Somehow, I expected higher worker consciousness. Then again, maybe he had to suck up to management for his supper.

So, I rewrote the ending. Here's the complete, revised fable:

Ken Wachsberger

The Fox, the Jackal, and the Stag: Workers' Version

The Fox, the Jackal, and the Stag went hunting one day with the Lion, and together they killed a Deer. When it came time to divide the Deer so that each could have his share, the Lion said to them, "My weak friends, the first part is mine because I am King of the forest; the second is mine because I am stronger than you are; the third is mine because I was the fastest of us all; and whoever touches the fourth part will be my enemy forever."

And so the Lion took for himself the entire Deer.

The Fox, the Jackal, and the Stag whispered to each other, "What he says is unfair. We worked just as hard as he did even though we contributed in different ways. We deserve our equal shares and to be treated with dignity.

But when the three presented their concerns to the Lion, he laughed and said, "Each of you is no match for my strength."

And he was right.

But together they were able to chase him away, and they did. Then the three enjoyed their individual shares and divided the Lion's share into three equal parts.

Moral: United we stand; divided we fall.

There's a moral to these two stories: The end of the story is what we make it.

THUMBS UP

SAYING GOODBYE TO TWO KEY INFLUENCES

Goodbye, Dad. You Will Always Be Missed

Posted on July 15, 2011

When you make it into your sixties and you still have your parents you sometimes have thoughts that they will live forever. I wasn't the only one who thought that about my dad, who died on July 5 and was buried one week ago today. "I can't believe your dad is gone." I heard that statement repeatedly during the week I spent with the family in Beachwood, Ohio, the eastern suburb of Cleveland that my pioneer parents helped build during the baby boom years and continued to lead in more ways than most people can remember.

"Shocked" was another word I heard repeatedly. The disbelief of friends and family is just one of many tributes to his life. He was 93, an age most people never attain, but he was clear of mind and healthy. He didn't seem to age. He was driving the day before he died. He was still visualizing the next way he was going to create order out of the chaos that we know as life, and do it in a way that would help the greatest number of people, as he had done his whole life.

During the forties, Beachwood school children would attend Fairmount School on Fairmount Boulevard until they reached the seventh grade and then transfer to the Shaker Heights school system, where they would remain until they graduated. But the baby boom put pressure on the Shaker Heights school system so in the early fifties they kicked us out.

Ken Wachsberger

Families on the south side of Beachwood wanted to secede from Beachwood and become part of Shaker. They put a proposal on the next ballot. My dad vehemently opposed the measure so he led the way to put another proposal on the ballot, that Beachwood raise the money to build its own schools including in that part of Beachwood.

He knew that both proposals couldn't win or residents would be building schools for kids who were living in Shaker. He was, of course, right. The proposal to secede was soundly defeated and residents voted to build their own schools. My dad served on the school board throughout the height of the baby boom years, and led the way in developing two new elementary schools, a middle school, and a high school. His name appears on plaques on all of them.

But far more important to my friends, he was the co-founder of the Beachwood Little League as well as a regular backer through his menswear store, the Oxford Shop, and a manager/coach. At the drop of a, well, bat, he would call a practice, I would get on the phone and call the members of my team, and we would meet at one of the baseball diamonds in the city for an afternoon practice. He was a mentor to my teammates and so many others, who all knew him never as Mr. Wachsberger but always just as Si. That's how everyone knew him.

My mom was no slouch during that period either, and still isn't. She was, among other activities, a regular member and leader of PTA. During my freshman year in high school, my dad was president of the school board, my mom was president of the PTA, and I was president of the junior high school student council. When I graduated, he was president again. At the ceremony, he handed me my diploma, which had his signature on it. I learned at the 90th birthday party that we threw for him that he was president when my brother Don graduated so he signed his diploma also. He wasn't taking any chances.

THUMBS UP

After 14 years, which included three terms as president, my dad retired from the school board, but not serving the community as an elected official must have given him fits so he ran for city council and won. He spent the next 24 years on the city council, including four terms as president. Among his many accomplishments, he created a law that prevented developers from cutting down trees that surrounded the site of new homes if they had reached a certain height. He also mentored the current mayor.

He died suddenly and painlessly in a way that is reserved for mortals who commune with angels during their lives. He had told Bob and my mom early in the day that his vision was blurry so they took him to the hospital. The doctors there were going to keep him a day or two because they thought he might have had pneumonia. He was also dehydrated according to one doctor who wanted him on IV fluids as soon as they got him to his room.

Don, who was there at the end, recalled,

> We had been talking to Dad about dinner and other small talk. He didn't like the dinner, but he had most of the two cookies. We asked him to read something, which he did pretty well, so we knew his eyesight was okay.
>
> Then while we were waiting for his hospital room to be prepared so he could be admitted for the night, his eyes rolled up, and he turned his head to the left. No sound. No grimace. Apparently no pain.
>
> We didn't know at that time that he had died, but he never regained consciousness. Soon after the doctors got into the room, they began to talk about not being able to detect a heartbeat, so it was pretty clear that he had passed away

Ken Wachsberger

when he had turned his head. About 25 minutes later, the two attending doctors came into the family room to tell Mom, Bob, and me that they were unable to revive Dad.

He died at Ahuja Medical Center. It is ironic, I suppose, because that's where his next volunteer project was going to be. He told me about it on a recent visit home. He was going to create a library there by writing letters to publishers around the country and asking them to donate books, as he had done at one of the inner-city schools in Cleveland where he and my mom tutored children. He already knew the name of the person at the hospital who he needed to talk to in order to bring his idea to life.

I don't know if he ever did talk to him, and I don't remember the exact details of the plan. I didn't always hear his words when he spoke to me. Sometimes I just felt his passion and let it feed me. It made me a better person.

In one of the karmic, zen moments that tie together so many parts of my family, he chose—and a part of me does believe he chose it—a special day to move on.

His father, my Grandpa Al, or Gramps as we knew him, died on June 21, 1990, the summer solstice. He was buried the next day, the birthday of his oldest grandson, my brother Don. A few years earlier, his wife, my Grandma Ida, died on the birthday of her oldest granddaughter, my cousin Barb. Six years after Gramps' death, on another June 22, my father's oldest grandson, my son David, read from the Torah and became a man according to our tradition.

My father died on July 5, David's birthday. I'm not nearly wise enough to tell you what that all means other than that it all comes together, the generations, life. As the family genealogist, I learned that life and death are connected by a line on a chart. It's also connected by shared anniversaries.

THUMBS UP

The time in Cleveland following his death was a surreal experience, filled with extreme sadness and extreme joy. Up, down, up, down. It was a testament to Judaism, whatever branch you follow, that every occasion is steeped in tradition and ritual that helps guide you through it.

We learned that Jewish funerals begin by focusing on the deceased but end by focusing on the living. The Mourner's Kaddish never mentions death. It is recited while standing as an affirmation of strength. At the home, during *shiva*, the period of mourning, the mourners are commanded to eat first to replenish their strength. Judaism always focuses on the positive. Life continues. The show must go on.

And so we buried my dad on Friday afternoon. The mayor, the rabbi, and the cantor all spoke to the 300 or so friends and relatives from Beachwood, Greater Cleveland, and around the country who came to pay their last respects. Their presence made the event a lot easier for all of us, especially my mom. After the funeral, he had a police escort to the cemetery under a sunny sky. Then we came to the house for an initial period of *shiva*.

Three hours later we all celebrated with my nephew Scott and his fiancé Diana at their rehearsal dinner. The next day was their joyous wedding. Then Sunday and Monday we sat *shiva*.

Friends wondered how we could celebrate a wedding right after a funeral but Jewish tradition demands no less. Besides, as we all knew, my dad would never have let us postpone it. He so looked forward to it himself. My mom was no less adamant. So, we felt grief and we felt joy, as was appropriate and natural for the two occasions. We just felt them out of the usual order.

I have no idea what people are thinking as they are about to die but I know my dad long insisted that he did not ever want to be confined to a rest home or be strung up on tubes. Maybe he thought that if he lived that would be his inevitable fate so he willed himself to go. But I know also that he was a practical person so I wouldn't be surprised if he figured transportation and lodging are expensive, out-of-towners will be coming in for the wedding anyhow, so if he died when he did he would save them the expense of another trip.

No one knows.

But I know that I want to call him a legend. I believed that for a long time. Perhaps that's just the perspective of a son. But I think I'm safe in saying he was a great man. An extraordinary man. I just happen to be fortunate to be his son.

He belonged to us—his beloved wife Shirley, who he adored; their four sons, Don, Ken, Jeff, and Bob; their two daughter-in-law, Judi and Emily; their three grandchildren, David, Scott, and Carrie; and now his granddaughter-in-law, Diana.

But he belonged to his community also. His imprint is everywhere—in the schools that he helped build, in the trees that beautify the city, in the Little League that he co-founded, the arts council that he and my mom helped co-found and that, my mom maintains, would have given way to age and exhaustion had not my dad almost singlehandedly revived it, at Montefiore where he kept the snack shop display cases full and fresh, with the children he and my mom tutored. And the volunteer hours that he and my mom devoted to more causes than likely any of us will ever be able to name.

Whether he was writing a letter to President Obama to share his views on how to run the country; or sharing financial advice with David, Scott, and Carrie; or playing Rummikub with whoever could fit around the kitchen table, he was so dynamic that, yes, we can be forgiven for not seeing the finish line that he was fast approaching.

THUMBS UP

He saw it, but he was too busy to dwell on it, and if the end of this adventure was near, he wasn't going to miss a second of it.

We miss him greatly and mourn for our loss but we don't mourn for him because he went out in style. He was a role model to everyone who knew him, a man of dignity, and we were fortunate for the time we had with him.

As Emily said, the earth is better because of him.

Ken Wachsberger

Goodbye to a Tough Broad

Posted on November 29, 2021

My mother, Shirley Pollack Wachsberger, died Sunday, November 21, two months after turning one hundred years old. We buried her the day before Thanksgiving.

Tough Broad

Mom was a tough broad. That's the term she used to describe herself when Dad died ten summers ago. It's what she was when she overcame paralyzing personal and social pressure to give up and instead earned her bachelor's degree in psychology when she was in her fifties because education was so important to her.

But Mom was also shy and polite to a fault. One holiday season, the story goes, Dad's mom baked a poppyseed cake for her. Mom hated poppyseed cake but she didn't want to hurt Grandma's feelings so she told her how much she loved it. Grandma baked her another one every year after that until Alzheimer's took away her recipe. Until the end, Mom always said she loved it. I don't know if Grandma ever saw her eat a piece after the first year.

She was gorgeous. At Glenville High School, where she graduated, two fellow classmates were writer Jerry Siegel and artist Joe Shuster, the creators of Superman. As Mom told the story, artist Shuster invited Mom to his studio to draw her. If it hadn't been for her shyness, Mom might have been the model for Lois Lane.

THUMBS UP

She was a community organizer, one of the pioneers who built Beachwood, the suburb on the east side of Cleveland where I grew up. She played a leading role, usually as president, both with my dad and on her own, in the Beachwood Arts Council, the PTA, the Montefiore Women's Auxiliary, American Field Service, and other community organizations. They taught prisoners and inner-city kids to read.

Always Learning

She was a voracious reader. I would call her every Friday to welcome her to the weekend. When I asked her what she was up to, she always said, "Nothing. Just reading."

She read everything I wrote starting with my days on the underground press, and so did Dad. Mom, in particular, was ready to hear a new viewpoint. She was outspoken and passionate and had been long before I came around.

In high school, according to family legend, she spoke out about the need to have classes that spoke to the concerns of women. The school responded by adding a cooking class. She knew it wasn't enough.

Mom was an early reader of *Ms.* Magazine. She used to tell me about how the issues always arrived with the covers torn. She was sure the sexist pig mailman was ripping them. She read the magazines from cover to cover in defiance.

Meanwhile, Dad's vote was going from Barry Goldwater in 1964 to Barry Commoner in 1980.

Ken Wachsberger

How Can I Rebel Properly?

During this period, my friends were all rebelling against their parents, but they loved my folks. I would say, "Yes, but," and try to show that I had rebelled against my parents, too, but I could never say it with conviction.

I hitchhiked one year, probably 1971, to Washington, DC, to participate in a women's rights rally. I hitchhiked with five women. On our way from Lansing, Michigan, where I lived, to DC, we spent a night on Edgewood. Mom made us all dinner, and breakfast the next morning. Then Dad drove us to the freeway. He gave me $20.

How could I rebel against them, like my friends? Do you see how they made me suffer?

Goodbye, Mom

Emily and I are grateful that we were able to see Mom the day she died. We were with her for an hour and a half, and she was awake and alert most of the time. Both of us said our last words to her. Emily thanked her for being such a great role model. I told her it was okay for her to let go. We told her that David and Carrie sent their love.

We were sad when we left. We both looked for reasons to be optimistic but neither of us expected to see Mom alive again.

Brother Bob called later that evening to say she went peacefully in her sleep. I like to think she heard my final words.

For her rich life and her dignified death, we can all be thankful.

THUMBS UP

TEMPLE BETH EMETH AND THE SANCTUARY MOVEMENT

Temple Beth Emeth Declaration in Support of Becoming a Sanctuary Congregation

In 2017, during the early Trump years, as the Sanctuary movement was moving into high gear, I accepted the call from my rabbi at Temple Beth Emeth in Ann Arbor to write the statement that would move the temple board to declare our support of the emerging movement in Washtenaw County. I accepted his call. This was my vision, which gained rapid support throughout the TBE community and led to TBE's board supporting sanctuary.

* * *

As an activist and devout member of the Reform Jewish community of America, Temple Beth Emeth in Ann Arbor, Michigan, declares itself to be a Sanctuary congregation, eager to face the resulting risks and accept the resulting obligations, to the best of our ability and with the best of intentions.

Declaring Our Sanctuary Status

In declaring our Sanctuary status, we join with those Jewish and other religious congregations that have declared similarly or will when they hear the call. We are part of a proud tradition that has roots in the Torah and more recently found voice in the 1980s when congregations and individuals throughout the country arose and united to protect refugees from oppressive conditions in Central

American countries, including Guatemala and El Salvador, whose military regimes were being financed with our tax dollars.

At the same time, we demand a halt to the hateful cries and harmful actions that are walling off constructive dialogue around the issue of immigration. We proclaim readiness to support efforts to change misguided laws that make this new Sanctuary movement a moral imperative. Sanctuary cannot be a permanent solution. Until that time comes when there is a permanent solution, however, we cannot sit on the sideline as observers.

Claiming Sanctuary status is not a partisan issue. The new Sanctuary movement has its roots in the administration of Barack Obama, when over two million immigrants were deported. Other congregations felt the call then.

We feel it now. No longer are only felons and dangerous individuals being deported. Homes and work places are being threatened. Schools are being monitored. Even immigrants who have begun the legal process of achieving citizenship and now carry green cards are being stopped and harassed. The intense hatred and irrationality that surround all debate today and prevent the finding of a just resolution require us to take an immediate, activist position, to pray that hard hearts will grow compassionate, and to affirm that, as long as the issue remains unsolved and the solution transitional, we will side with the most vulnerable and do our part to protect them.

Our History Demands It

Our history compels us to act in this way, for four initial reasons:

First, the prophetic mission of Reform Judaism is not only to pray for justice but to work for it, and to stand up to injustice when it gets in the way. Leviticus 19:33-34 guide our path: "When a stranger resides with you in your land, you shall not wrong him.... [He] shall

THUMBS UP

be to you as one of your citizens; you shall love him as yourself; for you were strangers in the land of Egypt."

In today's political environment, our work as a Sanctuary congregation must protect not only strangers but also long-time residents, taxpayers, and students, many brought to these shores as infants and knowing no other home than the United States, who are now being threatened with deportation back to a "home" they never knew. They are not strangers. They are our neighbors. Leviticus 19:18 says: "Love your neighbor as yourself." We shall.

Second, we are all immigrants. The majority of congregation members are four or fewer generations away from that same experience. Some are immigrants themselves. We remember the harsh conditions under which we lived in the shtetls of the nineteenth-century Old World and the countries of Nazi-occupied Europe during World War II. We have not forgotten our ancestors' expensive, dangerous journeys to America, being stopped at the border or turned back because of illness, perceived political leaning, educational level, religion, job readiness, poverty, and other arbitrary roadblocks that separated family members for long, lonely years.

Third, though many of us have found economic and social success in this country, and risen to positions of respect and authority, we can never forget our working-class roots. Our east European ancestors who escaped the pogroms and flooded the shores of New York and other immigrant-receiving ports in the late 1800s until World War I were laborers, craftsmen, artisans, peddlers, and small business owners who understood the need to work together despite petty differences. Drawing on their experiences in the shtetls and forced by conditions in the New World, they became leaders of the American labor movement, where strength was found in solidarity and unity.

Ken Wachsberger

Whether it is the Jewish watchword of one God or the working-class belief that we're all in this together, we are obligated to act in favor of Sanctuary. When one of us is victimized, we all are victimized. In building the Sanctuary movement, we must work to create a united network of Jewish Sanctuary congregations but we must reach far beyond our religious and ethnic borders as well.

Fourth, some say we are breaking a law. While that assertion leaves room for debate, it cannot be debated if one accepts the origin story of our faith that Judaism was born from peaceful civil disobedience when Abraham broke his father's idols and declared that there is but one God. The story of Purim, one of our most joyous liberation holidays, begins with Mordechai refusing to bow down to Haman. From these examples and others, we learn that unjust laws and outdated practices may be changed only when good people follow their consciences regardless of the consequences.

For these reasons and others not yet named, Temple Beth Emeth declares itself a Sanctuary congregation, ready to advocate for, support, educate the community about, and even house immigrants, refugees, and others who need asylum from deportation and other forms of unjust persecution until a just solution to the issue of immigration to the United States can be found.

THUMBS UP

A FINAL WORD OR TWO

Thank you for purchasing and reading *Thumbs Up: Memoir of a Joyful Organizer*. If you found any joy or intellectual awakening while reading it, or if you just got a good laugh, please be kind enough to post an honest review on your blog, through your social media networks, and at your favorite retailer so other readers can find it.

Then again, if you didn't find it helpful, go ahead and review it as well. (I just hope there are fewer of you.)

Ken Wachsberger

ABOUT THE AUTHOR

Ken Wachsberger, The Book Coach, has been writing and helping others to write better, through personal book coaching and editing, for over fifty years, going back to his work on the underground press of the Vietnam era.

Under Ken's gentle guidance, students, clients, and friends have

- worked through personal traumas
- prepared for life transitions
- made major purchases, and
- chosen their life paths

while writing more than they ever believed possible, and better.

His groundbreaking *Transforming Lives: A Socially Responsible Guide to the Magic of Writing and Researching* was the first textbook written to teach Ken Macrorie's I-Search paper.

Ken is known internationally as the editor of the landmark Voices from the Underground Series, about the Vietnam-era underground press.

As a member of National Speakers Association and National Writers Union, Ken helps speakers and others to write and publish the books they need for healing, to preserve their legacy, and to grow their professional credibility.

He can be reached at ken@kenthebookcoach.com or https://kenthebookcoach.com.

THUMBS UP

BOOKS WRITTEN AND EDITED BY KEN WACHSBERGER

Available as PODs and ebooks

- *Thumbs Up: Memoir of a Joyful Organizer*
- *You've Got the Time: How to Write and Publish That Book in You*, 2nd edition
- *Your Partner Has Breast Cancer: 21 Ways to Keep Sane as a Support Person on Your Journey from Victim to Survivor*
- *Never Be Afraid: A Belgian Jew in the French Resistance*, 3rd edition
- *Ken Wachsberger's Puns and Word Plays for the Job Seeker*
- *Voices from the Underground Series*

    Insider Histories of the Vietnam Era Underground Press, Part 1
    My Odyssey through the Underground Press
    Insider Histories of the Vietnam Era Underground Press, Part 2
    Stop the Presses! I Want to Get Off!: A Brief History of the Prisoners' Digest International

Other books by Ken include

- *Beercans on the Side of the Road: The Story of Henry the Hitchhiker*
- *Transforming Lives: A Socially Responsible Guide to the Magic of Writing and Researching*
- *The Ballad of Ken and Emily: or, Tales from the Counterculture*
- *The Last Selection: A Child's Journey through the Holocaust*

Ken Wachsberger

https://kenthebookcoach.com
http://www.azenphonypress.com
http://www.voicesfromtheunderground.com

www.ingramcontent.com/pod-product-compliance
Lightning Source LLC
Chambersburg PA
CBHW032025290426
44110CB00012B/669